$17⁵⁰

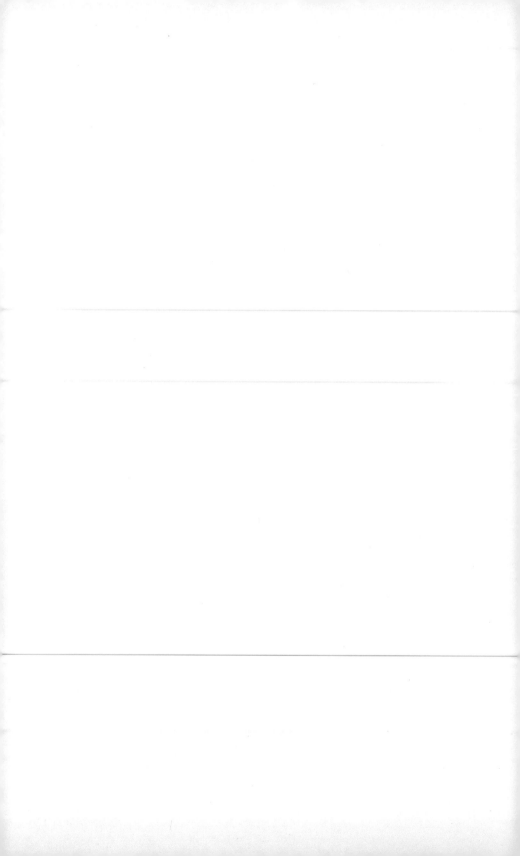

Baroque Music

Baroque Music

From Monteverdi to Handel

NICHOLAS ANDERSON

Preface by Nikolaus Harnoncourt

With 51 illustrations

THAMES AND HUDSON

To Alison

© 1994 Thames and Hudson Ltd, London

British Library Cataloguing-in-Publication Data

A catalogue record for this book is available from the
British Library

ISBN 0-500-01606-2

Printed and bound in Slovenia by Mladinska Knjiga

Contents

Preface

FOR THE MUSICIAN AS FOR THE LISTENER, how vital – and interesting –
is every conceivable scrap of information about music, about art,
about the place of art in life itself that we can lay our hands on. It is given
to only a few people, led or maybe even driven by a passionate interest,
and with the time available so to indulge themselves, to immerse
themselves in all the original documentation: the letters of composers,
painters, sculptors or architects, the writings of the great patrons,
instructional books, philosophical texts, prefaces to printed editions . . .
to say nothing of all the other material where the link to music may be
tenuous. Whole libraries have been written on music in all the languages
of Europe, across many centuries of our history. And only someone who
has consulted these myriad sources for himself, like Nicholas Anderson,
is truly in a position to construct an image of our beloved art, to form
opinions that are *genuinely* his own. . . . But how many others of us are in
that fortunate position? We, who, for whatever reason, cannot bring
unlimited dedication to our consuming passion, must be profoundly
grateful when someone else has done so for us. We can thus enjoy a
distillation of all such studies and a personal interpretation of them.

We may submit to our guide wholeheartedly, in almost blind trust –
but in the rarest of cases, as now, the summary that awaits us is gripping,
deeply informative. Here and there, the passion of the author is certain to
infect the reader as well . . . for we are cordially bidden to enter into the
dialogue.

NIKOLAUS HARNONCOURT

I

New thinking in Italy

No other period of music can boast the extent of change and influence of the Baroque. It was a period in which ideas and forms were developed to expand Western musical vocabulary and to express a wide range of emotions intelligibly as never before, and the effects are still being felt at the end of the twentieth century. In particular the years c.1590 to 1730 witnessed the re-evaluation of how music could enhance the effect of the spoken word, leading eventually to opera and song as we know them. The same period saw the emergence of instrumental music, and the structures required to deliver a textless discourse. Baroque sonatas and concertos in particular became a catalyst for succeeding generations in creating a whole philosophy of musical language: 'sonata form' as explored by Haydn, Mozart and Beethoven. The variety of ideas and forms in the Baroque gradually became governed by a common musical syntax, dictated by the growth of tonality with its liberating influence on improvisation, variation and other compositional demands. Yet for all this regularization, there remained a complex range of musical divergence from one European nation, or even city, to another, revealing the varying extent to which traditional genres were reshaped by the spirit of the new. The period is sometimes chastised for its formulaic tendencies, yet no era, before or after, contains music more elusive on the one hand or more passionate on the other. Its novelty and irregularity are aptly reflected in the obscurity of the word 'baroque' itself.

The derivation of 'baroque' is variously sought in the Portuguese *barroco* and Spanish *barrueco*, both used to describe an irregularly shaped pearl, in the Italian *barroco*, where it was applied especially to the architecture of Francesco Borromini, and lastly in mnemonic hexameters put together in the thirteenth century by William of Shyreswood. The word was largely synonymous with 'absurd', 'irregular', 'grotesque' and 'extravagant' until the late nineteenth century when it was first applied to a concept of styles within a period. In the history of painting 'Baroque' embraces the years roughly between 1580 and 1715. Baroque music encompasses a similar period but extends somewhat further into the eighteenth century. It is unwise to consider the Baroque style, either in painting or in music, as being an Italian invention, but Italy was the country where the style was formed, and from where it was disseminated throughout Europe.

The Counter-Reformation

The last decades of the sixteenth century in Italy were crucial to the formation of the many styles which make up the music and painting of the Baroque period. As a consequence of changing attitudes, personal sensibilities and modes of expression underwent an important shift. Among the fundamental reasons for this change were the Counter-Reformation, the proselytizing of the Jesuits, and an economic crisis which reached far beyond Italy. The Counter-Reformation marked the revival of the Roman Catholic Church in Europe. Stimulated by Protestant opposition, reform movements began in Italy during the early years of the sixteenth century but only became widely effective in Europe after the establishment of the Jesuit Order by Papal Bull in 1540. The ideals of the Counter-Reformation were embodied in the Council of Trent, summoned by Pope Paul III in 1537 but first convened at Trent in 1545; two further reassemblies took place in 1551 and 1562. Broken though it was by adjournments, from the session of this Council emerged not only the defined doctrine of the Roman Church but also a strengthened discipline brought about by a genuine desire for reform, a sense of the need for change and a new spirit of leadership.

The recently founded Jesuit Order was of particular importance in disseminating change. Autocratic, severe and dedicated, the Order set out to educate and to convert. Ignatius Loyola (1491–1556), the founder of the Jesuits, was quick to recognize values which had been assimilated by the young through the influence of the humanists: values in which culture took precedence over theology and freedom of thought over dogma. Loyola saw that any far-reaching changes in spiritual direction must be based on strict and systematic schooling. He offered himself to the Pope in 1540, and from then onwards the Jesuit influence was crucial in changing cultural attitudes.

The importance attached to feeling, to emotional involvement, which became a significant characteristic of the Baroque, stemmed at least in part from the Jesuits' teaching that by meditation on Christ's suffering human beings could share in Christ's agony and so gain spiritual strength. This concern with actuality, the wish to involve the spectator or the audience, to make him or her *feel* what they see and hear, is one of the fundamental distinctions between the Renaissance and the 'new' thinking of the post Counter-Reformation period. A vital characteristic of a Baroque work of art is that, by various means, it demands the emotional participation of the listener or onlooker.

In the 1550s Jesuits made their way into Germany, an important area in the campaign for the conversion of Protestants to the Catholic faith. Northern Germany at this time was an almost unbroken Protestant block, while Calvinism had been established in the Palatine and Lutheranism in Württemburg and Baden. It was in the Palatinate and, above all, in Bohemia that Catholicism met the strongest Protestant opposition; and it was in this area of central Europe that the seeds of the Thirty Years War were sown. The hardship and misery brought about by religious fanaticism are perhaps nowhere more clearly evident than in this war, fought largely in Central Europe between 1618 and 1648. The *primum movens*, Ferdinand of Styria, later Ferdinand II, was a Jesuit by education and persuasion; but the true participants were Austria and Spain, who represented the Catholics, and Germany, Scandinavia and England, who represented the Protestant cause. The issues were complex but an important outcome of the war was the stemming of further Jesuit advances and the preservation of a significant area of Central Europe for the Lutheran and Calvinist Churches. Italy, though not directly involved in the Thirty Years War, nevertheless had her own political, social and economic problems. There were two outbreaks of plague in the first half of the seventeenth century, a series of famines, and censorship of science and philosophy imposed by the Jesuits and by the Inquisition.

The social misery caused by disease, poverty, fanaticism and political unrest took their toll of the cultural and idealistic aspirations inspired by the Counter-Reformation and the Council of Trent. Rather than the ideal concept of universal harmony cherished during the sixteenth century, the goal became religious and intellectual harmony free from politics, fanaticism and moral zeal. There was a call for a new authority, a new approach, which was reflected in the arts and sciences of the period.

Few periods of history have been able to claim quite as many outstanding philosophers, scientists and men of letters as the seventeenth century. Among them were Galileo (1564–1642) who published his *Della nuove Scienze*; Johann Kepler (1571–1630) whose laws of planetary motion provided the basis for much of Newton's work; Francis Bacon whose *Advancement of Learning* was published in English in 1605; René Descartes whose *Compendium musicae* (1618) and *Les passions de l'âme* (1649) are closely allied with Baroque musical thought; Blaise Pascal

(1649) who attacked the Jesuits and contested Descartes' view of the supremacy of human reason; Isaac Newton whose *Philosophiae Naturalis Principia Mathematica* was published in 1687.

Although only the work of Descartes has direct bearing upon music these treatises illustrate the systematic and experimental spirit of the time. New sciences were being expounded which enabled educated people to embrace an altered concept of the universe. The misery caused by religious wars aroused a deep sense of scepticism towards ideas and theories connected with Church dogma, resulting in free-thinking, although by and large, seventeenth-century 'libertinism' – a word which at this period did not have connotations of loose morals – left the authority of the Church unchallenged.

The 'affections'

René Descartes (1596–1650) is an important figure in the early history of Baroque musical theory. Descartes was educated at the Jesuit school at La Flèche in Anjou from 1606 to 1612 – and 'the Societie of Jesus glorie in that theyr order had the educating of him,' observed the English antiquary John Aubrey. Descartes' *Compendium musicae* sets out both to define a relationship between physical and psychological phenomena in music and to apply scientific processes to aural responses; it was, in other words, a treatise on the mathematical basis of harmony. As an attempt to build a bridge between humanist thought of the previous century and the science of the seventeenth century it is important in that it argues that the 'new' values are not so much in opposition to the earlier ones as a development of them.

In *Les passions de l'âme* Descartes sets out to demonstrate that the human passions can be disciplined and their effects be controlled by reason. He distinguishes between six basic 'affections', that is to say emotions: admiration, love, hate, joy, sadness and desire. According to ancient physiology the 'affections' were derived from combinations of the four cardinal humours of the body – blood, phlegm, choler and melancholy. These humours correspond with the four temperaments, the four elements, and so on. Descartes emancipated himself from this traditional view by applying his own systematic and experimental methods. Theorizing of this kind was greatly admired in a century in which artists set out to exploit the emotions or 'affects', and was fundamental to the shift away from the Renaissance aim to 'represent' towards the Baroque desire to 'move'. Descartes' belief that he had found a rational, objective explanation for the passions contributed to the concept of the 'affections' which was central to the aesthetic of Baroque art.

Academies. Monody

It is in the wealth of literary polemics of the period, conducted between advocates of the new and adherents of the old, that we find a lively awareness of scientific and musical issues. Their dissemination, however, required centres for discussion, and academies were set up as the focal points. At such gatherings the vocabulary of rhetoric was learned and transmitted. The purpose of rhetorical discipline was to imitate human passions, and that is what musical rhetoric set out to achieve.

The earliest academies were formed in Italy during the Renaissance. At first they were chiefly concerned with reviving the traditions of the ancient classics; but their terms of reference soon widened, and by the middle of the sixteenth century a large number of academies existed in Italy whose members played an important role in the literary, dramatic, philosophical, scientific and musical thinking of the period. Italian academies became the model for those set up in northern European countries, notably in France.

One of the most important figures in the development of this new academicism was Giovanni de Bardi, who was born in Florence in 1534. Bardi was a nobleman and a critic, a poet, playwright and composer, and a key figure in the movement that led to early experiments in lyrical and dramatic monody. During the 1570s he was host to gatherings of noblemen, musicians, scientists and poets which became known as the Camerata dei Bardi. Stimulated by a renewed interest in ancient learning, Bardi and his circle pursued humanistic aims for which they sought expression in theoretical and aesthetic discussion, scientific experiment and a practical study of music. Their musical thinking was influenced above all by the humanist and historian Girolamo Mei (1519–94). Mei's correspondence with Vincenzo Galilei – father of the mathematician and astronomer, and patronized by Bardi – and with Bardi himself prompted the experiments with monody of Bardi's Camerata, and also the development of the first music dramas and the new recitative style. Mei's research into Greek music led Bardi to write his own discourse, which broadly reflected Mei's opinion that the counterpoint which character-ized the music of earlier generations was suitable neither for the expression of the feelings nor to render the meaning of the text.

Hardly less important for the development of monody was Galilei's *Dialogo della musica antica et della modernica* (1581–2) which also arose from Mei's suggested reforms. The views held by Bardi, Galilei and their radical friends of the Camerata were, however, at odds with those of others, such as Monteverdi in Mantua and Gesualdo in Naples. Both composers were demonstrating that Baroque ideals could satisfactorily be expressed in polyphonic writing.

In the teaching and dissemination of musical rhetoric the Italian academies played a vital role. Rhetorical concepts and oratorical figures were applied to almost all the formal and expressive techniques of the Baroque. Baroque music aspired towards an expression of words in music comparable with impassioned rhetoric. This was the fundamental means by which composers aimed to 'move' as opposed to 'portray' or 'represent' the affections. Several attempts were made to organize music composition in rhetorical terms, and this concept remained vital until the decline of the Baroque period, although the enormous variety of musical techniques presented a problem both of terminology and definition to theorists and composers engaged in the systematic transformation of rhetorical concepts into musical equivalents.

Science, philosophy, and discussions conducted at aristocratic gatherings – the academies and camerate already mentioned – all provided stimulus for a new approach to music, painting and architecture, but it was ideals held in common that gave the new style momentum, and patronage which provided the means to realize the aspirations of the new thinking.

The chief patrons of the arts during the Baroque period were the Church, the nobility, and increasingly, later on, the municipality. Noble employment or sponsorship was the most widely practised patronage at this time. Patronage dictated the composition and performance of music, and assured a composer of at least a respectful acknowledgment of his art by his public. A patron's status and surroundings played a vital part in determining the nature, size and purpose of a composition. Composers would normally carry out their duties either by commission or under contract. Music was written and assembled into collections according to a composer's desire to dedicate a piece or set of pieces to his patron, or to someone from whom he desired to receive patronage.

The political, social and economic changes of the period were to have both broad and specific implications for musical life. In particular the growth in volume and range of patrons' musical requests could be amply served by the flexibility of Baroque designs and idioms. But first, music had to expand the means by which its language could enhance rather than obscure the text, and in so doing, created a veritable explosion of emotive possibilities: the catalysts of 'modern' music.

2
The development of Baroque style

Manifestos

W E HAVE SEEN FROM A BRIEF SURVEY of the political, social and artistic changes which occurred during the latter half of the sixteenth century that Italy was the fountain-head from which the 'new thinking' emerged. Italy dominated European architecture, painting, sculpture and music throughout the seventeenth and first half of the eighteenth century. The Baroque was a period of stylistic inconsistency but the treatises, manifestos and prefaces through which scientists, philosophers and musicians sought to express their points of view assist us in understanding its artistic aims.

One of the earliest and most important of the manifestos was written by the Italian composer Giulio Caccini (*c*.1545–1618). Caccini's preface to a collection of his own strophic songs with basso continuo together with madrigals was published in 1602 under the title *Le nuove musiche* – The New Music. Caccini was a member of the informal academy mentioned earlier which met at the house of Giovanni de Bardi in Florence – indeed it was probably he who coined the name Camerata dei

Caccini's 'Sfogava con le stelle', as printed in his *Le nuove musiche* (1602)

13

Bardi for the group. Besides being a composer Caccini was a noted singer, instrumentalist and teacher; he taught music to several members of his own family, and apart from a short visit to Rome as Bardi's secretary in 1592 he remained in Florence, in 1600 moving to the court of the Medici as musical director.

Caccini and other artists and men of learning associated with Bardi embraced humanistic ideals. Their discussions were both theoretical and aesthetic, taking into account a practical study of music. 'I have endeavoured,' wrote Caccini in the preface to *Le nuove musiche*:

> to bring a kind of music by which men might, as it were, speak in harmony, using in that kind of singing . . . a certain noble nonchalance of the song, passing now and then through certain dissonances, holding the bass note firm, except when I did not wish to observe the common practice, and playing the inner voices on an instrument for the expression of some passion . . .

Caccini tells us that the Camerata received such pieces as he describes enthusiastically, and that when he tried them out before a select gathering in Rome he was urged to

> continue the enterprise I had begun, all telling me that they had never before heard harmony of a single voice, accompanied by a single stringed instrument, with such power to move the passion of the soul [*muovere l'affetto dell'animo*].

The importance of Caccini's preface, and of the sentences quoted in particular, is that not only do they outline the 'new style', the *stile rappresentativo*, the so-called 'monodic' style, but they also clearly state that this style was intended to engage the passions. To do so was one of the prime aspirations of the Camerata, and indeed, one of the principal unifying artistic aims of the Baroque period.

Caccini also discussed another issue of significance, the nature and function of improvised ornamentation, which he believed should be placed at the service of the text. By adhering to principles which he laid down, singers might both avoid that 'laceration of the poetry' by which he characterized the old style, and succeed in appealing to the sensibilities. He aimed, in short, to respect the rhythm and cadences of ordinary speech, a type of expression to which he applied the term *sprezzatura*.

Caccini's preface provides us with a firm foundation for a survey of Baroque music, in that it clearly expresses a new practice, a new style and a new outlook influenced by some of the greatest thinkers of the time.

The 'modern style': basso continuo and tonality

Both the preface and the music of *Le nuove musiche* draw attention to the principal resources of the 'new style': monody, tonality, chromaticism, dissonance, recitative – all of which are inseparable from that most important element of music of the Baroque period, the basso continuo, or thorough-bass. A musical score as written, Caccini explains in his *Le nuove musiche*, was only an outline of what was required in performance. Whereas in the Renaissance the independent parts or voices were customarily of equal importance, the new style emphasized melody and bass, the latter acting as a foundation for additional melodic and harmonic material. The essence of Baroque texture is therefore to be found in the basso continuo, which implies the harmonies of all the parts, usually notated precisely by means of figures. The figures represent the harmonies and intervals to be played above the bass; by converting or 'realizing' these figures, a composer's harmonic prescription can be brought to life.

The term 'basso continuo' seems to have first been used in Italy around 1600, when it referred to the organ part of an ensemble. An important early use of both term and practice occurs in the collection *Concerti ecclesiastici ... con il basso continuo* (1602) of Lodovico Viadana (*c*.1560–1627), the earliest publication to include basso continuo, the *stile moderno*, with sacred vocal music.

While the 'realization' of a figured bass is a precise matter the arts of ornamentation and improvisation are not. The weight of responsibility borne by a keyboard continuo player is therefore considerable, for not only is he or she required to interpret correctly the figures written by the composer but also, as occasion arises, to ornament and to improvise within the boundaries of good taste as it was understood at the time.

With the emphasis of bass-supported melody as a central principle in Baroque composition came a gradual shift from modality towards tonality. The age-old modes used in Gregorian chant, scarcely changed through the sixteenth century, could no longer act as an intervallic vocabulary for a new style of music of the seventeenth century dependent on chords for its direction. But composers had first to get used to new possibilities of melodic freedom, including dissonance, before a system of chordal successions could be developed. Initially the tonic acted as an anchor for brief excursions to close diatonic chords such as the dominant, the fifth above the tonic. Only later in the century did tonality expand to include the type of formulae which both encircle the established tonic key and allow for a broad range of modulation to new key areas.

As tonality developed so various group forms began to take shape in which two or more distinct movements, displaying contrasting tonality and rhythm, nevertheless represented a coherent interdependent group structure. A number of basic formal schemes became established during the Baroque period: recitative and aria; the bi- or tri-partite scheme of a French overture; prelude and fugue, toccata and fugue; the symmetrical four-movement pattern of the *sonata da chiesa* or church sonata and the three- or four-movement scheme of the instrumental concerto.

It would be mistaken to suppose that all aspects of this new style of expression went unchallenged. In the first place the polyphonic writing of the Renaissance did not simply vanish with the swing of fashion towards vertically-orientated harmony. Not only did various systems of polyphonic modes play a complex part in the development of tonal harmony, but polyphony itself continued to thrive throughout the Baroque period. It influenced, above all, a tradition of imitative counterpoint which reached its highest artistic level with the fugues of Bach, while being subjected itself to a degree of reshaping. The organizational potential of tonal schemes allowed for a new contrapuntal complexity.

First and second practices: Monteverdi and madrigals

Writers and composers used a variety of terms to make the distinction between 'old' and 'new' practices, polyphony and tonality. Monteverdi called the two styles *prima prattica* and *seconda prattica*. However, the distinction concerned not only style and aim in composition but also the relative importance of text and music. Indeed, Monteverdi regarded the domination of text over music which characterized the 'new' style as the fundamental distinction between the two practices. 'By First Practice he understands the one that turns on the perfection of the harmony,' writes Monteverdi's brother, Giulio Cesare, in a manifesto printed with the *Scherzi Musicale* (1607):

> that is, the one that considers the harmony not commanded, but commanding, not the servant, but the mistress of the words, and this was founded by those first men who composed in our notation music for more than one voice, was then followed and amplified by Ockeghem, Josquin Desprez, Pierre de la Rue, Jean Mouton, Crequillon, Clemens non Papa, Gombert and others of those times, and was finally perfected by Messer Adriano with actual composition and by the most excellent Zarlino with most judicious rules.

Such distinctions though lucid in theory are seldom clear-cut in application. Late fifteenth- and early sixteenth-century music in Italy is often characterized by an interplay and interrelation of styles which, in accordance with the very nature of artistic change, were obliged to find means of co-existence. Much of the polemical writing of the time shows how tenaciously adherents of old and new held their ground, and a reconciliation between old and new had to be found.

Both Claudio Monteverdi and his brother published prefaces to madrigal books in support of the 'second practice', but it is in a vigorous controversy between Monteverdi and Giovanni Maria Artusi (c.1540–1613) that the issues of technique and composition are most clearly laid out. At the simplest level the issues reflect the changing attitudes of two generations: Artusi the older, more conservative composer versus Monteverdi the younger and more rebellious.

Monteverdi accepted the advances of concerted instrumental music, improvised counterpoint, ornamented singing, the use of dance rhythms, and the enlarged vocabulary of chromaticism blended with the diatonic scale. Artusi, on the other hand, viewed these innovations as corrupt, and in his dialogue *L'Artusi, overo Delle imperfettioni della moderna musica* (1600) he criticized innovations in several of Monteverdi's madrigals, though without mentioning the composer by name. 'The texture was not unpleasing,' states one of the two interlocutors of the dialogue,

> But ... insofar as it introduced new rules, new modes, and new turns of phrase, these were harsh and little pleasing to the ear, nor could they be otherwise; for so long as they violate the good rules – in part founded upon experience, the mother of all things, in part observed in nature, and in part proved by demonstration – we must believe them deformations of the nature and propriety of true harmony far removed from the object of music, which as Your Lordship said yesterday, is delectation.

After the dialogue's publication Artusi received letters defending the unnamed composer, and answered them in a second book (1603). Not until 1605, when Monteverdi replied to his critic in a letter published with the fifth book of madrigals, was the composer's identity revealed.

In the years leading up to the turn of the seventeenth century it was, above all, the madrigal form by which Italy judged her own prowess in music and by which she was judged in other European countries. Madrigals are of all 'musical works those most worthy of respect', wrote the Italian composer Domenico Mazzocchi (1592–1665). The number of madrigal collections published in Italy between c.1580 and 1620 is considerable, and in them we find many valuable insights as to the means by which the first and second practices came to terms with each other. One of the earliest composers to explore the musical techniques and forms of expression which soon were to be termed 'second practice' was the Flemish born Cipriano de Rore (c.1515–65). Although in his church music de Rore adhered to tradition, in his later madrigals he showed a range of techniques, complementing the various images of the texts. The essence of de Rore's progressive outlook is variety – rhythmic variety, tonal variety and modal variety. By his abandonment of polyphonic homogeneity in favour of colouring nuances of the text, de Rore won the admiration of composers of later generations, including Monteverdi.

No less significant to these younger composers were the madrigals of Carlo Gesualdo, Prince of Venosa (c.1560–1613). An important collection of these in a Genoese edition of 1613 was in circulation throughout the seventeenth century. Gesualdo's bold counterpoint and pervading chromaticism were carefully studied by later composers, and moulded the image of the seventeenth-century madrigal. In a letter of 1706 Alessandro Scarlatti informs us that he often took pleasure in performing and studying the madrigals of Gesualdo. The German composer Heinrich Schütz, writing from Dresden in 1632, asks that copies of madrigals by Gesualdo and his Neapolitan disciples be sent to him from Italy; and Girolamo Frescobaldi directed performances of Gesualdo's madrigals on viols in the Roman household of the Barberini family.

Madrigal poems and libretti

Several extensive anthologies of madrigal poetry, printed in Italy in the late sixteenth and early seventeenth centuries, were of significance to composers. The two poets most frequently set by Italian madrigalists and monodists were Giovanni Battista Guarini (1538–1612) and Giovan Battista Marino (1569–1625). Guarini was a diplomat and courtier whose pastoral poetry caught the imagination of writers and composers in many European countries. His finest work was Il pastor fido (1584), a tragi-comic pastorale whose success brought the pastoral vogue in Europe to its height. Guarini's theories of tragi-comedy would influence both the style and content of opera libretti; and Il pastor fido, in particular, with its two pairs of lovers, pair of villains, unmasking of false identities and changing fortunes, became a model for Venetian opera libretti.

Marino was a Neapolitan whose Rime became one of the most successful anthologies of the period. Marco da Gagliano, Salomone Rossi, Ascanio Mayone, Frescobaldi, Sigismondo d'India, Kapsberger, Schütz and many other composers turned to Marino's madrigal poetry.

Concision of form, subtlety of expression, easily recognized 'affections' and symmetry were among its virtues, and helped to establish the genre of *poesia per musica* (poetry enhanced by music). Marino's mythologically based poem 'Adone' reflected the new thinking of the time in attempting to 'move' or involve the passions of its readers.

The heroic poems of two earlier Italian writers provided composers with an abundance of stories which lent themselves to musical treatment. *Orlando furioso* by Ludovico Ariosto (1474–1533) was published in its first version in 1516 and became especially popular with musicians, and above all with the madrigalists of the last decades of the sixteenth century. The first complete edition of *Gerusalemme liberata* by Torquato Tasso (1544–95) was published in 1581 and soon became a rival to Ariosto's poem. Like *Orlando furioso*, *Gerusalemme liberata* was written in the 'ottava rima' long associated with the epic. The large number of libretti based on episodes from these two great poems bears witness to their popularity among opera composers of the seventeenth and eighteenth centuries.

Madrigals and solo songs

Music for solo voice with instrumental accompaniment rapidly supplanted the polyphonic madrigal during the first two decades of the seventeenth century. The main forms adopted by composers in the new style outlined by Caccini in his *Le nuove musiche* (p. 14) were the continuo madrigal and the monodic aria.

The monodic style of instrumentally accompanied songs for solo voice flourished in Italy during the first three decades of the seventeenth century, after which it began to yield to the chamber cantata. Monodies were usually secular songs which fell into two principal schematic patterns. One of these was the 'strophic' or 'stanzaic' song in which all the stanzas or verses of a text are sung to the same music. In *Le nuove musiche* Caccini terms this type of song an 'aria'. The other, which Caccini termed 'madrigal', was a through-composed song in which new music was provided for each stanza. The strophic song lent itself to formal variety, above all that of the 'strophic variation'. This scheme, set within the framework of a fixed melodic harmonic pattern in the bass though it might vary rhythmically, enabled composers to elaborate the vocal melody of the first strophe in subsequent strophes, so permitting greater emphasis on certain words and phrases in the text and thereby a greater expressive intensity. Orpheus's song 'Possente spirto' in the third act of Monteverdi's opera *Orfeo* (1607) provides a fine example of the 'strophic variation', whose origins lie in the vocal and instrumental variation-techniques of the sixteenth century. Instruments commonly used for accompanying solo songs at this time included the harpsichord and various members of the lute family.

Monteverdi: The 'affections' expressed

Italian music of the seventeenth century is dominated by the genius of Claudio Monteverdi (1567–1643). Monteverdi was born in Cremona, and received his earliest musical education from Marc'Antonio Ingegneri (c.1547–92), *Maestro di cappella* of the cathedral. His first publication, *Sacrae cantinunculae*, a volume of three-part motets, appeared in 1582, when the composer was fifteen years old. His first set of madrigals was printed in 1585 and was followed by a second book in 1590, at about the time he was establishing contact with the Gonzaga family at the court of Mantua. By 1592 he was settled at the Mantuan court where he held the post of *Suonatore di vivuola*, an imprecise title indicating a viol or violin player. As well as taking part in the weekly concerts given by the Duke's small but virtuoso band, Monteverdi worked on a third set of madrigals which was published in 1592, and which proved popular enough to be reprinted two years later. His abilities seem to have been recognized, for in 1595 he was among the courtiers chosen to accompany Duke Vincenzo on his expedition to Austria and Hungary against the Turks. It must therefore have been all the more disappointing for Monteverdi when, following the death of the *Maestro di cappella* Giaches de Wert in 1596, the post went to another, longer-serving court musician, Benedetto Pallavicino. Pallavicino's death in 1601 prompted Monteverdi to write to the Duke requesting the post, and it was granted in the same year. Monteverdi published a fourth book of madrigals in 1603, a fifth in 1605 containing his reply to Artusi (p. 17), and his *Scherzi musicali* in 1607. Monteverdi's first opera, *Orfeo*, was produced before the Accademia degli Invaghiti in Mantua in February 1607. Later in the year he returned to Cremona, where he was profoundly affected by the death of his wife, Claudia de Cattaneis, formerly a singer at the court of Ferrara. She had borne him three children, one of whom, a daughter, died soon after birth. In the autumn of 1607 Monteverdi returned to Mantua where it was planned to stage his second opera *L'Arianna* during Carnival. In the event another opera, *La Dafne* by Marco da Gagliano, was substituted, and *L'Arianna* was eventually performed in 1608 in celebration of the return to Mantua of the heir-apparent, Francesco Gonzaga, after his marriage to Margaret of Savoy in Turin. *L'Arianna* was a success, and its celebrated lament much admired. It was also for the Gonzaga wedding that Monteverdi wrote his ballet, *Il ballo della ingrate* (1608).

These successes marked the close of a fruitful period in Mantua, and Monteverdi returned to his native Cremona for a year, weary and dispirited. Both his father and he attempted vainly to secure his release from service at the Mantuan court, and by 1610, though not yet released from Mantua, Monteverdi was looking for other employment. In 1612 Duke Vincenzo died and Francesco, to whose wedding celebrations Monteverdi had so richly contributed, dismissed him without warning. He returned once more to Cremona, and in the following year (1613) was appointed *Maestro di cappella* to the Venetian ducal chapel of S. Marco.

Three madrigal collections were published during Monteverdi's Venetian period. The earliest, the sixth book, probably completed at Mantua, appeared in 1614; in his new sphere of influence as *Maestro di cappella* Monteverdi found himself able to dispense with patronage and published the collection without a dedication. The seventh book was published in 1619, and the eighth, the celebrated *Madrigali guerrieri et amorosi* which contains *Il ballo delle ingrate* and the *Combattimento di Tancredi e Clorinda*, appeared in 1638. The immense variety in form and expression within the eight books reflects, not only the diversity of Monteverdi's genius, but also formal developments which had been taking place in Italy during the first three decades of the century.

Compared with these later collections, to which we shall return, Monteverdi's first three madrigal books are conventional. Book I, in particular, shows indebtedness to his teacher, Ingegneri, who had also taught another great madrigalist, Luca Marenzio (1553–99). Book II contains several pieces in which Monteverdi's expressive powers became apparent, especially 'Ecco mormorar l'onde', in which he tenderly and evocatively portrays Tasso's dawn breezes. Book III includes settings of texts mainly by Guarini, but also two groups of madrigals from Tasso's *Gerusalemme liberata* containing passages of recitative-like declamation. Books IV and V represent the greatest stylistic advance on previous publications, for they contain pieces utilizing all the newest techniques such as musical rhetoric and expressive harmony and melody which reflect Monteverdi's concern for the text. We have already mentioned the criticism levelled by Artusi at Monteverdi, which was prompted by the dissonant, contrapuntal character of several of the madrigals in these books. Here we find a musical rhetoric used not merely in the illustration of poetic images but also in shading textual detail. Effectively this represented a new concept of vocal music. In 'Svogava con le stelle' (Book IV) Monteverdi's harmonic colouring and declamatory freedom complement the passionate nature of Rinuccini's text, while 'Si ch'io vorrei morire', also from Book IV, consists of stylistically contrasting episodes where chords and tonal affirmation alternate with dissonance, chromaticism and counterpoint in an innovatory manner.

In the last six pieces of Book V Monteverdi makes a fundamental break with the traditional madrigal form by writing obligatory basso continuo parts. In the remaining three books and in the *Scherzi musicali* all the madrigals have a basso continuo, and in the seventh and eighth books an additional dimension is created by the use of instrumental ritornelli. These reprises provided yet another contrast between different musical elements, while at the same time increasing the dramatic potential of the emerging chamber monody. The psychological insight which Monteverdi brings to the settings of the texts of his later madrigals in duet form was unprecedented, and this aspect of his genius, combined with a fluent handling of forms both new and old, resulted in music of virtuosity, dramatic intensity and expressive depth.

Monteverdi was among the earliest composers to use solo voices (as for the opening of 'Ecco mormorar l'onde', in Book II) and to adopt basso continuo in five-part madrigal polyphony; but not until the seventh book, to which Monteverdi gave the title *Concerto*, did chamber monody finally prevail over madrigal polyphony. The diversity of the contents of this book not only reflects the versatility of Monteverdi's style but also reveals the variety of literary genres to which he turned. As '*Concerto*' implies, the emphasis is on pieces written in 'concertante' style. In the opening work, 'Tempro la cetra', four sections of a text by Marino are declaimed by a tenor solo voice, accompanied by a strophic bass and linked by an instrumental ritornello whose last repetition leads into a short ballet. Other notable compositions include 'Ohimè dov'è il mio ben', an 'ottava rima' by Tasso which Monteverdi sets as a duet in four sections for two sopranos, whose virtuoso variations derive from the *romanesca* bass theme ('*romanesca*' being a famous sixteenth-century harmonic pattern first found in Spanish lute books); 'Con che soavita' in which he vividly sets a Guarini text for solo soprano with an instrumental accompaniment of strings, lutes, harpsichords and organ; 'Chiome d'oro', a canzonetta for two sopranos with two violins and basso continuo; and, concluding the seventh book, 'Tirsi e Clori', which Monteverdi had written for Mantua in 1615 and which he called *Ballo Concertato con voci et instrumenti à 5*.

Nearly twenty years separated the publication of Monteverdi's seventh book, the *Concerto* of 1619, and the appearance of the eighth, *Madrigali guerrieri et amorosi*, in 1638. This book, too, contains pieces in a diversity of styles. We have already noted the significant place of rhetoric in the development of Baroque music; in his preface to the eighth book Monteverdi enters into the art of oration, and writes of certain recognizable 'affections'. He notes that the three 'affects' of wrath (*ira*), humility or prayer (*humiltà* or *supplicatione*) and temperance (*temperanza*) have only two equivalents in music: the *stile molle* of humility and the *stile temperato* of temperance. The 'affect' of anger or warlike passions is so far missing in music. Monteverdi therefore introduces a third style, which he calls the *stile concitato*, that by rhythmic subdivisions of repeated notes was capable of evoking emotions of agitation and terror, and was intended to complement the 'affect' of bravery described by Plato in Book 3 of his *Republic*: 'Take that harmony which in tone and accent imitates men who bravely go into battle.' The most celebrated application of *stile concitato* occurs in Monteverdi's setting of stanzas from the twelfth canto of Tasso's *Gerusalemme liberata*, the *Combattimento di Tancredi e Clorinda*, where he moves the listener with a vivid musical representation of the two opposing affects of humility (*stile molle*) and anger (*stile concitato*). Also in Book VIII, *Il lamento della ninfa* for soprano, two tenors and a bass, and *Il ballo delle ingrate* both contain vividly contrasting musical images, whose skilful handling reflects the maturity of Monteverdi's distinctive style.

The *Scherzi musicali* of 1632 and the *Madrigali e canzonette* were to be published as Monteverdi's ninth book in 1651, after the composer's death. The most celebrated piece from the second collection of *Scherzi musicali* is the duet for two tenors, 'Zefiro torna'. The poem is by Rinuccini, and is not to be confused with the Petrarch text which Monteverdi had already affectingly set as a five-part madrigal in the sixth book. 'Zefiro torna' is built upon a concise bass motif, of two measures. Although the 'ostinato' bass recurs a great many times, Monteverdi uses this unifying device to great effect; monotony is avoided by means of the expressive subtlety with which contrasting affects are portrayed. 'Zefiro torna' and 'Armato il cor', also for two tenors, seem to have enjoyed popularity in Monteverdi's lifetime; both were imitated by the German composer Schütz, and both were included in the posthumous publication *Madrigali e canzonette* (unauthorized by the composer).

The affecting mood-changes that distinguish Monteverdi's madrigals are also a key to the success of composers' settings of pastoral poems, such as Guarini's *Il pastor fido*, while the combination of monologue, dialogue, and chorus with continuous music stimulated the growth of opera as a framework ideally suitable for the accommodation of music and dance, rhetoric and spectacle – indeed all artistic impulse.

3
Italian innovations: opera, instrumental and sacred music

The birth of opera

THE PRECURSORS OF OPERA were the *intermedi* and related forms in which music, either for singing or dancing, played an intermittent or episodic part in an otherwise spoken entertainment. Among the most celebrated *intermedi* were six performed in Florence in 1589 at the marriage of Duke Ferdinand I of Tuscany. These consisted of singing, dancing and instrumental pieces performed with elaborate stage machinery and lavish costumes. Five years later, in 1594, a further step was taken towards the creation of a drama with continuous music, or *dramma per musica*; this was a madrigal cycle by the Modenese composer Orazio Vecchi (1550–1605). Vecchi called his madrigal-comedy, *L'Amfiparnaso*, a '*commedia harmonica*'. The music is written in a five-voice madrigal texture.

The earliest attempts to reach a musically continuous dramatic style were made largely by those composers and poets who were associated with the thriving Camerate of the time, mentioned in previous chapters. Among the first such experiments for which the music has survived is a work which is difficult to classify entitled *Rappresentatione di Anima et di Corpo*. Its composer was a Roman, Emilio de' Cavalieri (*c*.1550–1602), who had already attempted the setting of two texts to music in his short pastorales, *Il Satiro* and *La disperazione di Fileno*, performed at the Tuscan court in Florence in 1591. *Rappresentatione di Anima et di Corpo* was first performed in Rome in 1600 in the Oratory of Sta Maria in Valicella. Its subject, a dispute between the body and the soul, and its place of performance, have often led to the work being classified as an oratorio, but the nature of the drama is more closely related to opera. Cavalieri approached his task according to his understanding of the aesthetics discussed by the Camerate. He adopted a system of extended recitative interspersed with vocal solos, or *canzonette spirituali*, and choruses singing in continuo style with figured bass instrumental parts.

The entire production was mounted with scenery, costumes and dancing. Cavalieri's aims are clearly outlined in the work's preface which was written by Alessandro Guidotti:

Let the singer have a beautiful voice with good intonation, well supported, and let him sing with expression, soft and loud, and without passagework; and in particular he should express the words well, so that they may be understood, and accompany them with gestures and movements, not only gestures of the hands but other gestures that are efficacious aids in moving the affections. The instruments also should be well played, and their numbers be more or less according to the place – theatre or hall – which to be proportionate to this recitation in music should not seat more than a thousand persons . . .

And to give some idea of the instruments which have served in a similar situation for rehearsal, a double lyre, a clavicembalo, a chitarrone, or theorbo as they say, all together make a good effect: as do likewise a sweet-toned organ with chitarrone. And Sig. Emilio [Cavalieri] would approve of changing the instruments according to the *affetti* [expression] of the performer . . . The Sinfonie and Ritornelli can be played with a great number of instruments; and one violin, which plays the soprano, will make a fine effect.

Opera in Florence and Mantua.
Peri's Euridice, Monteverdi's Orfeo

Some months after the performance in Rome of Cavalieri's *Rappresentatione di Anima et di Corpo* an event took place in Florence of even greater significance to the creation of *dramma per musica*. This was the performance on 6 October 1600 of *Euridice* as part of the celebrations of the wedding by proxy of Henry IV of France to Maria de' Medici. The music was by Jacopo Peri, the libretto by Rinuccini and the direction by Cavalieri. All three had been members, along with Caccini and da Gagliano, of Count Bardi's Camerata in Florence. Bardi himself had left for Rome in 1592, but the group continued to meet at the house of Jacopo Corsi, a Florentine amateur poet and musician. Corsi had previously enlisted the help of Peri and Rinuccini in setting to music Rinuccini's tragi-comic pastoral poem, *Dafne*, first performed at Corsi's palace in 1597 and twice subsequently. In the *stile rappresentativo* of that work, poet and composer attempted, in Peri's own words, to achieve 'a harmony surpassing that of ordinary speech but falling so far below the melody of song as to take an intermediate form'.

Whereas only fragments of *Dafne* have been preserved, *Euridice* may be considered the first opera to have survived complete. More than any other of the earlier experiments in *dramma per musica*, *Euridice* became a model for composers. Like Cavalieri's *Rappresentatione di Anima et di Corpo* it consists of recitatives, airs, choruses and dances in which Peri once again sought a path between singing and speech, as he himself explained:

> I knew also that in our speech we intone certain syllables in such a way that a harmony can be built upon them, and in the course of speaking we pass through many that are not so intoned until we reach another that permits a movement to a new consonance. Keeping in mind those manners and accents that serve us in our grief and joy, and similar states, I made the bass move in time with these, faster or slower according to the affections. I held it fixed through both dissonances and consonances, until the voice of the speaker, having run through various notes, arrived at a syllable that, being intoned in ordinary speech, opened the way to a new harmony.

From Peri's declared aims we see that the *dramma per musica* was primarily a literary form and only secondarily a musical composition during this period of its development. In *Euridice* both poet and composer aimed at economy, consistency and simplicity of expression. Their achievements are affectingly demonstrated in the poignant account by the messenger, Daphne, of the death of Eurydice, 'Per quel vago boschetto'. Peri does not succeed in maintaining the strong tonal focus of its opening passages but the subtly contrived illusion of speech-rhythm in this narrative monody is effective. The score of *Euridice* consists only of singing parts and figured continuo bass making provision for instrumental realization.

Two years after the performance of Peri's *Euridice* another member of the Florentine Camerata, Giulio Caccini, whose *Le nuove musiche* is discussed in Chapter 2, performed his own version of Rinuccini's libretto. However it was Peri's setting, not Caccini's, that became the model for composers of a lyrical *dramma per musica* at this time. Outstanding among such composers was Monteverdi, whose genius lifts his first work in this form, *La favola d'Orfeo*, beyond the range of the experimental Florentine operas of Peri and Caccini. Nevertheless, many ingredients of Monteverdi's recitative style were acquired from Peri's *Euridice*, and in both operas the illusion of speech-rhythm is skilfully maintained.

The text of Monteverdi's *Orfeo* is by Alessandro Striggio (*c*.1573–1630), who like Monteverdi was employed at the court of Mantua.

Striggio's libretto keeps more closely to events as recounted in the classical legend than does Rinuccini's, and there is greater emphasis on its tragic element. Fable and myth dominated the subjects chosen by librettists during the first half of the seventeenth century. Ovid was among their most important sources but it was the pastoral poems of Tasso, Ariosto and Guarini, above all, that provided material for the fashionable tragi-comical pastorals. Peri's *Euridice* and Monteverdi's *Orfeo* are both representative of this fashion.

Orfeo was first performed on 24 February 1607 at the ducal palace of Mantua, where it was appreciatively received by an audience of connoisseurs. The production included dancing as well as a chorus of singers, approaching forty in number. Although the larger size of the orchestra is one of the features which immediately distinguishes Monteverdi's opera from Peri's, both works, and indeed all early seventeenth-century operas, were essentially understood as 'singers' music'. The difference between Monteverdi's *Orfeo* and works by others is essentially Monteverdi's superior dramatic gifts and his successful fusion of music and text to create a convincing opera as we understand the form today. Only with the opening of theatres, the establishment of opera companies and the development of the concerto grosso principle, which we shall consider in a later chapter, did the orchestra begin to assume a more important role. Nevertheless, in *Orfeo* Monteverdi attempts to organize a substantial group including trombones, cornetts, recorders, violins, a harp and continuo instruments for the first time, thus signposting a path for the future development of the orchestra.

Following the success of *Orfeo* Monteverdi wrote his opera *Arianna* (1608), of which only a celebrated lament, 'Lasciate me morire', has survived (p. 65). Giovanni Battista Doni (1595–1647) in his *Annotazioni sopra il Compendio de' generi, e de' modi della musica* (1640) writes of three types of dramatic monody: the narrative, recitational and expressive. Quoting Arianna's lament as an example of the expressive style, he goes on to describe it as 'the most beautiful composition that has yet been seen in stage and theatrical music'. Monteverdi himself clearly thought well of it, for he subsequently arranged the melody as a five-part madrigal and later again used it for a sacred text. The *Lamento d'Arianna* was based on the lament of Olympia from Ariosto's *Orlando furioso*. His model, in turn, was taken from the lament of Arianna in Ovid's *Heroides* which circulated widely in translation. Spectators would therefore have been familiar with the literary tradition behind this scene-type, the lament of the woman protagonist.

Prefaces and manifestos of the time are largely agreed on points of style in their advice to singers, affording us a valuable insight to the aspirations of the early Florentine opera composers, as well as providing a useful summary of the character and function of *stile rappresentativo*. Da Gagliano, for example, advises in the preface to one of his own operas:

> ... in such affairs the music is not everything, but many other things are necessary, without which harmony, no matter how excellent, would be of little use. In this respect many people are deceived, for they wear themselves out making *gruppi, trilli, passaggi* and *exclamazioni* with no regard for their purpose or whether or not they are apropos. I certainly do not intend to deprive myself of these adornments, but I want them to be used in the right time and place, as in the choral songs such as the *ottava* stanza 'Chi da' lacci d'amore vive disciolto', which is put in this place so we can hear the grace and the disposition of the singers ... But where the sense does not demand it, leave aside every ornament, so as not to act like that painter who knew how to paint cypress trees and therefore painted them everywhere. Instead, try to pronounce every syllable distinctly so the words are understood and let this be the principal aim of every singer whenever he sings, especially in performing on the stage, and let him be persuaded that real pleasure is increased by understanding the words.

Roman opera: court patronage and grand spectacle

During the thirty years or so between Monteverdi's Florentine operas and those which he composed for Venice the scene of *dramma per musica* shifted from Florence to Rome. The most influential patrons of Roman opera were the Barberini family, the ruling house from the time of the election of Matteo Barberini as Pope Urban VIII in 1623. As in the Florentine operas pastoral subjects were favoured, but productions were more lavish and greater emphasis was placed on the visual aspect of the drama. Machines and elaborate scenery were features of early Roman opera, recalling not so much the simple pastorals of Peri, Gagliano and Caccini as their predecessors, the Florentine *intermedi*. Clarity, integrity and directness of sentiment, which had been the aspirations of the early Florentine composers, gave way in Rome to extravagant scenic effects and dramatic irrelevancies. Recitative, which had been the vehicle, *par excellence*, for moving the hearers' affections in Florentine opera, now became little more than a means of linking the somewhat disparate attractions that comprised Roman opera.

The principal composers of opera at Rome in the 1630s were Domenico Mazzocchi (1592–1665), Marco Marazzoli (*c*.1602–62),

Stefano Landi (*c.*1586–1639) whose opera, *Sant' Alessio*, inaugurated the Barberini Teatro Quattro Fontane, probably in 1631, Loreto Vittori (*c.*1590–1670) and Luigi Rossi (1598–1653). Outstanding among the composers patronized by the Barberini family was Luigi Rossi whose opera *Il Palazzo incantato d'Atlante* (1642) enjoyed a great success at the Carnival season. The librettist was Giulio Rospigliosi (1600–69), who had also provided Landi with the libretto for *Sant' Alessio* as well as writing two comic operas, *Chi soffre speri* (1637), with music by Mazzocchi and Marazzoli, and *Dal male il bene* (1653), with music by Antonio Maria Abbatini (*c.*1610–*c.*1679). A revival of *Chi soffre speri* with scenic effects by the great architect Gian Lorenzo Bernini (to whom Pope Urban VIII had entrusted the furnishing and decoration of St Peter's) took place in 1639.

Venetian opera: Monteverdi and Cavalli

Five years after the inauguration of the Teatro Quattro Fontane in Rome an event of comparable importance in the history of opera took place in Venice. This was the re-opening of the Teatro San Cassiano as an opera house in 1637; but whereas in Rome the proprietors of the theatre were the ruling family, in Venice it was the aristocracy and influential merchant class who exerted control. Although visual extravagance was an important element in Venetian opera, a greater emphasis was placed on the music. San Cassiano opened with a performance of *Andromeda*, produced jointly by the librettist Benedetto Ferrari (1597–1681) and the composer Francesco Manelli (1595–1667).

The leading figures in the early period of Venetian opera were Monteverdi and his gifted pupil Cavalli. Monteverdi wrote four operas for Venice but the music of only two has survived: *Il Ritorno d'Ulisse in patria* (1641) and *L'Incoronazione di Poppea* (1642). In these operas Monteverdi is concerned above all with human relationships. Apart from the prologue, the libretto of the first, by a Venetian nobleman, Giacomo Badoaro (1602–54), is based on Homer's account of the Ulysses story in the *Odyssey*. It gave Monteverdi an opportunity for vivid characterization, for instance in the finely shaded portrayal of Penelope, or in representing the wittily affected mannerisms of Eurymachus, the page. It is in his last opera, *L'Incoronazione di Poppea*, however, that the truth of Monteverdi's psychological insight in the portrayal of both tragedy and comedy is most evident. In this opera myth is abandoned in favour of history, which Monteverdi handles on a variety of levels with realism and deep humanity. Recitative, aria and duet alternate and merge into one another with a subtlety which reflects the changing emotions of the characters. Comic and serious scenes follow each other with a fluency that mirrors life itself, while Monteverdi's powers of musical characterization and his compassion combine to create a vivid dramatic masterpiece.

The most successful of Monteverdi's successors in Venetian opera was Francesco Caletti (1602–76) who adopted the name of Cavalli after his first patron, Federico Cavalli, one-time Venetian governor of the small town of Crema where Cavalli was born. Cavalli's early musical life was centred on S. Marco in Venice where his teacher, Monteverdi, was *Maestro di cappella*. Cavalli became second organist there in 1639, the year in which his first opera, *Le nozze di Teti e di Peleo*, was staged at the Teatro San Cassiano. Within the following decade he produced a further eight operas for this theatre, among them *Egisto* (1643), *Ormindo* (1644), and *Giasone* (1648/9) which was played more than any other of his operas during his lifetime.

While in the later operas of Monteverdi drama, music and staging achieved a balanced synthesis, in those of Cavalli and his generation the aria became increasingly the most important element. As yet, however, there was no set pattern of alternating recitative and aria. Natural speech-rhythms are characteristic of Cavalli's recitative – nearly all of it 'semplice', accompanied only by continuo – just as with Monteverdi's operas, and the influence of the concertato madrigal is strong; but the dramatic monologue, such a vital component in the earliest operas, now began to yield to more songful, arioso passages, sometimes unified by a single basic rhythm. Cavalli's music is subtly responsive to the texts, and rapidly changing moods or situations are vividly portrayed, just as with Monteverdi. The librettists with whom Cavalli collaborated most frequently were Giovanni Faustini (*c.*1619–51) and Nicolo Minato (*c.*1630–98). Between them they provided Cavalli with stories ranging from the mythological to real heroic events. Cavalli wrote almost thirty operas, mostly for Venice, although many were performed in other Italian cities as well. His activities in Paris between 1660 and 1662 followed on from his most productive period, and will be discussed in a later chapter.

Cavalli's operas effectively define Venetian opera between the years 1640 and 1660, and only in the figure of Cesti may we recognize any serious rival. Pietro Antonio Cesti (*c.*1623–69) was born in Arezzo, and joined the Franciscan order in 1637. His first operatic venture was *Orontea* which was successfully performed at the Teatro Santissimi Apostoli in Venice in 1649. Although some scenes in Cesti's operas are almost entirely set in recitative, the alternating recitative and aria pattern was further strengthened. Cesti's melodies are often tinged with melancholy, though he was gifted in handling comedy. His later operas, however, are of a different character, and in all but one or two instances were conceived as court entertainments rather than for public performance in the theatre. Cesti's *Il pomo d'oro* is one of the most celebrated examples of Baroque court opera on a grand scale. It was composed to celebrate the marriage of the Emperor Leopold I of Austria and the Infanta Margherita of Spain, and was performed at the Viennese court in 1667. Among its notable features were an unusually large instrumental ensemble (an earlier but smaller counterpart of which we can find in Monteverdi's court opera *Orfeo*) and no less than twenty-four different stage sets (p. 66).

Opera in Germany

Opera was not long in spreading beyond its native Italy, and performances of Italian opera are recorded in Salzburg as early as 1618. The subdivision of Germany into petty dukedoms and principalities, each favouring different elements of imported artistic styles, precluded any unified development. Among the most important centres for the cultivation of Italian opera, and foreign musical styles generally, were Vienna, Dresden, Brunswick, Weissenfels and, later, Hamburg. Unlike other centres, however, Hamburg succeeded in establishing opera in the vernacular, and while arias were usually sung in Italian, recitative was generally in German.

Opera in Hamburg was established by Gerhard Schott (1641–1702), who together with the celebrated Hamburg organist Johann Adam Reincken (1623–1722) and Johann Theile (1646–1724) built an opera house on the Gänsemarkt which opened in 1678. This was the first public opera house to be established outside Italy. Schott himself intermittently acted as its director, in the early years funding it partly from municipal resources and partly, perhaps, from personal assets. During the late seventeenth century Hamburg's trading prosperity enabled it to acquire the political importance that Venice had previously enjoyed, and during the following century the city was to become one of the most important bourgeois musical centres in Europe. The establishment of mainly German-language opera nevertheless met obstacles arising indirectly from internal political unrest and directly from the open condemnation of stage entertainments by the Pietist branch of the Lutheran Church. An effort to reach a compromise with the Church is reflected in the choice of subjects of the early Hamburg operas, which were predominantly sacred. The first of these was the work of Theile, a former pupil of Schütz (p. 43). Theile's *Adam und Eva* was first performed in 1678 and was followed by several operas based on sacred texts by German composers, as well as by adaptations of Italian and French libretti. Hamburg bourgeois opera was in no sense a national opera, but an entertainment aimed at a society of wealthy businessmen, foreign diplomats and the cosmopolitan element to be found in any international trading centre. It depended for its well-being on box-office receipts and so needed to cater for a wide variety of artistic taste.

The cosmopolitan Hamburg outlook is still reflected in the operas of composers of the following generation, notably Reinhard Keiser (1674–1739) and Georg Philipp Telemann (1681–1767). Keiser's earliest operas were performed at the Brunswick court during the early 1690s, but in 1695 he moved to Hamburg which was to be his main sphere of activity for the remainder of his life. In 1702 he assumed directorship of the Theater am Gänsemarkt, but during a period of absence from Hamburg between 1718 and 1723 he was supplanted by Telemann who arrived as the city's new music director (1721), taking over the administration of the theatre in addition to his prescribed duties.

Keiser occupies a commanding position in German Baroque opera by virtue of his prolific output and the skill with which he enlivens the plots of his libretti. This skill can be seen above all in his dramatic handling of recitative and his resourceful, imaginative deployment of instrumental textures, well displayed in scenes such as that at the beginning of the second act of *Croesus* (1710, revised 1730). The models which Keiser took for his operas were varied and include French *tragédie lyrique* and *opéra-ballet*; but more important was Italian opera, above all the seventeenth-century Venetian opera models afforded by Steffani. Agostino Steffani (1654–1728) was one of the most gifted Italian composers resident in Germany during the late seventeenth and early eighteenth century. He lived at the Munich court for twenty-one years, after which he entered the service of Duke Ernst August of Hanover. The Duke shortly after established a permanent Italian opera company and appointed Steffani *Kapellmeister*. Between 1689 and 1697 Steffani wrote some half-dozen operas for Hanover, all of which were staged in Hamburg by the turn of the century.

The opera which resulted from these models was a dramatic entertainment of a distinctive character comprising a rich variety of musical forms, and situations both serious and comic. Hamburg audiences liked to understand all that they heard, and so a tradition was established that recitatives, which narrate the story, were translated into German while arias and set pieces remained in their original language, almost invariably Italian. Such adjustments often required considerable rearrangement, and together with the occasional insertion of extra dances and comic scenes to suit the taste of the Hamburg public, resulted in an entertainment substantially different from a composer's original conception.

During Telemann's directorship of the Theater am Gänsemarkt (1722–38) Keiser contributed several more operas, but in 1728, doubtless hampered by Telemann's forceful presence, he took up an appointment as *Kantor* of the cathedral, and thereafter directed his energy towards the production of sacred vocal music.

Hamburg opera thrived under Telemann's supervision. Not only did he continue to stage operas by other composers – notably Handel, fifteen of whose operas, including *Agrippina, Amadigi, Tamerlano* and *Radamisto*, were seen there between 1715 and 1734 – but he also contributed works of his own. The most successful of these was *Der geduldige Socrates* (1721), one of the earliest wholly comic operas to be staged in Hamburg. As in Keiser's operas there is a great diversity of formal structure in the arias and vocal ensembles, and an even greater variety of instrumental accompaniment. A notably effective scene, the 'Adonis Festival' which begins the third act, bears no direct relationship to the plot and shows us that German opera of the period resists conformity to its Italian model. With the intermezzo *Pimpinone* (1725), antedating Pergolesi's more celebrated *La Serva Padrona* by eight years, Telemann more consistently demonstrates his skill with comic opera.

Opera in Austria, Poland and Spain

Further south, Viennese court opera was mainly provided by Italians, notable among whom was the Venetian Antonio Caldara (*c*.1670–1736). Caldara became *vice-Kapellmeister* in 1715 and remained in the post for the rest of his life. He provided the court not only with a prodigious number of operas, mainly with texts by Zeno and Metastasio, but also with oratorios at the rate of at least one a year for the court's Lenten schedule. Indigenous composers of opera included the court *Kapellmeister* Johann Joseph Fux (1660–1741). Though chiefly remembered as a theorist, Fux was a prolific composer who provided the court with some twenty stage works and a considerably larger quantity of sacred music. Both the operas, such as the attractive *Dafne in Lauro* (1715), and the oratorios contain music which justify the words of the contemporary

German theorist and composer, Johann Adolph Scheibe (1708–76), when he wrote that 'although [Fux] was the most profound contrapuntalist, nevertheless he possessed the skill of writing lightly, appealingly and naturally ...'.

Italian influence also reached the *dramma per musica* of Poland and Spain, to east and west of Europe respectively. Throughout the seventeenth century opera in Poland was a court entertainment, cultivated above all through the enthusiasm of King Wladislav IV (1632–48). It was performed by musicians of the royal chapel at Warsaw, many of whom were Italian, rather than by Italian travelling companies. Between 1635 and 1648, the most productive period, no less than ten dramatic works were produced whose text and music were written at Warsaw. However opera in seventeenth-century Poland was invariably in Italian, and favoured themes of love and heroism expressed mainly through recitative; indeed, it was in almost every sense an Italian phenomenon.

Only two operas were performed in Spain during the seventeenth century. One of them, *La purpura de la rosa*, was written to celebrate the marriage of Princess Maria Teresa to Louis XIV in 1659; the other, *Celos aun del aire matan*, was performed late in 1660, or during the following year. The librettist in each was the great Spanish dramatist Calderón (1600–81). The composer of the earlier work has not been identified, but the music of the later opera was by Juan Hidalgo (*c*.1612–85). Both were performed in the Buen Retiro palace near Madrid. Music dramas thereafter gave way to plays which were partly sung and partly spoken, and which became known as *zarzuelas*. It has been well argued that *zarzuelas* were not uniquely Spanish products, but were rather in the tradition of Italianate operas diluted by the spoken word.

Italian instrumental forms. Frescobaldi

As in opera, so too in instrumental music did the Italians lead the way in the development and dissemination of new forms during the seventeenth century. We have seen that during the early years of the century vocal polyphony and monody were practised side by side; similarly with instrumental music around 1600, which made use of imitative contrapuntal pieces such as the ricercare, canzona, capriccio and fantasia, as well as adopting newer techniques associated with monody, such as basso continuo. Although the development of vocal and instrumental forms is closely related at this time, each had problems of its own which had to be solved in different ways. Instrumental composers needed to find ways of

Caricature of Girolamo Frescobaldi
by Bernini, drawn around 1640–45

sustaining a piece without the aid of a text as well as establishing an idiomatic style capable of diversity. The search for an eloquent means of expression is reflected in the variety of forms with which composers experimented during the early decades of the seventeenth century (though the inconsistency with which they applied their terminology creates confusion well into the following century, when, for instance, there is frequently no formal distinction signified by the terms 'sonata', 'concerto' and 'sinfonia', as applied by Italian composers to their music). Among the most important types of instrumental composition during the early Baroque were the canzona, the theme with variations (ostinato/ chaconne/passacaglia), the ricercare and the dance; but in each of them we may frequently find the distinguishing character of one of the others.

Perhaps the greatest Italian keyboard instrumental composer of the first half of the seventeenth century was Girolamo Frescobaldi (1583–1643). Frescobaldi was born in Ferrara but in 1608 was appointed organist at St Peter's, Rome, and apart from occasional leaves of absence, notably between 1628 and 1634 when he served at the ducal court in Florence, he remained in this post for the rest of his life. Although he wrote madrigals, arias, vocal and instrumental canzoni and masses, his reputation was founded on his keyboard virtuosity and on his compositions for organ and harpsichord. In the prefaces to his *Toccate e partite* (1615) and *Fiori musicali* (1635) Frescobaldi provides instructions for the performer, and from these we learn that he attached great importance to the emotional responses of the individual player.

Imagination and expressive freedom were essential prerequisites for an effective realization of his virtuoso and often experimental keyboard style. The individual character of Frescobaldi's instrumental music is strongly accentuated in the toccatas, correntes and partitas, or variation sets on popular tunes, contained in the 1615 collection, as also in its second, revised edition of 1616, where Frescobaldi added further variations to the three existing sets and included an additional set of variations on the celebrated 'La Follia'.

Development of the violin. The early sonata

Generally speaking, seventeenth-century composers specified the instrumentation required for the performance of their music. The specifications might often be of a general nature amounting to little more than a recommendation, and in many cases we cannot be certain as to the exact nature of the prescribed instrument. Instrumental idiom nevertheless became an important consideration in determining formal and interpretative aspects of a piece of music, and is of vital significance where bowed string music is concerned.

Although the first description of the four-stringed violin is found in a French treatise – the *Epitome musical* (1556) of Philibert Jambe de Fer (*c*.1515–*c*.1566) – it was northern Italy that fostered the earliest developments of the violin, for it was not only the centre of violin-making but also the home of the principal violin composers and virtuosi. In an environment where composers, instrument-maker and players were in constant touch it was hardly surprising that a rich exchange of ideas took place, resulting in a rapid expansion of technique and repertory. Even as early as 1619, Praetorius could write in his *Syntagma Musicum* that, 'since everyone knows about the violin family, it is unnecessary to indicate or write anything further about it'.

Two composers who made important contributions to the early development of the violin were Monteverdi and Marini. Independent violin parts occur in several of Monteverdi's madrigals in the *Scherzi musicali* and in his opera *Orfeo*, where idiomatic figurations occur well before the form of the violin sonata was established. Biagio Marini (1587–1663) further explored violin technique, notably in his *Sonate, symphonie . . . e retornelli*, Opus 8 (1629). Here, as with the violin music of his contemporaries, we find a deliberate attempt to imitate the expressive qualities of the human voice while at the same time exploring the instrument's technical potential. Tremoli, graded dynamics, double or even on occasion treble-stopping, and a fertile rhythmic and melodic invention contribute towards the brilliant, even at times passionate character of Marini's music. This pioneering spirit and search for new forms of expression should not, however, be seen in isolation but be understood rather as aims and aspirations of the seventeenth century in general.

The idiomatic, more virtuosic approach to violin-writing developed by composers such as Marini, Giovanni Battista Fontana (d.1630), Carlo Farina (c.1600–c.1640), Francesco Turini (c.1589–1656), Salomone Rossi (c.1570–c.1639), Giovanni Paolo Cima (c.1570–c.1622), Tarquinio Merula (c.1594–1665) and others played a significant part in the establishment of new forms, the most important of which was to be the sonata, discussed in Chapter 6. Although the term 'sonata' applied to an instrumental piece of music had been in use before the turn of the seventeenth century it was only by about 1650 that it began to signify a form distinct from the multi-sectional canzona from which it evolved. In the earlier decades of the century the terms 'sonata' and 'canzone' were synonymous when used to describe music for small ensembles, usually of strings, accompanied by a keyboard instrument; Merula's title *Canzoni overo Sonate concertate per chiesa e camera* (1637) is an instance of this usage.

Sacred music: old style versus new. Polychoral effects

Sacred music of early seventeenth-century Italy, like secular music, was strongly influenced by innovations of the period. At the root of the stylistic variety of sacred music throughout the century were the two fundamentally opposing practices termed *stile antico* and *stile moderno*. The concept of *stile antico* or 'old style' as one written in imitation of Palestrina's polyphony was especially upheld in Rome, where a traditional outlook among some musicians led them to regard the parity of vocal strands as an established foundation on which to base a church music idiom.

Venice, on the other hand, was more progressive in outlook. Here the developments which had taken place in church music style during the late sixteenth century influenced techniques in the seventeenth. Above all, there was the Venetian interest in polychoral effects and in the *stile concertato* or concerted style. The influential Flemish composer Adrian Willaert (c.1490–1562) had been an early exponent of antiphonal effects while occupying the post of *Maestro di cappella* at S. Marco in Venice. His antiphony, however, was conservative compared with that of Giovanni Gabrieli (c.1553–1612). Gabrieli was one of the most gifted and original exponents of polychoral techniques. His characteristic style features the deployment of *cori spezzati* (broken choirs), in which two and often more groups of singers were positioned in different parts of a building; the singers were furthermore frequently supported by and contrasted with instrumental groups, creating colourful spatial effects.

By the end of the sixteenth century the festive character of Venetian *cori spezzati* had attracted Roman composers. These remained loyal to the Palestrina tradition, up to a point, but introduced polychoral techniques to create a monumental effect, with vast assemblies of voices and instruments in opposition, sometimes referred to as 'colossal baroque'. Among the Roman composers who wrote in this style were Orazio Benevoli (1605–72), his pupil Ercole Bernabei (*c*.1621–87) and Virgilio Mazzocchi (*c*.1597–1646). One opponent of the new Roman outlook was the composer and writer on music, Marco Scacchi (*c*.1600–81). In 1643 Scacchi published an attack on the sacred compositions of one Paul Siefert, working in Danzig. Scacchi's polemic, entitled *Cribrum musicum ad triticum Syferticum*, criticized Siefert for the introduction of techniques incompatible with *stile antico*. While Scacchi was not opposed to developments in music – on the contrary he regarded diversity of style as one of the great virtues of the new music – he argued for the equal dignity but different functions of *stile antico* and *stile moderno*. A mixture of the two, he maintained, resulted in compromise and a departure from correctness.

In a letter to the German composer and organist Christoph Werner, and later in his *Breve discorso sopra la musica moderna* (1649), Scacchi attempts a classification of the styles which had gained wide acceptance in many European countries. Broadly these fell into three categories: *stylus ecclesiasticus* (church), *stylus cubicularis* (chamber) and *stylus theatralis* (theatre), with a variety of subdivisions. Scacchi's classification was taken up by his pupil Angelo Berardi, and by Christoph Bernhard (1628–92), who was at the Dresden court with Schütz. It also provided Fux in his celebrated treatise *Gradus ad Parnassum* (1725), and Johann Mattheson (1681–1764) in *Der vollkommene Capellmeister* (1739) with the basis for their own musical divisions. These treatises serve to illustrate the continuing opposition between *stile antico* and *stile moderno* – that struggle between tradition and progress, as some writers have seen it – which remained a vital issue throughout the Baroque period, from the *prima* and *seconda prattica* outlined by Monteverdi early in the seventeenth century to Mattheson's theoretical writings of the mid-eighteenth century.

Among the first Italian composers to adopt the *stile moderno* in church music was Lodovico Viadana (*c*.1560–1627). His *Cento concerti ecclesiastici* (1602) is the earliest known sacred vocal publication to include a basso continuo. Although the ideals of *prima prattica* were, in part, upheld – as, for instance, in the four-voice concerti which can be performed unaccompanied – Viadana's collection with its basso continuo is modern in outlook.

It is in the sacred music of Monteverdi, however, that we find the most ample accommodation of past forms with new developments. In 1610, while Monteverdi was at Mantua, he published a famous collection of sacred works which he dedicated to Pope Paul V, entitled *Sanctissimae virgini missa senis vocibus ad ecclesiarum choros ac Vespere pluribus decantandae – cum nonnullis sacris concentibus ad sacella sive principum cubicula accommodata* (Mass to the Most Holy Virgin for Six Voices for Church Choirs, and Vespers for Many Voices, together with Some Sacred Harmonies Suitable for Chapels or Princes' Chambers) – popularly known as 'the Monteverdi Vespers'. The component parts of this impressive publication are a mass, vesper psalms, two settings of the Magnificat, and motets. The *Missa de cappella* for six voices is freely modelled on themes from a motet, *In illo tempore*, by the Flemish composer Nicolas Gombert (*c*.1495–*c*.1560). This contrapuntal work adheres to the austere discipline of *stile antico* or *prima prattica* and is to this extent both academic and archaic. In the vesper psalms, by contrast, Monteverdi introduces a mixture of styles which are in the main forward-looking; here, he combines concertato elements with those of plainsong, contrasts instrumental with vocal idioms and solos with ensemble and chorus. The motets of the collection are, in comparison, more consistently rooted in the *stile moderno*, revealing in their vocal virtuosity the influence of opera. Especially striking is the opening responsorium, 'Domine ad adiuvandum me', in which Monteverdi has added an opposing six-part vocal texture to the radiant instrumental toccata of his Mantuan opera, *Orfeo* (1607).

Towards the end of his life and some twenty-eight years after he had been appointed *Maestro di cappella* at S. Marco, Venice, Monteverdi published a second collection of sacred music, *Selva morale e spirituale* (1641). Here as in the 1610 collection he included music composed in a diversity of styles, ranging from *stile antico* to psalm settings in concertato manner. A further collection was published posthumously in Venice in 1650, consisting mainly of a mass and psalms.

By the time the newest musical trends had penetrated the conservative church tradition in Italian cities, other European countries and Germany and France in particular had begun to assimilate the principles of *stile moderno* into their own established conventions.

4
Seventeenth-century Germany: Lutheran hymnody, Italian virtuosity

B Y THE BEGINNING OF THE SEVENTEENTH CENTURY the influence of the Italian Baroque had already affected musical tradition, not only in southern Germany and the Habsburg-ruled lands of Austro-Bohemia but also in the north and central regions. From the time of Hans Leo Hassler (1564–1612), a Nuremberg musician and pupil of Andrea Gabrieli in Venice, German composers had travelled to Italy to imbibe Baroque art at the source. However, the political and religious turmoil which erupted in the Thirty Years War (1618–48) fragmented development in all branches of the arts. As a result of this bitter, protracted conflict the Protestant areas of north and central Germany became further divided from the south, where, following the Peace of Westphalia in 1648, the Habsburg dynasty was compelled to accept the failure of efforts to reunite Germany in the Catholic faith.

While broadly speaking, Catholic composers in the southern German-speaking lands embraced the Italian style – what better example was there for them to follow than that set by Rome – Protestant composers further north were exposed to the more evenly divided influences of Italy and of France, who had played a significant role in protecting the German dukedoms and principalities from Habsburg encroachment. A major challenge to Protestant composers was to find a means of preserving the Lutheran hymnody within the context of new techniques from Italy, and to a lesser extent from France. The successful fusion which subsequently took place between the Lutheran chorale and the Venetian concertato style in a society dominated by Lutheran theology resulted in what the historian Manfred Bukofzer has termed 'the most original German contribution' to the history of Baroque music.

Italian influence: Praetorius, Schein, Scheidt

German sacred music during the first half of the seventeenth century is dominated by four great composers, all of whom, in different ways, experimented with and developed Italian techniques within the German and Lutheran tradition. The earliest is Michael Praetorius (1571–1621). In his nine-part series of chorales *Musae Sioniae*, published between 1605 and 1610, Praetorius applied a wide diversity of techniques to the German hymn; there are polychoral settings ranging from eight-part works for two choirs to settings for two voices, as well as simple homophonic harmonizations. Even greater stylistic advances can be seen in Praetorius's later collection, *Polyhymnia caduceatrix et panegyrica* (1619), where he drew upon ideas contained in the most up-to-date Italian techniques in compositions for two-, three- and four-voice concertato vocal groups, with choirs of instruments and voices. They may be seen in his setting of three verses from Luther's Christmas hymn 'Von Himmel hoch, da komm' ich her', where the writing achieves richness and variety in texture and in expression, and as the use of continuo suggests, is progressive in style.

Praetorius's three-part *Syntagma musicum*, a product of his last years, written between 1614 and 1618, attempts a systematic approach to the theory and practice of music, including in the second volume detailed information concerning the wide range of instruments available in his day. The third volume deals with the many-voiced concertato compositions of the kind collected in the *Polyhymnia caduceatrix*: 'and it is not unwelcome to the ears when the same part as that of the singer in an ensemble is played by the instrumentalist an octave higher or lower on cornetts, fiddles, flutes [recorders], trombones, or bassoons'. Praetorius's music is appealing in its diversity of forms, ranging from modest four-part hymn settings to pieces for as many as twelve voices, but with the work of his younger contemporary, Johann Hermann Schein (1586–1630), the *stile moderno* reaches its first peak of excellence in Germany.

Schein like Praetorius was the son of a pastor; his musical training included a period as a soprano in the Hofkapelle of the Elector of Saxony at Dresden, followed in 1603 by four years at Schulpforta, a school near Naumburg specializing in music and the humanities. Afterwards Schein went on to study law and the liberal arts at Leipzig University. His subsequent appointments included *Kapellmeister* to Duke Johann Ernst the Younger at Weimar and *Thomaskantor* at Leipzig, where he succeeded Sethus Calvisius (1556–1615) in the autumn of 1616.

Schein was equally active in the spheres of sacred and secular music, but apart from a colourful collection of instrumental dances, *Banchetto musicale* (1617), his chief interest was in writing for the voice. Schein's first collection of sacred music, *Cymbalum Sionium sive Cantiones sacrae* (1615), contained choral works without basso continuo but of

Portrait of Johann Hermann Schein, composer in the *stile moderno*

considerable stylistic variety. His next publication, however, *Opella nova, geistlicher Concerten ... auff italiänische Invention componirt* (1618), reveals both a more modern outlook and greater personal means of expression: each of the sacred concertos is composed for three to five voices with basso continuo, and Schein's attempt to illustrate the meaning of the words with evocative harmonies gives the collection a distinctive character. A second collection of *Opella nova* (1626) differs in that rather less than half the pieces are based on hymns, the remainder being settings of biblical texts. The songs of the second book, settings for three to six voices with instruments and basso continuo, are often longer, more elaborately scored and more colourful in their interpretation of the words.

Two further publications during Schein's lifetime reflect progressive and traditional influences respectively. The *Fontana d'Israel, Israelis Brünlein* (1623) contains in all but one instance settings for five voices and continuo of texts largely drawn from the Old Testament. As the full title of the collection tells us, the pieces are composed in the 'Italian madrigal manner', and according to the preface may be performed 'either alone with singers and instruments or with organ or harpsichord'. Schein's last collection of sacred music was the *Cantional oder Gesangbuch Augspurgischer Confession* (1627), a vast anthology of Lutheran hymns in four-part harmony with the melody in the soprano line. Such anthologies as these had been assembled by German composers since the end of the sixteenth century. Schein introduced continuo figures in the bass part for the use of 'organists, instrumentalists and lutenists', wrote new harmonizations for many of the hymns, and included forty-one hymns in which he himself provided the melody, the harmonization and the text.

A comparable diversity of styles appears in the music of Schein's contemporary Samuel Scheidt (1587–1654). Unlike Schein, Scheidt excelled in keyboard writing – he had been a pupil of the great Netherlands organist, composer and skilled contrapuntalist, Jan Pieterszoon Sweelinck (1562–1621) – and was a gifted composer of sacred vocal music. He published seven collections of sacred music, of which the earliest was the *Cantiones sacrae* (1620) containing eight-voice polychoral motets without basso continuo. It is uncertain whether Scheidt intended instrumental doubling in all these works, but he specifically calls for it in one of them. Almost half are settings of German chorales while the remaining texts are drawn from Luther's German translation of the Bible. Although Scheidt's stylistic vocabulary in the *Cantiones sacrae* reveals a mixture of German, Italian and Netherlands influences – Sweelinck's own *Cantiones sacrae* had appeared in the previous year – that of his second publication, *Pars prima concertuum sacrorum* (1622), is more pronouncedly Italian. Here there are sinfonias, instrumental obbligati, doubling of vocal parts and basso continuo throughout. Scheidt's remaining sacred vocal publications were four volumes of *Geistliche Concerten*, scored for a small vocal group with continuo (1631–40), and the *Liebliche Krafft-Blümlein* (1635), containing twelve 'concertos' for two voices and continuo.

Schütz: life, sacred music

Scheidt remained closer to Lutheran hymnody in his vocal music than did the greatest of the early Baroque German composers, Heinrich Schütz (1585–1672). Schütz received his early education at the Collegium Mauritianum, which had been founded by Landgrave Moritz of Hessen-Kassel. According to an account by Martin Geier, electoral court chaplain at Dresden, who appended a somewhat unreliable biographical sketch to his funeral oration for the composer, in 1598 the Landgrave stayed at an inn at Weissenfels owned by Heinrich's father, Christoph Schütz, where the boy's singing so pleased him that 'His Noble Grace was moved to ask the parents to allow the lad to come with him to his noble court, promising that he would be reared in all good arts and commendable virtues'. At first reluctant, Christoph Schütz eventually acceded to the proposal and took his son to the Landgrave's court at Kassel in 1599.

After leaving the Collegium Mauritianum Schütz enrolled at the

University of Marburg where he studied law. Landgrave Moritz, however, had other plans for his talented protegé, and around 1609 financed Schütz's first visit to Venice where he studied with Giovanni Gabrieli. Schütz returned to Kassel probably in 1613, but in the following year went to the Dresden court at the request of the Elector Johann Georg I of Saxony. In 1615 Schütz once more returned to Dresden, becoming a permanent member of the Elector's household in 1617. Some two years later came his appointment as court *Kapellmeister*, a post which he held for fifty-three years until his death in 1672. Schütz's fame grew rapidly, and before the mid-seventeenth century he enjoyed an international reputation. His life, nevertheless, was far from easy. His first and bitterest blow came in 1625 when his wife, in her mid-twenties, died after barely six years of marriage leaving him with two young daughters. According to the oration delivered at her funeral Schütz 'never knew or heard a more lovely sound or song than when he heard the voice and word of his precious wife'. In 1630 his close friend Schein died – Schütz visited him on his deathbed, and at Schein's request published the motet *Das ist je gewisslich wahr* (SWV 277) in his memory – and in the following year he lost both his father and his father-in-law. In 1638 the elder of his two daughters died, and in 1655 the younger. In addition to this succession of personal losses Schütz had to contend with deteriorating work conditions at Dresden. The number of musicians was reduced as an effect of the Thirty Years War (p. 68), and those who remained were either ill-paid or not paid at all. As Schütz approached old age (p. 67), all his requests to be released from the full burden of official duties were ignored. 'Since the electoral Kapelle has gone completely to ruin in these parlous times, and I have in the meanwhile grown old,' wrote the composer in 1645, 'it is now my only wish that I might henceforth live free from all regular obligations.' Only with the death of the Saxon Elector Johann Georg I in 1656 were Schütz's requests answered. The new Elector, Johann Georg II, bestowed on him the title of senior *Kapellmeister*, granted him a pension and expected only occasional visits to the court each year. Schütz died on 6 November 1672 and was buried in the Frauenkirche in Dresden.

In 1619 Schütz published his first collection of sacred music: *Psalmen Davids sampt etlichen Moteten und Concerten* (SWV 22–47), the Psalms of David; his only previous publication (1611) had been a set of Italian madrigals (SWV 1–19), written at Giovanni Gabrieli's instigation as an exercise in unaccompanied five-part vocal writing. Venice, above all, was the source of inspiration behind the polychoral works which comprise the *Psalmen Davids*. Of the twenty-six pieces the greater number are settings of complete psalms, in Luther's translations, for at least two four-part choirs supported by instruments and basso continuo. An assured feeling for structure, harmonic variety, sensitive treatment of the texts, vivid colour in performance and, not least, the skill with which Schütz accommodates the speech-rhythms of the texts are all notable features of this music, and are displayed, for example, in the setting of Psalm 100: 'Jauchzet dem Herren alle Welt' (Make a joyful noise unto the Lord, all ye lands) (SWV 36). In his preface to the *Psalmen Davids* Schütz outlines a performance practice of his works, recommending a moderate tempo so that 'the words of the singers may be intelligibly recited and understood'. Here as throughout his sacred music, Schütz stresses his strong commitment to German and Lutheran tradition.

The *Cantiones sacrae* (SWV 53–93, 1625) reveal a different kind of expressive writing, no less Italian than that of the *Psalmen Davids*, but closer in spirit to the madrigal than to larger concertato techniques. The texts are Latin rather than German, and Schütz set these for four-part vocal texture with continuo. The monodic declamation and often extreme affective dissonance which Schütz employed to colour the words are more suited to small- than to large-scale concertato ensembles.

Like the *Cantiones sacrae*, Part I of Schütz's next publication contained settings of Latin texts. These were the *Symphoniae sacrae* (SWV 257–76), published in Venice in 1629. Schütz had paid a second visit to Venice in 1628, partly to escape the economic hardships of the Dresden court. This time he met 'the noble Monteverdi', who 'guided him with joy and happily showed him the long-sought path'. In the dedication to the Elector Johann Georg of Saxony which prefaced Part I of the *Symphoniae sacrae*, Schütz refers to some changes in composing methods which had taken place between his four-year stay as Gabrieli's pupil (*c.*1609–13) and his present visit.

> Staying in Venice as the guest of old friends, I learned that the long unchanged theory of composing melodies had set aside the ancient rhythms to tickle the ears of today with fresh devices. To this method I directed my mind and energies, to the end that, in accordance with my purpose, I might offer you something from the store of my industry ...

One aspect of the change in style which Schütz mentions was a shift away from the larger polychoral techniques reflected in *Psalmen Davids* towards smaller concertato units. In Part I of the *Symphoniae sacrae* the pieces are set for three voices, with various though specified wind and stringed instruments with continuo. In Part II (SWV 341–67), published in 1647, an even stricter economy of means prevails. In the third part (SWV 398–418), published in 1650, however, the pieces are larger in scale though the instruments are not always precisely named. In these later books Schütz makes use of the *stile concitato* – the style expressive of agitation and anger – an oblique tribute to Monteverdi, who as we have seen in Chapter 2, introduced it in his eighth book of madrigals (1638); and he pays the composer direct tribute in revisions in Part II of *Armato il cor* and *Zefiro torna e di soavi accenti.*

Schütz's *Musicalische Exequien* (SWV 279–81), published in 1636, had been composed as a requiem for the funeral of Prince Heinrich Posthumus von Reuss. The work is striking in its musical organization, drawing upon contrasting techniques of single and double choral settings and small-scale vocal ensembles with continuo accompaniment. An unusual feature in Schütz's music is the quotation of hymn tunes in each of its three components: concerto, motet and canticle. They would have been familiar to his audience and thus have acted as signposts to an understanding of the text. The first part of this work is cast in the form of the Lutheran *Missa*, consisting of a Kyrie and Gloria; the second section, a motet for two antiphonal choirs, uses the motto of the Prince's funeral oration as its text, while the concluding section, the Nunc dimittis, is set for two opposing choirs in three and five parts.

The *Kleine geistlichen Concerten* (Small Sacred Concertos) which Schütz brought out in two parts in 1636 (SWV 282–305) and 1639 (SWV 306–37), call upon modest resources. That only a small solo vocal ensemble with continuo is required is a direct reflection of the devastation wrought by the Thirty Years War with its effect on the finances and number of musicians of the Elector's court at Dresden. In 1631 Johann Georg had entered into an alliance with King Gustavus Adolphus of Sweden, and in so doing, caused the war to spread through Saxony. Its effect was catastrophic above all in the sickness and famine which ensued. Schütz remarks in the preface to the *Kleine geistlichen Concerten* on 'the evil of present times, adverse to the liberal arts', adding that the terrible effect of war had paralyzed musical life. The form of the concertos varies from solo monody in *stilo oratorio*, as Schütz termed it, to solo ensemble.

Schütz's *Geistliche Chor-Music* (SWV 369–97) of 1648 is an extensive collection of motets in five to seven parts with continuo, published with a partly didactic purpose. In a detailed preface Schütz expresses a fear that younger composers, acquainted only with basso continuo techniques, may no longer be familiar with traditional polyphonic discipline. He provides by way of example a wide variety of styles in motet composition, emphasizing the continuing merits of vocal polyphony.

Probably dating from the same period of Schütz's old age is *Die sieben Wortte Jesu Christi am Kreuz* (SWV 478). This deeply affecting work in a forward-looking dramatic style for five-part vocal and instrumental ensemble was first published in 1885, three centuries after the composer's birth. Its symmetrical framework of opening and closing choruses, followed and preceded respectively by brief and harmonically poignant 'symphonies', encloses a grief-laden account of Christ's death on the Cross. The role of the Evangelist is taken, not by one voice, but by solo treble, alto and tenor voices, as well as, in three instances, by a vocal quartet of treble, alto, tenor and bass. The words of Jesus, set in a style recalling the Italian madrigal lament, are sung by a tenor, while the thieves on the left and right of the Cross are sung by a tenor and bass respectively. The German text of this deeply contemplative work, imbued with mysticism and dramatic force, is drawn from the four Gospels but also contains two stanzas of the hymn 'Da Jesus an dem Kreuze stund'.

The great works of Schütz's last years include a Christmas History (SWV 435), comparable in its modern outlook and dramatic treatment to *Die sieben Wortte, Zwölff geistliche Gesänge* (SWV 420–31), and three Passions. Each of the Passions is set *a cappella*, that is, without instrumental accompaniment, in accordance with liturgical custom at Dresden. One of the most impressive features of these powerfully dramatic works is Schütz's use of an unmeasured, monodic declamation for the Evangelist's role and for those of the other *dramatis personae*. The result is an ingenious blend of plainchant recitation and more coloured operatic recitative, through which Schütz arrives at a strikingly natural and, at times, dramatic presentation of the German text.

When Schütz died in 1672 he had long been regarded in Protestant Germany as an outstanding composer. 'When Schütz's songs resound, Saxony rejoices,' wrote the lyric poet, Paul Fleming; and another German musician referred to him in 1657 as '*Parentem nostrae Musicae modernae*'. Schütz's published music spans over half a century, providing a fascinating picture of old and new styles in composition and a rapprochement of polyphony and Italian monody. Above all, by introducing Italian developments in music to Germany he laid the foundations of eighteenth-century German sacred music.

Schütz's contemporaries

In Catholic south Germany a comparable distinctive indigenous German contribution to church music was non-existent; this was largely because Rome was the centre and the model for Catholic church music. Furthermore, the south German courts favoured Italian musicians who followed in the tradition of the great masters of technique, Orlande de Lassus (1532–94), who had spent nearly fifty years at the court of Duke Albrecht V of Bavaria at Munich from 1556 until his death, and Giovanni Pierluigi da Palestrina (1525–94). Catholic and Protestant music did, however, find a meeting ground in collections of *stile antico* motets which circulated in Germany. Two of these were of particular importance for the quality of the music: the *Florilegium Portense* and *Promptuarium musicum*. The earlier, *Florilegium Portense*, first appeared in 1603 but was published in a larger edition with continuo in 1618. The compiler Erhard Bodenschatz (1576–1636) mainly included German composers, though Lassus and the Slovenian Jakob Handl (1550–91) were also represented. In 1621 Bodenschatz brought out a second part in which Italian composers were favoured, among whom were Giovanni Gabrieli, Marenzio, Agazzari, Vecchi and Viadana. *Florilegium Portense* seems not to have run into subsequent editions, but the facts that surviving copies appear to have been frequently re-bound, and that it was among the books later used by J.S. Bach at the Thomasschule in Leipzig testify to its importance. The second of the motet collections, the *Promptuarium musicum*, was a three-part anthology assembled by Abraham Schadaeus (1566–1626), issued in 1611, 1612 and 1613, and set out according to the liturgical year. Here there was a stronger emphasis on Italian music, German composers seldom featuring in it. The settings are for five to eight voices with Latin texts. These volumes containing a vast treasure-house of old Roman, Venetian and German repertory were used almost throughout the Baroque period in Germany, providing a valuable musical heritage to *Kantors* and composers alike.

As well as composers of the stature of Schütz, Schein and Scheidt there were lesser figures who nevertheless made individual contributions to the development of the chorale concertato. In the north of Germany there were Schütz's pupil Matthias Weckmann (c.1619–74), Thomas Selle (1599–1663), Franz Tunder (1614–67) and Christoph Bernhard (1628–92). Weckmann's most important post was that of organist of the Jacobikirche in Hamburg, which housed one of the finest organs in Germany. His cantatas follow in the tradition of concerted music for solo voices, choir and instruments established in Germany by Schütz, but he gives the instruments greater prominence, and treats the voices with greater virtuosity. Thomas Selle was educated in Leipzig where he was influenced by Schein who was *Thomaskantor*. Selle himself eventually became *Kantor* of the famous Johanneum school in Hamburg and civic director of the church music. The quality of Selle's music is variable, but his feeling for instrumental colour infuses his church music with a

48

pleasing variety of sonority, displayed above all in his St John Passion, which is perhaps the first Passion to include instrumental interludes.

Tunder was organist of the Marienkirche at Lübeck from 1641 until his death in 1667. It is possible that he began the evening concerts or 'Abendmusiken' which became celebrated under his successor and son-in-law Dietrich Buxtehude. Only a small amount of music by Tunder has survived, but his chorale cantatas and arias possess an affecting, intimate quality. Tunder's treatment of chorale cantatas, above all the dependence on chorale melody and the variety with which it is presented verse by verse, makes him a significant composer for the development of the Lutheran church cantata.

Christoph Bernhard had been a pupil of Carissimi and was an able composer – in 1670 Schütz requested a funeral motet from him, and it was performed at the great composer's funeral in 1672. Bernhard succeeded Selle as *Kantor* of the Johanneum in Hamburg but his contribution to seventeenth-century music theory is of greater significance. His *Tractatus compositionis augmentatus* (An Augmented Treatise on Composition) takes up the classification of styles already begun in Marco Scacci's *Cribrum musicum* (1643); but where Scacci's terms related more to occasion and location, Bernhard attempted a strictly stylistic division based on the relationship between words and music, place of performance and types of dissonance used. His three distinct styles are *stylus gravis* (*stylus antiquus*) for church use, where music is master of language; *stylus luxurians communis* for vocal and instrumental chamber pieces both sacred and secular; and *stylus luxurians teatralis* for theatre productions, where language is master of the music. The writings of theorists such as Scacchi, Athanasius Kircher (1601–80), Bernhard, Johann Mattheson and others serve to underline, not only the Baroque composers' awareness of the diverse functions which the music of their day was able to perform, but also, by their very variety, that Baroque music was not governed by any single system of classification or exclusive doctrine.

The central German school of mid-century composers included Andreas Hammerschmidt (*c.*1611–75), three Leipzig *Thomaskantors* who spanned the years between Schein and Bach's predecessor at Leipzig, Johann Kuhnau: Tobias Michael (1592–1657), Sebastian Knüpfer (1633–76) and Johann Schelle (1648–1701), and several members of the Bach family. Hammerschmidt was a prolific and successful composer who spent most of his life as organist at St Johannis, Zittau. He wrote and published sacred music, and also contributed to the solo secular repertory of the time. Of the three *Thomaskantors*, Knüpfer was perhaps the most original; his compositions were almost entirely sacred, and possessed distinction not only in their skilful, sometimes dramatic handling of voices but also in their contrapuntal mastery and colourful instrumentation. Schelle, too, composed chiefly sacred music, further developing the sacred cantata. He showed a leaning towards colourful, often stirring instrumental effects for textual illustration. The chorale cantata *Vom Himmel kam der Engel Schar* is a resonant example of his musical imagination and his varied treatment of chorale melody in each verse.

The seventeenth century witnessed the emergence of a remarkable dynasty of musicians, crowned with the genius of its most illustrious member, Johann Sebastian Bach. The musical members of the Bach family spanned a period of two hundred years, roughly from 1600 to 1800. They belonged to Thuringia, an area of central Germany close to the Harz mountains, the most important towns of which were Arnstadt, Eisenach, Erfurt, Gotha, Mühlhausen and Weimar. Among the chief occupations of a town musician in seventeenth-century Germany were those of organist, teacher and *stadtpfeifer*, or town piper, to which we should add an aptitude for the craft of instrument-building demonstrated by many of the Bachs. The multifarious gifts and extraordinary musical versatility demonstrated by this family were recognized throughout the region. An entry in the Eisenach town chronicle relating to Johann Ambrosius Bach (1645–95), father of J.S. Bach, records, for example, that 'in 1672 the new director of town music played at Easter upon the organ, the violin, the trumpet and the kettledrums, and also sang, something which has never been known in the history of Eisenach'.

While J.S. Bach's musical forbears are too numerous to consider individually, a few deserve mention. Earliest is Johann Bach (1604–73), whose motet *Unser Leben ist ein Schatten* (Our life is but a shadow) paints an affecting picture of the frailty of human life. Johann Bach's younger brother Heinrich (1615–92) was also an able composer, if we are to judge by the few pieces by him that survive; but Heinrich's two sons, Johann Christoph (1642–1703) and Johann Michael (1648–94), were notably accomplished composers, skilled above all in the art of the chorale motet. Johann Christoph, the most original of J.S. Bach's ancestors, proves himself a musician of striking imagination in pieces such as his vocal concerto *Es erhub sich ein Streit* (And there was war in heaven). The work is scored for double choir, four trumpets, timpani, strings and continuo, and was highly regarded by subsequent generations of the family. Evidence of this is provided by J.S. Bach's son, Carl Philipp Emanuel, who in 1775, long after his father's death, recalled: 'This composition in 22 parts is a masterpiece. My beloved father once performed it in a Leipzig church and everyone was astonished by the effect it made.'

The principal German composer working in the south in the seventeenth century was Johann Erasmus Kindermann (1616–55). Kindermann worked in Nuremberg but may have visited Venice, where he could have encountered Monteverdi and Cavalli. Kindermann was a teacher, composer and organist, and his music encompasses many of the instrumental and vocal forms of the time. Among his most interesting works are four cantatas in concertato style in which he makes effective contrasts between a central solo movement and two choral ones that frame it. The cantata *Wachet auf, ruft uns die Stimme* is an attractive example. In its outer movements the cantus firmus or melody, sometimes in broken phrases, is taken up in various strands of the vocal texture in an imaginative, often florid manner, while lively string figurations and distinctive harmonic modulations add further character to the work.

The continuo Lied

Several of the composers whom we have discussed in connection with sacred music also made an important contribution to the secular repertory. In vocal music one form enjoyed popularity above all others: continuo Lied, or figured-bass song. The stimulus was provided by Italy whose continuo madrigals and 'dramatic' monodies, of the kind both included and explained in Caccini's *Le nuove musiche* (p. 13), had begun to impress themselves on a wider audience. One of the earliest and most important German composers to introduce Italian music into Germany was Hans Leo Hassler. In 1601 Hassler published his *Lustgarten neuer teutscher Gesäng, Balletti, Gaillarden und Intraden*, a collection of part-songs and dances in which the Italian influence is strong, and especially that of Giovanni Giacomo Gastoldi (c.1555–1622). One song, 'Mein Gmüt ist mir verwirret', eventually became linked to the words of Paul Gerhardt's Lutheran hymn 'O Haupt voll Blut und Wunden', and was incorporated by Bach in his St Matthew Passion. *Lustgarten* stimulated similar collections by Christoph Demantius (1567–1643), Erasmus Widmann (1572–1634) and Melchior Franck (c.1580–1639) who had been Hassler's pupil.

The combination of current styles in Hassler's music influenced the next generation of German composers in its development of the strophic figured-bass song. As with the sacred music composers of this period, the chief exponents of the Lied may be grouped by geographical location. The most important figures in the north of Germany were Schütz's cousin and disciple, Heinrich Albert (1604–51), and Thomas Selle; outstanding in central Germany were Schein, one of the earliest composers of figured-bass songs, Schütz's pupil Caspar Kittel (1603–39), Hammerschmidt and Adam Krieger (1634–66); in the south there were Sigmund Theophil Staden (1607–55) and Kindermann. Notable among the poets and song-writers was Martin Opitz (1597–1639), whose treatise *Buch von der deutschen Poeterey* (1624) was widely disseminated among musicians and writers. Opitz's verse was popular with composers and his German adaptation of Rinuccini's *Dafne* was set by Schütz, though the score has not survived. Opitz had a powerful influence on poets of his generation such as Johann Rist (1607–67), who was also a theologian and composer, and Paul Fleming (1609–40). A further poet of importance in the history of the continuo Lied was Simon Dach (1605–59). Dach formed a fruitful partnership with Heinrich Albert who set many of his poems to music. The continuo Lied reached a high-water mark in the songs of Adam Krieger. In many of them as, for instance, the robust 'Der Rhein'sche Wein', dance-like five-part ritornelli break up the sequence of verses; and there are engaging examples of the genre, too, in the songs of Albert, whose simple but affecting melodies complement the direct, homely sentiments of the texts. The continuo Lied was later to enjoy a vogue in the compositions of Johann Valentin Görner (1702–62) and Telemann.

German instrumental music

Even more varied than the vocal forms developed in Germany in the seventeenth century were the instrumental forms, in which dance music played a large part. The most important keyboard instrument was the organ, and its literature in north and central Germany was influenced both by English and Netherlands music of the previous century. One of the most significant figures in the development of north and mid-German organ music was the Amsterdam composer Sweelinck, whose pupil Scheidt's three-volume *Tabulatura nova* appeared in 1624. Its title signifies that it was the first keyboard collection to appear in open score – that is, with each voice or strand of the texture placed on a separate staff. The first and second parts of *Tabulatura nova* contain a mixed repertory of psalms, fugues, toccatas, echoes, *passamezzi*, canons and secular songs. Several sets of variations are based on songs and dances from England, France and the Netherlands. The third part contains works for liturgical use based on a cantus firmus. In a preface Scheidt provides the intending performer with instructions, emphasizing that the chorale melody, the cantus firmus, should be clearly heard at all times.

The Thirty Years War contributed to the prevention of any continuous development in German organ music after Scheidt, and it was not until the second half of the century that a north German school flourished, with composers such as Tunder, Weckmann, Buxtehude, Lübeck, Reincken, Böhm and Brühns. South German organ music took Italy as its model and, more particularly, the music of Andrea Gabrieli and Claudio Merulo (1533–1604).

The growing assimilation of national styles: Froberger and his contemporaries

A strong personal idiom can be discerned in the keyboard music of Johann Jacob Froberger (1616–67). Froberger was the greatest German harpsichord composer in the first half of the seventeenth century. Around 1637 he was appointed court organist at Vienna, a post which he held for some twenty years, but which did not prevent him from travelling. His first journey was to Rome in 1637, where he studied with Frescobaldi. He remained there for about four years before returning to Vienna and his musically gifted employer, Emperor Ferdinand III. A longer period of travel seems to have taken place between 1645 and 1653; during these years Froberger visited Italy once more, the Low Countries, England and France. He returned to Vienna in 1653, remaining court organist until the Emperor's death in 1657. As a mark of respect and affection for his employer, Froberger composed a rhapsodic three-section *Lamentation faite sur la mort très douloureuse de Sa Majesté Imperiale, Ferdinand le troisième*. Its title, its choice of key – F minor, which was only rarely used by keyboard composers at this time – and its unmistakable strain of personal sadness testify to the warm rapport that had existed between the two men.

Italian influence in Froberger's music can be found in the contrapuntal canzonas and ricercares and in the toccatas, while the dances of the harpsichord suites owe more to the arpeggiated figurations of the French lute school, which were taken over by the mid-seventeenth-century French harpsichord composers such as Chambonnières and Louis Couperin. Froberger's earlier keyboard suites contain only three movements: allemande-courante-sarabande; to this grouping he added a gigue, which in his autograph suites is placed between the allemande and courante. Many years after Froberger's death, however, an Amsterdam publisher brought out further suites, asserting that he had placed the dances '*en meilleur ordre*' (in better order); in this publication (*c*.1697) the gigue comes at the end of the sequence, but we cannot be certain whether or not this was Froberger's own intention. Froberger is important for his fine and individually expressive compositions, but particularly for his assimilation of diverse styles, through which he forges a link between those of Italy, France, Germany and the Netherlands.

Gifted keyboard composers working in Austria and southern Germany who also provided a link between Frescobaldi and late Baroque style include the Italian-born Alessandro Poglietti (?–1683) and Johann Kaspar Kerll (1627–93). Poglietti was successor to Froberger as organist at the Vienna court, and a celebrated teacher who published his didactic *Compendium oder kurtzer Begriff, und Einführung zur Musica* (1676) for the guidance of his pupils. He was also a composer with an individual keyboard style, found at its most original in his Toccatina *Sopra la Ribellione di Ungheria* (1671). This is a suite inspired by an uprising against Habsburg persecution of Hungarian Protestants; here and in his cycle of movements, *Rossignolo*, dedicated to the Emperor Leopold I, Poglietti displays his particular talent for programmatic effects, imitative of war and nature respectively. Kerll was first employed as organist in Vienna by Archduke Leopold Wilhelm who sent him to Italy to study with Carissimi and perhaps also Frescobaldi. In 1656 Kerll was appointed *vice-Kapellmeister* at the Munich court, becoming *Kapellmeister* a few months later. In 1673 he returned to Vienna and became organist first at St Stephen's Cathedral, then in 1677 at the Vienna court. Kerll was an imaginative composer of sacred vocal music as well as of keyboard pieces; the *Modulatio organica super Magnificat* (1686) containing both a strict polyphonic and a freer, improvisatory element, is among his most impressive achievements in solo keyboard composition, above all for the high quality of the fugal writing.

Two important collections of instrumental ensemble music appeared in Germany during the second decade of the seventeenth century. The earlier was Praetorius's *Terpsichore* (1612) containing four- and five-part settings of French dances, the later the *Banchetto musicale* (1617) of Schein. Praetorius's pieces were acquired from dancing masters who would have given instructions on how to dance them, while Schein's were stylized and musically interrelated five-part pavanes, galliards, courantes and allemandes, with a unifying thematic pattern. The latter idea had its roots in the previous century, when a pair of contrasting dances, slow and fast, had thematic material in common. Schein extended the practice to embrace all the dances in a suite, unifying them not only thematically but also tonally. To the four movements listed above he added a *tripla* or *nachtanz* – a reworking of the allemande, but in triple rather than duple time. The pieces could be played on any group of instruments, though

54

Schein expressed a preference for viols. *Banchetto musicale* was the last of his collections in the *prima prattica* style, that is, without basso continuo.

Rosenmüller, Schmelzer and Biber

The three composers of the German mid-Baroque who made the most important contribution to instrumental chamber music were Johann Rosenmüller (*c.*1619–84), Johann Heinrich Schmelzer (*c.*1620–80) and Heinrich Ignaz Franz von Biber (1644–1704). Rosenmüller was born in Saxony but spent the greater part of his active musical life in Italy, where he was at one time a trombonist at S. Marco, Venice, and at another, composer to the Ospedale della Pietà which was later to become celebrated through Vivaldi's assocation with the institution. Rosenmüller's suites and sonatas are impressive both for their harmonic invention and for the fine quality of their craftsmanship, above all apparent in the last collection of sonatas, published in Nuremberg in 1682. Towards the end of his life Rosenmüller returned to Germany, becoming *Kapellmeister* at Wolfenbüttel, and providing with his compositions a valuable channel for stylistic influence from Italy to north Germany.

Schmelzer was an Austrian who after holding varied posts as a musician, became *vice-Hofkapellmeister* (1671), and briefly, *Hofkapell-meister* (1679) of the Vienna court. He was a versatile composer who excelled above all in instrumental forms, where he incorporated elements of local colour from the folk music of Hungary, Bohemia, Croatia, Poland and Austria. His finest instrumental compositions are contained in his *Sacroprofanus concentus musicus* (1662) and the *Sonatae unarum fidium* (1664). The earlier set contains sonatas scored for two to eight instruments in which the contrasting sonorities of strings and brass are frequently called into play. The six *Sonatae unarum fidium*, on the other hand, are for violin and basso continuo, requiring virtuoso technique and betraying Italian influence in their idiomatic writing. In these sonatas above all, Schmelzer contributed to both the technical and stylistic development of the solo sonata in Germany. Like the musically gifted Leopold I, Kerll and later Biber, Schmelzer made important contributions to sacred vocal music in Austria, exploiting in particular the concertato style with its possibilities for contrast between large choral combinations and rich-textured instrumental groups.

Biber was a Bohemian, and both an outstandingly imaginative composer and a celebrated violin virtuoso. Though he seldom travelled his music was widely disseminated, spreading his reputation well beyond the boundaries of central Europe. During the 1660s Biber was employed by the musical Count Liechtenstein-Kastelkorn of Olomouc, at Kroměříž in Moravia. By the autumn of 1670, however, he had left the Count to take up a post at the court of Max Gandolph, Prince-Archbishop of Salzburg, where he subsequently became *vice-Kapellmeister* (1679) and *Kapellmeister* (1684). In nearby Vienna the musical Emperor Leopold I quickly recognized Biber's talents, eventually granting him the title which raised him to noble rank.

Biber's compositions are varied in form and include operas, sacred vocal music with instruments, solo sonatas and pieces for instrumental ensemble; outstanding in the last category are a *Battalia* for solo violin and strings, a *Serenada* (Nightwatchman's Call) with the surprising appearance of a solo bass voice toward the conclusion; a Balletto, *Fechtschule* (Fencing School) for strings, and a six-part anthology *Mensa sonora* (1680), consisting of suites and chamber sonatas – all striking examples of Biber's pictorial and colourfully imaginative style. His finest achievement, however, is the solo music which he wrote for his own instrument, the violin, and above all the sixteen *Mystery Sonatas* dedicated to his patron Max Gandolph (*c.*1676) and the posthumously published *Harmonia artificiosa-ariosa* (1712). With the exception of the first *Mystery Sonata* (or *Rosary Sonata* – Biber explains in the dedication that the subject of each sonata is a section from the Catholic devotion known as the Rosary) and the concluding unaccompanied *Passacaglia*, all the pieces of these two sets demonstrate Biber's unparalleled exploration of scordatura. Scordatura, or retuning of one or more strings, not only facilitates certain fingerings but also enables the performer to achieve sonorities impossible on an instrument tuned in conventional fifths. Biber makes considerable demands upon the player with tunings employed in the *Mystery Sonatas* to illustrate the fifteen central events in Christian history, and these further have an important function for the polyphonic texture. The music itself evokes a wide range of emotional responses, with exuberant south German Baroque flamboyance on the one hand and an affecting, contemplative intensity on the other. Both moods are to be found in the expressive Aria with Variations from the fourteenth *Mystery Sonata*, while the unaccompanied *Passacaglia*, occupying a detached position, seems to represent an even more profound act of contemplation.

The pieces contain an emotive writing which would eventually become the hallmark of French musical expression, where again, current fashions were tailored to suit indigenous taste.

5
French music of the grand siècle

'THE MOST HONOURABLE THING we can say of a man is that he does not understand the court; there is scarcely a virtue which we do not imply when saying this.' So wrote the first social critic in French literature, Jean de la Bruyère (1645–96), in his famous work *Caractères* (1694). We shall have to put aside La Bruyère's ironic observation, however, if we are to understand anything of the cultural life of France in the seventeenth and early eighteenth centuries since the court played a vital part in almost all artistic endeavour during the reigns of Louis XIII (1610–43) and Louis XIV (1643–1715).

Paris, like Florence, fostered, through humanist influence, the establishment of academies during the late sixteenth century. One of the earliest and most important to the subsequent history of French Baroque poetry and music was the Académie de Musique et de Poésie, founded in 1571 by Jean Antoine de Baïf (1532–89) and Joachim Thibaut de Courville (d.1581). Baïf was interested in the combination of story, music and dance in the ancient Greek manner and, in pursuit of his aims, evolved his *vers mesurés à l'antique*. These verses adopted the metres of Greek and Latin verse and were set to music by musicians of the Académie. Baïf's system was rigid, but in the hands of the ablest musicians of the Académie, such as Claude Le Jeune (*c*.1528–1600), rules were modified to benefit both words and music. The *musique mesurée à l'antique* which resulted had a significant part to play in the development of both the *air de cour* and the *ballet de cour* of the following century.

Ballets *and* airs

The earliest and most successful work reflecting the aspirations of Baïf to unite poetry, music and dance was *Circé, ou le Ballet Comique de la Reine*, which was performed at the Petit-Bourbon palace in Paris on 15 October 1581. It was occasioned by the marriage of Marguérite de Vendemont, the Queen's sister, to the Duc de Joyeuse. Several artists had a hand in the creation of *Circé*, but the overall supervision lay with Balthasar de Beaujoyeux (*c*.1535–*c*.1587). Beaujoyeux was an Italian by birth who adopted French nationality, becoming a successful ballet-master at the courts of Charles IX (1560–74) and the last of the Valois branch of the Capetian dynasty, Henri III (1574–89). The music of *Circé* was the work of two composers, Lambert de Beaulieu (fl.1576–90), and Jacques Salmon (*c*.1545–90). The surviving material includes several choruses, a small number of vocal solos and some instrumental dances.

The *ballet comique*, or ballet in the manner of a play with unified plot, had little direct influence on subsequent ballets during the following thirty years or so and died out after 1620. Around 1600, however, a significant development took place in the treatment of *récits* in ballets, for whereas formerly they had been spoken, now they were more often sung, bringing the *ballet de cour* a step nearer to opera. A typical ballet of the early years of the seventeenth century consisted of dances, pantomime and *récits*, which were not recitatives but more in the nature of an air or dramatic arioso.

In the years leading up to the middle decades of the seventeenth century, unified plot in ballet gave way to a succession of scenes linked by an idea common to all but which did not amount to continuous dramatic action. These were *ballets à entrées*, in which mythology and allegory, lavish costumes and stage sets were brought together in a fashion which illustrates both Baroque ornateness and the contrasts and paradoxes – the grotesqueries and elegance mingled – that characterize so many aspects of the period. In these respects the *ballets à entrées*, in which music and dancing were the most important elements, foreshadow the *opéra-ballets* of the early eighteenth century. A *ballet à entrées* of particular interest, since an elaborate account of its preparation and performance has survived, is the *Grand Bal de la Douairière de Billabahaut*, in which Louis XIII himself danced. In this ballet, staged at the Hotel de la Ville in Paris on 25 February 1626, the four corners of the world, each with its own dances, *récits* and *entrées* send representatives to the 'Dowager's Ball'. There is no unity of plot but the four tableaux, whose grotesque element is evident from the appearance of the ugly dowager, provided the spectators with an entertaining choreographic spectacle.

A component of the sixteenth- and early seventeenth-century ballet which enjoyed wide currency in its own right was the *air de cour*. The first collection of such pieces was printed in 1571 by the Paris publishers Adrian Le Roy and Robert Ballard under the title *Livre d'airs de cour miz sur le luth par Adrian le Roy*. Although the songs in this publication, where the term *air de cour* appears for the first time, were for solo voice with lute accompaniment, most of those which appeared before 1600 were for four or five voices. In his preface Le Roy explains that *air de cour* is a new term for what had previously been known as *vaudeville* or *voix de ville*. The early *airs de cour* possessed simple melodies and uncomplicated polyphonic structure, were secular in content and strophic in form.

One of the most celebrated early composers of *airs de cour* was Pierre Guédron (1565–1621) who succeeded Claude le Jeune at the court of Henri IV as composer of the *Chambre du roi* in 1610. Guédron's *airs* and *récits*, some of which show a marked Italian influence – he was among the first in France to employ basso continuo, albeit tentatively, as opposed to accompaniment in lute tablature – were published in a series of sixteen books of *Airs de différents autheurs mis en tablature de luth*, printed between 1608 and 1643. Other composers represented in this important collection are Antoine Boesset (*c*.1587–1647) and Jacques Mauduit (1557–1627). Several books of *airs* by Etienne Moulinié (*c*.1600–after 1669), published between 1624 and 1635, also make an important contribution to the genre. Towards the middle of the seventeenth century, lute tablature gradually yielded ground to the basso continuo as accompaniment to *airs de cour*. At about this time, too, the term *air de cour* was gradually abandoned in favour of *air sérieux* or, simply, *air*. The most important figures in the later history of the *air* were Pierre de Nyert (*c*.1597–1682) and Michel Lambert (*c*.1610–96). Nyert was foremost a singer who had travelled to Italy where he familiarized himself with Italian monody. When he returned to France in 1635 he entered the court of Louis XIII and influenced both Lambert and another composer, Bénigne de Bacilly (*c*.1625–90). Lambert was widely praised for his *airs*, and according to that champion of French music Lecerf de la Viéville (1647–1710), there was neither Frenchman nor foreigner in Paris who did not wish to study with him. Lambert succeeded Jean de Cambefort (*c*.1605–61) as *Maître de musique de la chambre du Roi* in 1661. His *Airs à une, II, III et IV parties* (1689) include parts for two violins and basso continuo, and reveal him above all as a gifted composer of poignantly affecting melodies.

Italian influence on French music

During the first half of the seventeenth century France, though by no means bereft of original musical talent, had no figures to match the stature of Monteverdi or Luigi Rossi in Italy. Italian developments in music, though cautiously received by the rationalists of the French classical tradition, nevertheless play an essential role in the development of French Baroque music. Marin Mersenne (1588–1648), in his *Harmonie universelle* (1636), criticized the conservatism of his fellow-countrymen which he claimed prejudiced them against new ideas. Mersenne was a Jesuit priest who had studied at the Jesuit college at La Flèche, there meeting Descartes with whom he formed a lifelong friendship. Mersenne's *Harmonie universelle* is one of the most important French sources of musical information in the seventeenth century, much of its interest lying in his attempt to differentiate between French and Italian music.

Although Italian music and musicians had played a part in French musical life in the sixteenth and early seventeenth centuries – Rinuccini and Caccini had both stayed at the French court of Henri IV – it was not until Cardinal Mazarin (1602–61) succeeded Cardinal Richelieu as prime minister of France in 1642 that Italian opera was introduced to the French court. Mazarin, himself an Italian who had been sent to Paris as papal legate in 1634, was a shrewd politician with a love of Italian music. It was largely through his artistic zeal and political influence that Cavalli's *Egisto* (1646) and Rossi's *Orfeo* (1647) were performed at court. Both productions incurred enormous expense which Mazarin met through taxation, the first of several unpopular fiscal measures that eventually led to the first *Fronde* or revolt of 1648. Mazarin was as yet undeterred, and in 1654 *Le nozze di Peleo e di Theti*, an opera by Carlo Caproli (*c.*1615–*c.*1695), was staged at the Petit-Bourbon, where Louis XIV himself danced in the ballets which followed each act. Although the music is lost, the work retains historical significance as an attempt to integrate the ballets with the main part of the opera. Two more Italian operas, both by Cavalli and both with danced *entrées* by Lully, were given in the following decade. The earlier was *Xerse*, performed in honour of the marriage of Louis XIV to the Infanta Maria Theresa of Spain in 1660; *Ercole amante* followed in 1662, but by then Mazarin was dead and only the prodigious expense already incurred ensured a performance. The production proved financially disastrous and the work was indifferently received.

Lully

The decline of Italian culture at the French court following Mazarin's death in 1661 approximately coincided with the rise to fame and power of another Italian, Jean-Baptiste Lully (1632–87). In his own musical sphere Lully was no less astute a politician than his compatriot, and his career reflects a close relationship between politics and the arts in seventeenth-century France. Lully was born in Florence but as a youth in 1646 accompanied the Chevalier de Guise to Paris where he joined the household of Mlle Montpensier, niece of Louis XIII. He became one of her *garçons de chambre* as well as studying music with Nicolas Métru (d.*c.*1670). Mlle Montpensier was a courageous participant in Frondist affairs, and when the movement came to an end in Paris in 1652 she was exiled outside the city. Lully sought release from her household, and returned to Paris at the end of that year. In February 1653 the *Ballet de la nuit*, with text by Isaac de Benserade (1613–91) and vocal music by Jean de Cambefort (*c.*1605–61), included Lully and Louis XIV among the dancers (p.68). Within a month the King had appointed the young musician to replace the Italian Salami Lazzarini as *Compositeur de la musique instrumentale du Roi*. This decade saw a fresh flowering of the court ballet, and between 1658 and 1681 Lully and Benserade collaborated in more than twenty such works. Benserade's poetry, which reflected not only the characters portrayed but also those who performed them, was particularly suited to the requirements of court ballet, of which the first was the *Ballet de Cassandre* (1651); but his sharp wit made him formidable enemies, notable among them Racine and Molière.

In 1661, following the death of Cambefort, Louis XIV appointed Lully *Surintendant de la musique et compositeur de la musique de la chambre*, a position created under Henri IV in 1592. By the end of the year Lully had received his *Lettres de naturalité* and in July 1662 he married the daughter of the composer Lambert. The following ten years saw crucial developments both in Lully's career and in the formation of his style. During this period he collaborated with Jean-Baptiste Molière (1622–73), one of the greatest geniuses of the French theatre, in a succession of highly original *comédies-ballets* in which Molière integrated songs and dances with the action of his plays. The idea of working music into the body of the action was not Molière's invention for, as we have already seen, a similar attempt had been made in Caproli's *Le nozze di Peleo e di Theti*; but the skill with which he fused the two elements, so that music and dancing both complemented and enhanced the action, had never been seen before. Initially Lully must have seemed to Molière an ideal partner, since not only was he a composer of proven ability but he had been a dancer, or *baladin*, and according to his ardent admirer Lecerf de la Viéville, was possessed of a ready wit. The first *comédie-ballet* of 'Les deux grands Baptistes', as Molière and Lully became known, was *Le Mariage forcé* (1664), and the last and greatest of all was *Le bourgeois Gentilhomme*, performed at Chambord in 1670. By then, however,

Lully's consuming ambition and the King's love of music and ballet were acting against the dramatist Molière's interests. A contemporary report of *Le bourgeois Gentilhomme*, for instance, refers to it as 'a ballet composed of six entrées accompanied by comedy'. A brilliant partnership came to a close, and Molière was obliged to seek another collaborator in the young Marc-Antoine Charpentier. Lully, meanwhile turned his attention to developments taking place within the sphere of newly founded French opera.

French opera: Lully's monopoly

In 1669 Pierre Perrin (*c*.1620–75), supported by the finance minister Jean-Baptiste Colbert (1619–83), was granted a 'Privilège' or licence to establish *académies d'opéra* for the performance of operas based on Italian models but employing French rather than Italian texts. In 1671 the Académie d'Opéra in Paris staged *Pomone* with texts by Perrin and music by Robert Cambert (*c*.1627–77). Described by the witty man of letters Saint-Évremond, not quite accurately, as the 'first French Opera to appear on the Stage', *Pomone* was well received and ran for 146 performances. Perrin himself was not so fortunate; his two business associates, the Marquis de Sourdéac and a financier, Bersac de Champeron, embezzled the receipts and Perrin was thrown into gaol. Lully, who had previously expressed the view that the French language was unsuited to large works of this kind, now saw a chance to turn matters to his advantage. At the suggestion of Colbert, he negotiated with the newly impoverished Perrin for the 'privilege', acquiring it in March 1672. In August 1672 a new royal 'privilege' not only enabled Lully to establish an Académie Royale de Musique but also gave him the power to restrict performances of any work that was sung throughout. Further restrictive measures followed; in September a new licence gave Lully proprietorship over all verses, texts, and entire works for which he had provided the music; and in April 1673 an ordinance limited the number of musicians who were allowed to appear outside the auspices of the Académie to two singers and six instrumentalists – and these musicians, furthermore, were not to be members of the Académie. Among those who suffered most from Lully's monopolist practices were Molière and his recently acquired collaborator in *comédie-ballet*, Charpentier. Charpentier's inscriptions on the three manuscript versions of Molière's *Le Malade imaginaire* (1673) indicate the progressive effects of Lully's measures on his rivals. For the 1673 production, we read '*Le Malade imaginaire avant les défenses*'; for a 1674 revival, it is '*avec les défenses*' (restrictions which limited Charpentier to two voices and six instrumentalists), and for a revival in 1685, we read '*rajusté autrement pour la troisième fois*' – revised for the third time.

Lullian tragédie en musique *or* tragédie lyrique, *and recitative*

Comédie-ballet was some way from the *tragédies en musique* which were to establish French opera and Lully's European reputation; yet with its effective blend of music, poetry and dance it may be regarded, along with the *ballet de cour*, the pastorale, the *tragédies à machines* and imported Italian opera, as a significant precursor of serious French opera. Molière's contribution to the form of *tragédies en musique*, or *tragédie lyrique* as it later came to be known, should not be underestimated. Lully was undoubtedly influenced by the skill with which Molière fused the elements of comedy and ballet (the 'silent comedy' to which the playwright once refers) and Molière's verse provided Lully's subsequent librettist, Philippe Quinault (1635–88), with a model of poetry suitable for musical adaptation.

Although Molière's chief theatrical interest was in comedy, he collaborated with Pierre Corneille (1606–84), Quinault and Lully in a *tragédie-ballet*, *Psyché* (1671). This work, though with spoken dialogue as opposed to recitative, contains many ingredients of *tragédie lyrique*, such as overture, integrated dances, and airs, so forming a significant link between *comédie-ballet* and serious French opera. Indeed, *Psyché* with added recitative and other small adjustments later became a *tragédie lyrique*. In this work, however, Lully collaborated with one librettist only, Thomas Corneille (1625–1709), younger brother of the celebrated dramatist, Pierre.

Lully's first *tragédie lyrique*, *Cadmus et Hermione*, was performed on 29 April 1673. Quinault, the librettist, based his story on ancient myth, while Lully in his divertissements and comic scenes drew upon much that he had learned through his partnership with Molière. The same is true of Lully and Quinault's second opera, *Alceste* (1674), but in subsequent *tragédies lyriques* such as *Thésée* (1675) and *Atys* (1676), comic scenes were first reduced and then banished as being unsuited to their serious context. *Cadmus et Hermione* marked the beginning of Lully's collaboration with Quinault, which lasted, with a two-year interruption, until *Armide* in 1686 (p. 70). During this fourteen-year period Lully perfected an opera style in which earlier forms of entertainment were assimilated and a newly developed recitative was modelled on the declamation of French classical drama. The style proved both popular and enduring. The form of Lullian *tragédie lyrique* consisted of a prologue – invariably a royal panegyric – and five acts.

Reason, logic and order were fundamental to French thinking during the seventeenth century, and the need for system, balance and regularity is reflected in Lully's operas as in almost all French art of the period. French classical drama contained the order and regularity required to make French opera successful, and according to Lecerf de la Viéville, it was to Racine's mistress, Marie Desmares-Champmeslé, that Lully turned in order to learn the best manner of tragic declamation. La Champmeslé, it was claimed, had been taught by Racine himself. Recitative occupies a central position in Lullian opera, being, as the French writer Romain Rolland observed, 'the very heart of his work'. There are two distinct types of recitative in Lully's *tragédie lyrique*: the *récitatif simple*, accompanied by basso continuo, which carries forward the action, and the *récitatif à noté* or *obligé*, accompanied by the orchestra, which contained an expressive element transcending mere musical commentary. 'Nothing is more agreeable than our recitative,' Lecerf tells us; 'it is a perfect balance between ordinary speech and musical art'; and he quotes Lully as having said that he wished his recitative to be an accurate reflection of the speaking voice.

Although the letters patent of the Académie Royale de Musique refer to the production of operas similar to 'those that are given in Italy', similarity between Lully's operas and those of his Italian contemporaries hardly extends beyond the principle of setting the entire drama to music and a basic division into acts and scenes. The recitatives were inspired by French declamation, but no less French in derivation is the spirit of the *airs*, choruses and dances. The *airs*, of which several types may be found in Lully's operas, are directly related to the *airs de cour*. The *air de cour*, as we have already seen, had not been unaffected by Italian influence, but in Lully's operas, though often expressive of deep feeling, it is not used in the Italian manner as a vehicle for strong passions, and though ornamented, it does not follow the Italian model in the use of coloratura.

The orchestra had a notably important role in French musical drama of the early and mid Baroque, being required to play the overture, to accompany *airs*, choruses and certain recitatives, and to provide the music of the divertissements containing a wide variety of dances, above all minuets, bourrées, gavottes, sarabandes and chaconnes, as well as to supply the various other descriptive symphonies which form an integral part of French opera.

Left: The philosopher René Descartes, whose Compendium musicae *(1618) and* Les passions de l'âme *(1649) contributed to the concept of the 'affections'*

Above: Monteverdi, the composer of madrigals, sacred music and operas in the 'new style', whose genius reconciled the 'first' and 'second practices'. Below: the score of Monteverdi's celebrated lament, 'Lasciate me morire' – all that survives of his opera Arianna *(1608)*

Left: Bernini's Apollo and Daphne, *1622. The legend of Daphne's transformation into a laurel to escape her pursuer was chosen for the earliest Florentine opera,* Dafne *(1597), and later attracted Handel*

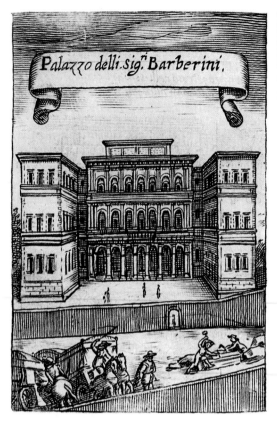

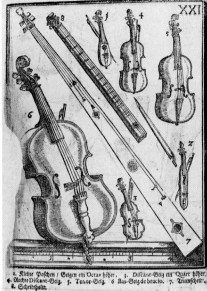

2. Kleine Poschen / Geigen ein Octav höher. 3. Discant-Geig ein Quart höher.
4. Rechte Discant-Geig. 5. Tenor-Geig. 6 Bas-Geig de bracio. 7. Trumscheit.
8. Scheidtholtz.

*Left: The palace of the Barberini, the most
influential patrons of Roman opera*

*Above: Praetorius's Syntagma musicum (1614–
18) offered a systematic approach to the theory
and practice of music, and included information
about most of the instruments of the day*

Lodovico Burnacini del.

left, below: A lavish set for Cesti's opera Il pomo d'oro, *performed at the Viennese court (1667)*

right: Heinrich Schütz, the greatest of the German early Baroque composers. This portrait painted about 1650 shows him in his middle sixties, and he was to live for a further twenty years

below: An autograph page of Schütz's Resurrection Story *(1693), including an 'affective' accompaniment of* viole da gamba

The 'Grand European War Ballet', an engraving of 1643. Germany of the early and mid Baroque suffered musically just as in the other arts from the chaos and privations of the Thirty Years War (1618–48)

right: Jean-Baptiste Lully, the figure who created and then monopolized French opera between 1672 and his death in 1687

opposite, below: Both absurdity and elegance were striking features of early Baroque musical entertainments. left: The comic dame as 'leader of the country music' in the Ballet des fées de la Forêt de Saint Germain *(1625). right: Louis XIV dancing* The Sun *in the* Ballet de la Nuit *(1653). Not only the King but also his future court musician, Lully, danced a part in this entertainment*

below: Borromini's prayer-hall or oratorio *alongside the Chiesa Nuovo in Rome (to which it was added in 1640). The building in which the music was performed gave the mid-Baroque musical form its name. Cavalieri's* La Rappresentatione di Anima e di Corpo *was first performed in the 'new church' in 1600*

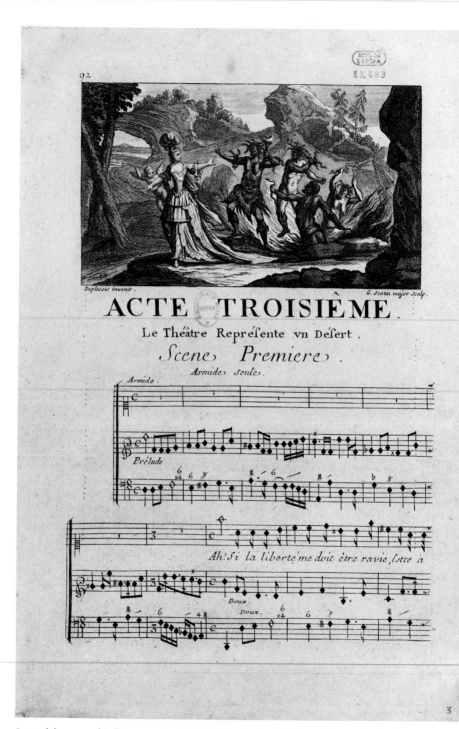

Page of the score of Lully's opera Armide (1686), the last in which he collaborated with the librettist Quinault. The story is based on an episode of Tasso's Gerusalemme liberata (Jerusalem Delivered)

Right: Frontispiece of Jean-Henri d'Anglebert's Pièces de clavecin, a remarkably varied publication including organ pieces, a table of ornaments, arrangements of dances from Lully's operas as well as a short treatise on accompaniment

Title page of the opera Alcyone (1706) by Marin Marais, one of the most musically striking works to be staged in France between Lully's death (1687) and the first opera of Rameau (1733)

Set design for Marc-Antoine Charpentier's Opera Médee *(1693). The scene is the Act III musical climax, in which Medea prepares the poisoned robe for Creuse, and summons monstrous demons to assist her*

Michel-Richard Delalande (or de Lalande), a great favourite of Louis XIV after the death of Lully in 1687

Arcangelo Corelli, whose definition and refinement of musical forms in the mid-Baroque were admired in Italy, France, Germany and England, and whose compositions served as models for later generations of Baroque composers

Musical organization at court

Since the reign of Louis XIII French court music had been organized in three divisions: *Musique de la Chambre, Musique de la Chapelle Royale* and *Musique de la Grande Ecurie*. Under Louis XIV (1645–1715) these divisions grew in size and importance, with some of the positions held by the *musiciens du roi* attracting high salaries. The musicians of the chapel comprised mainly singers but also organists, string players and wood-wind players. The *Grand Ecurie* ('Great Stable') musicians were woodwind, brass and percussion players, while keyboard, woodwind and string players comprised the King's chamber musicians. Almost any of the players of one category might be expected to reinforce those of another, resulting on occasion in a band of imposing proportions. As early as 1609 twenty-two string players were employed at court; and in 1626 Louis XIII formally established what was, in effect, the earliest standardized orchestra, the '24 Violons du Roi' which became attached to the King's chamber music. From this time onwards the violin's prestige increased and Mersenne, who describes the distribution of players in the '24', refers to it as 'The King of Instruments' (1636). Around 1648 Louis XIV created another group of string players which he put in Lully's charge: the *Petits Violons*. Both groups were based on a five-part string texture. Each of the five parts was played by instruments of the violin family, and the division of labour from top to bottom was accordingly: six *dessus* (violins), four *haute-contre* (viola tuning), four *taille* (viola tuning), four *quinte* (viola tuning), and six *basse de violon*; later in the century 7-4-4-2-8 became the norm. We can see from this that an unusual feature of the French string band was the absence of a second violin, and that the three middle parts, the so-called *parties du milieu* or *parties de remplissage*, were tuned as the modern viola, though size of instrument and playing registers differed. Often, though, the violins divided where the violas rested, to form the typical trio textures.

Opera orchestra, the French overture

The 24 *Violons du Roi* or *Grande Bande*, and the *Petits Violons*, also known as the *Violons du Cabinet*, were largely associated with court functions, and it is not clear to what extent, if at all, they were involved in the opera orchestra of the Académie Royale de Musique; we can be certain, however, that his successful experiments with the *Petits Violons* were of assistance to Lully, both in the achievement of standards of performance which became renowned beyond France and in developing his technique as a composer. In Lully's opera orchestra, as with the 24

73

Violons du Roi and the *Petits Violons*, the five-part string band formed the nucleus. In addition, a variety of woodwind, brass and timpani was customarily present in his *tragédies lyriques*. Although we do not have precise information concerning the details of Lully's opera orchestra at this period, early eighteenth-century sources inform us that by then it consisted of some forty-eight players. In Lully's operas these were divided, like his vocal choruses, into *grand* and *petit choeur*. The *grand choeur* played the overture and the 'symphonies', and accompanied the larger choruses; the *petit choeur*, centred on the harpsichord, mainly accompanied solo *récits* and consisted of between nine and eleven players. One source, the *Lettres historiques sur tous les spectacles de Paris* (1719), lists the instruments of the *petit choeur* as follows: harpsichord, two basses de violes; two basses de violons; two theorboes; two *dessus* de violons and two flutes. Lully's woodwind instruments included flutes and recorders, oboes and bassoons, all of which had recently undergone technical improvements. Flutes, oboes and recorders appear frequently in pastoral scenes while oboes and bassoons provide a characteristic trio texture; oboes and bassoons furthermore might double the string parts in the purely orchestral pieces. Trumpets and drums are generally reserved for martial or ceremonial scenes.

Lully's fame was founded on his instrumental dance airs, his ballets and *comédies-ballets*, his *tragédies lyriques*, his achievement as an orchestral disciplinarian and also on the definitive establishment of a form which was to permeate many types of Baroque composition throughout Europe – the French overture. As early as 1640, in the *Ballet de Mademoiselle*, the first *entrée* is called *Ouverture*, and the idea of pairing a slow opening piece of music with a subsequent faster one goes back to the previous century. It was not until 1658, however, in Lully's ballet *Alcidiane*, that we find those distinctive features – the sharply dotted rhythm, followed by a faster fugal section which returns us to the opening idiom – which from then onwards became characteristic of the French overture. For a century afterwards the French overture, in a variety of formal contexts, held its place as one of the major Baroque forms. As late as 1768, Jean-Jacques Rousseau in his *Dictionnaire de Musique* writes that '*Les ouvertures des opéras français sont presque toutes calquées sur celles de Lully*'.

Lully's successors, the opera of Charpentier

While Lully was alive he had no operatic rivals in France. His various restrictive measures prevented productions other than his own from being mounted in Paris or elsewhere. Following his death on 22 March 1687, however, opera was carried forward by several gifted composers, among whom were Pascal Collasse (1649–1709), Marin Marais (1656–1728), André Campra (1660–1744), André Cardinal Destouches (1672–1749), Henry Desmarest (1661–1741) and Marc-Antoine Charpentier (1643–1704). All these composers wrote *tragédies lyriques* in the Lullian manner, to varying acclaim.

Collasse, who had been Lully's secretary during the last decade of his life, and who composed the inner parts of some sections of his operas where Lully had written soprano and bass framework only, scored a success with his *tragédie lyrique, Thétis et Pélée* (1689). Marais, too, was successful with his *Alcide* (1693), for which Lully's son provided the libretto, and *Alcyone* (1706, p. 71). Campra's *Tancrède* (1702) was much admired, and was to be described by Rameau as a 'masterpiece', while Destouches shows individuality in his harmonies and declamation and in his colourful use of the orchestra. Desmarest was one of Lully's most gifted pupils, and like Destouches gave greater flexibility to recitative than we find in the opera of his teacher. A modest number of sacred compositions, mainly 'grands motets', perhaps more consistently illustrate Desmarest's talents, with their well-sustained vocal ensembles and effective polyphony.

Charpentier's two full-scale serious operas are of considerable interest. The earlier was a religious drama, *David et Jonathas* (1688), commissioned by the Jesuit Collège Louis-le-Grand. Here, for the first time, Charpentier was able to draw upon the large forces required for a music drama but hitherto denied him by Lully's monopoly. Charpentier's affective dissonances and striking chromaticisms give heightened harmonic interest to the more predictable Lullian textures, and he treats themes such as jealousy, warfare and death in a vividly imaginative way.

David et Jonathas was followed by Charpentier's operatic masterpiece, *Médée* (1693). This *tragédie lyrique* which ranks among his supreme achievements was written for the Académie Royale de Musique and printed in 1694. The Euripides-based libretto by Thomas Corneille is not as weak as some writers have suggested; it gave Charpentier an opportunity for some powerful and individual characterization, notably in his portrayal of Medea. The chilling modulations of her great monologue at the close of Act III (p. 72), as she prepares the poisoned robe for Creuse, are far removed from the musical language of Lully and his contemporaries. The powerful impact of scenes such as this are not to be encountered again until Rameau's first opera, forty years later. From among a wealth of fine music in *Médée* one might mention vigorous martial airs and rondeaux, varied choruses, and an affecting, deeply felt air for Creon's daughter, Creuse, as she dies in agony. Throughout this work Charpentier's colourful use of the orchestra and his rich harmonic invention derived from French and Italian stylistic traits make for a high level of musical interest. *Médée*, however, was not a success; it was given ten performances and then largely forgotten. Some connoisseurs admired it, among them Sébastian de Brossard (1655–1730); this discerning musician and author of the first French music dictionary blamed the failure on '*les Caballes des envieux et des ignorants*'.

Sacred music

Developments in sacred music during the first half of the seventeenth century were conservative in comparison with the changes taking place in French musical drama. Although little early seventeenth-century French sacred polyphony has survived it seems that the shift away from *stile antico*, or polyphony, to *stile moderno* or monody, occurred only gradually. Settings of the Ordinary of the Mass adhered to *stile antico*, and the *ceremoniale parisiense* (1662) further encouraged conservatism by warning against the inclusion of instruments other than organ in church music. Some ecclesiastical establishments were more conservative than others; the Paris convents and the Jesuit institutions, for instance, were receptive to new musical trends, as we have already seen with Charpentier's sacred *tragédie lyrique, David et Jonathas*.

Music at the Chapelle Royale, on the other hand, developed along separate lines, reflecting the taste of the King. In 1663, the period in which he began to express his personal views on music, Louis XIV appointed four *sous-maîtres* in charge of the chapel music. They operated in quarterly shifts, and were responsible for training the choir and providing music for all religious ceremonies. The appointments went to Henry Dumont, Gabriel Expilly, Pierre Robert and Thomas Gobert. In 1678 the King further expanded the chapel music by the appointment of four organists, Nicolas Lebègue, Guillaume Nivers, Jean-Baptiste Buterne and Jacques-Denis Thomelin. Following the death of two *sous-maîtres* and the retirement of two others, the King held a competition in 1683 through which he selected four replacements: Pascal Collasse, Guillaume Minoret, Nicolas Coupillet and Michel-Richard Delalande; Charpentier had also entered the competition, but was prevented by illness from taking part in the final test, and never subsequently held a court appointment. (The King, however, thought sufficiently well of him to award him a pension.)

The development of *stile moderno* can best be seen in several of the smaller musical forms such as motets, hymns and psalm paraphrases which incorporate elements of the Italian solo motet, the Italian concertato manner and the *airs de cour*. Two composers whose music adopted aspects of *stile moderno* in France during the first half of the century are Guillaume Bouzignac (before 1592–after 1641) and Etienne Moulinié. Both musicians came from southern France where progressive Italian currents in composition were strong. Bouzignac never went to Paris, and his entire work remained in manuscript. Moulinié, who spent most of his life in Paris, shows skill in counterpoint and is imaginative in his treatment of voices.

The grand motet. *Dumont and Delalande*

An important figure in the development and establishment of *stile moderno* in French church music was Henry Dumont (1610–84), who was born near Liège in Belgium as Henry de Thier, but changed his name to Dumont as a young man. Dumont made significant contributions both to the *petit motet* for two and three voices with continuo and to the *grand motet*. To perform the *grands motets*, according to Brossard: 'it is necessary to have five solo voices that constitute the *petit choeur* including soprano, haute-contre (high tenor), two tenors and bass; five parts of the same distribution for the *grand choeur* and five instrumental parts ... Thus one should have a rather large group of performers ...'.

Lully, too, has left us fine examples of the *grand motet*, of which a vigorous setting of the *Te Deum*, a *Dies Irae* and a *Miserere* deserve mention. The *Te Deum* was first performed at Fontainebleau in 1677 and subsequently in 1679 and 1687. It was on this occasion, it is traditionally believed, that Lully inflicted upon himself a fatal injury to the foot with the long stick he was using to beat time. All the evidence, however, shows that Lully conducted with a scroll, so that the foot injury must have been sustained in some other way. Of the *Miserere*, Mme de Sevigné wrote to her daughter in 1672 that 'during the *Libera me* there were tears in every eye. I cannot believe that there is music different from this in heaven itself.' Dumont's *grands motets* provided models for the next generation of composers of sacred music, the most gifted and successful of whom were Michel-Richard Delalande (or de Lalande, or Lalande) and Campra.

Delalande (1657–1726) was among the most talented French composers of his time. We know little of his early life and almost nothing of his formal education in music. During the mid-1660s he became a member of the choir at the church of St Germain-l'Auxerrois; in 1679, following the death of Charles Couperin, Delalande was engaged as organist of St Gervais in Paris until Couperin's son, François, became old enough to take up the post inherited from his father. Delalande, as we have noted, was one of four *sous-maîtres* appointed by Louis XIV to the Chapelle Royale in 1683 (p. 72). Almost from the start he was a favourite of the King, who gradually gave him full control of music, and referred to him in 1704 as *'nostre bien aimé Richard Michel de Lalande'*. He was appointed *Surintendant de la musique de la chambre* in 1689, then *maître* in 1695, and finally, *compositeur* in 1709.

Sixty-four *grands motets* by Delalande have survived, among which his *De profundis* is an outstandingly expressive example. In this work many of the diverse elements of his style are on display, ranging from the architectural grandeur of his homophonic choruses to the profound intimacy and tenderness of the utterances found especially in the *récits* and in the *airs* with obbligato instruments.

Charpentier's sacred music

No less than in his music for the stage, Charpentier proved himself a gifted and innovative composer in the sphere of sacred music, where he was also considerably more prolific. Marc-Antoine Charpentier was born in Paris in 1643. As a young man he went to Rome where he may have studied with Carissimi, one of the greatest Italian mid-Baroque composers of sacred music. Probably during the early 1670s Charpentier returned to Paris and shortly afterwards joined the musical establishment of Marie de Lorraine, Duchesse de Guise. In 1673 Charpentier began an association with Molière's *comediens français*. The association lasted for thirteen years although Molière himself died during one of the first performances of *Le Malade imaginaire* (1673). Some time around 1680 Charpentier took charge of the Dauphin's musicians for whom he composed both sacred and secular music. During the 1680s and 1690s the composer was commissioned for a variety of works by churches, convents and Jesuit foundations. In 1698 Charpentier took up his last appointment, that of *Maître de musique* of the Sainte-Chapelle du Palais in Paris, a post which he held until his death in 1704.

Charpentier's rich legacy of sacred music includes eleven masses, several settings of the Magnificat, over eighty psalms and over two hundred motets. Among the motets there are some thirty-six which fall into the 'oratorio' category (Chapter 6). In these and in his masses Charpentier proves himself capable of expressing a wide range of emotions. A masterpiece of the small oratorio or dramatic motet type is

Le reniement de St Pierre for soloists, chorus and continuo. (Charpentier, however, never used the term 'oratorio', nor does it appear to have been used by any other French composer at this time.) The concluding passages of this work with their anguished harmonic progressions must surely rank among the most pathetic and grief-stricken utterances in the literature of French church music. Charpentier was a master of such poignant writing, skilfully introducing it to his many *Leçons de ténèbres* (tenebrae settings) and in two outstanding compositions of his last years, the dramatic motet *Judicium Salomonis* and the mass for soloists, choruses and orchestra, *Assumpta est Maria*.

French early Baroque instrumental music

There remains to be considered the development of instrumental music. In the early part of the seventeenth century the most widely used instrument for domestic and intimate music-making was the lute. Its

Lute-player, engraving from Bonanni, *Gabinetto Armonico* (1722)

popularity was closely connected with the vogue for the *air de cour*. Among the chief exponents of the lute in France during this period were members of two families, the Gallots and the Gaultiers. Ennemond Gaultier, or 'le vieux Gaultier' (1575–1651), was the most prolific composer among them, and perhaps the greatest celebrity, both as a teacher and as a performer. He held an official court appointment and played before Charles I (1625–49) at the English court. His cousin, Denis Gaultier (1603–1672), was also a gifted composer whose most important work, *La rhétorique des dieux*, was published around 1652. Both cousins excelled in the expression of pathos, which they pioneered in the form of the *tombeau*, a characteristically French musical-poetic tribute to the departed. The idiom of these compositions, sometimes in memory of a deceased friend, was taken up by the early school of French harpsichord composers who further developed the form. The most important member of the Gallot family was Jacques Gallot (d.*c.*1690), a pupil of Ennemond Gaultier who like his teacher excelled in the art of the *tombeau*.

The most significant figure in the early history of French organ music was Jehan Titelouze (1563–1633). His music like that of his younger Italian contemporary, Frescobaldi, reveals a subtle harmonic language. Several composers following Titelouze made important contributions to the development of the French organ repertoire. The *Fugues et caprices à quartre parties* (1660) of François Roberday (1624–80), though conservative, are influenced by styles outside France. In this anthology Roberday acknowledges the composers whose themes he developed into fugues, and he also included pieces by Frescobaldi and Froberger. Roberday's scoring was laid out in such a manner that the music could also be played by a variety of four-part instrumental ensembles. Music of greater significance can be found in the organ pieces of Louis Couperin (1626–61), one of the most gifted and fascinating keyboard composers of the *grand siècle*. Couperin was one of the earliest French composers to specify the registration that he required for the performance of his pieces. The close relationship between French organ music and particular instrumental colours is a distinctive feature during the Baroque, and indeed right up to the present day.

The high-water mark of French Baroque organ music was reached during the last decades of the seventeenth century with Nicolas Antoine Lebègue (*c.*1631–1702), Guillaume Gabriel Nivers (*c.*1632–1714), André Raison (before 1650–1719), Nicolas de Grigny (1672–1703), Louis Marchand (1669–1732) and François Couperin (1668–1733). Grigny, Marchand and Couperin in particular maintain a level of musical interest that is only intermittently achieved by their contemporaries, and their contribution to the French repertory would remain unrivalled throughout the following century.

The composer generally recognized as founder of the French harpsichord school is Jacques Champion, Sieur de Chambonnières (c.1601–72). Chambonnières developed a style in harpsichord writing akin to the lutenists' *stile brisé* – that is, a 'broken', arpeggiated texture. The close relationship between lute and harpsichord writing during the mid-seventeenth century can be observed in the *préludes non mesurés* or 'unmeasured preludes' contained in most composers' keyboard collections at this time. This manner of writing, characterized by semibreve notation without regular bars and without time signature, leaves the shaping of the rhythm to the performer. Movements customarily associated with the seventeenth-century harpsichord suite include the allemande, courante, sarabande and gigue, though other dances including menuets, galliards, gavottes, loures, passepieds, canaries and chaconnes are almost as frequently encountered.

After Chambonnières, the leading figures of the early French harpsichord school were Louis Couperin, already mentioned as a composer for organ, Jean-Henri d'Anglebert (1635–91) and Gaspard Le Roux (d.c.1707). Louis Couperin's music, amounting to over one hundred and thirty pieces, is distingushed by its fine craftsmanship and expressive nobility. Couperin and d'Anglebert have provided many fine examples of the *préludes non mesurés*, but it is perhaps in the chaconnes that Couperin excels. These stylized dances handed down from the *ballet de cour* were in the form of a rondeau with a recurring refrain. Couperin's resonant sonorities, the grandeur which he imposed upon the design and a pervasive melancholy all together create a remarkably powerful impression. D'Anglebert and Le Roux were less prolific than Couperin but their music is of comparable merit. D'Anglebert's *Pièces de clavecin* (1689) was a significant publication containing a wide variety of forms for harpsichord and organ, a comprehensive table of ornaments, arrangements of dances from Lully's operas and a brief treatise on accompaniment. An unusual feature of Le Roux's pieces is their adaptability as ensemble music for two melody parts and figured bass. The composer also envisaged performance on two harpsichords, and included his own versions for six of the pieces in his only collection, published in 1705. Two further important harpsichord composers of the *grand siècle* should be mentioned: Lebègue, better known today for his organ pieces, and Elisabeth-Claude Jacquet de la Guerre (c.1666–1729), whose earliest harpsichord pieces, found only recently, were published in 1687 and dedicated to Louis XIV.

Instrumental ensemble music

The role of instrumental ensemble music in seventeenth-century French opera and ballet has been mentioned earlier in the chapter, but such music is important in its own right, and a fine collection of such pieces was assembled by Delalande for entertainment at court. His *Symphonies pour les Soupers du Roi* are dance suites of particular charm whose music originated in his *opéra-ballets*. It is in his three *Caprices ou Fantaisies*, however, that Delalande's gifts as an orchestral composer are most apparent. The Caprice in G minor, '*que le Roi demandoit souvent*', is the most striking, and contains passages of sustained beauty.

In the first half of the century ensemble music unconnected with the court consisted chiefly of fantasies for viols. An important early collection of these by Eustace Du Caurroy (*c*.1549–1609) was published by Pierre Ballard in Paris in 1610. Other composers of viol music included Nicolas Métru (*c*.1610–*c*.1663), Louis Couperin and Dumont. Throughout the century the viol was the favourite instrument for chamber music, while violins with their brighter tone and power of rhythmic articulation were preferred for opera and dance. Though solo music for bass viol was being written and published well into the eighteenth century, little in the way of viol consort music appeared after the 1660s. Among the last such pieces to be written was Charpentier's affecting *Concert pour quatres parties de violes* which dates from about 1680; even here there are indications that Charpentier may have had members of the violin family in mind. The increasing popularity of the violin was general, and the growing sophistication of music written for it was exemplified in France by François Couperin's trio sonatas, written during the last decade of the century, and Marais's *pièces en trio*, published in 1692.

France was late in adopting the sonata, which as we shall see in the following chapter had been developed in northern Italy from early in the seventeenth century. Couperin was one of the first French composers to experiment with this 'foreign' form, and Corelli was his chief source of inspiration, though the French predilection for the *air* is often apparent. During the 1690s, when according to the contemporary French lexicographer, Sébastien de Brossard, 'every composer in Paris ... was madly writing sonatas in the Italian manner', Couperin's mastery of the trio sonata is displayed in pieces such as *La pucelle*, *L'astrée*, *La superbe* and *La Sultane*. Charpentier's Sonata for eight instruments of the early 1680s, like his cantata *Orphée descendant aux enfers*, ranks among the earliest and most impressive of its kind in France. Consideration of the French sonata, however, belongs to the late Baroque, and to a later chapter.

6

The Italian mid-Baroque: oratorio, cantata, sonata, concerto

D URING THE FIRST HALF OF THE SEVENTEENTH CENTURY opera rapidly established itself as one of the major Baroque forms, influencing the development of other types of vocal music, sacred and secular. Among these were the oratorio and the cantata. We have already considered the ambivalent position of Cavalieri's sacred drama, *Rappresentatione di Anima et di Corpo*, which had been performed in Rome in 1600. Its staging, with scenery, costumes and dancing, allows us to think of the work as an opera, yet its sacred inspiration, its performance in the oratory of the Chiesa Nuova, its static drama and its lack of human interest count against its being regarded as wholeheartedly representative of the genre. Although Cavalieri's staged drama with music did not set a fashion, its up-to-date musical style was influential in the subsequent development of large-scale sacred compositions intended for performance in oratories.

The oratorio, as a musical form, originated in Rome, taking its name from the oratories or prayer-halls in which it was performed. Not until 1640, however, do we find documented use of the word to describe a musical composition. By the 1660s the term was established in connection with musical settings of dramatic texts based on the Bible or other sacred sources. In the mid-sixteenth century the Italian religious leader and saint Filippo Neri (1515–95) founded a group which, in 1575, became recognized by Pope Gregory XIII as an official community. It was known as the Congregazione dell'Oratorio and its meeting place was the church of Sta Maria in Vallicella, popularly called the Chiesa Nuova, having been built by Neri on the site of an older church of the same name. Not until 1640, however, did the Chiesa Nuova have its own oratory, designed by the great Baroque architect Francesco Borromini (p. 69). Until this was completed the Oratorians used various halls in the neighbourhood of the Chiesa Nuova.

One of the most important composers to provide music for the Oratorians in the late sixteenth century was Giovanni Animuccia (*c*.1500–

71). His two volumes of *laude spirituali* intended, as he put it, 'for the consolation and needs of many spiritual and devout persons, religious and secular alike' formed the roots of early oratorio. It was Cavalieri's *Rappresentatione di Anima et di Corpo*, however, that established the new, monodic style in music for the oratories.

An illuminating account of the performance of oratorio is provided by the French writer and bass viol player André Maugars (*c.*1580–*c.*1645), who travelled to Rome during the late 1630s and gave an account of his musical impressions in the S. Marcello Chapel in his *Response faite à un curieux sur le sentiment de la musique d'Italie escrite à Rome le premier octobre 1639*, published in Paris the following year:

There is still another kind of music which is not performed in France … called *Stile recitativo.* … This admirable and ravishing music is heard only on Fridays during Lent, from three to six o'clock. The church is not nearly as big as the Sainte Chapelle in Paris. At the end is a spacious rood screen with a medium sized organ, very sweet and very suitable for voices. At the two sides of the church there are two small galleries where the best musical instruments were located. The voices began with a Psalm in the form of a Motet and then the instruments played a very good Sinfonia. The voices after this sang a story from the Old Testament in the form of a spiritual drama, like that of Susanna, of Judith and Holofernes, of David and Goliath. Each singer represented a personage of the story and perfectly expressed the force of the words. Then one of the most celebrated preachers recited the Exhortation. When this was finished the music recited the Gospel of the day, like the story of the Good Samaritan, the Feast at Canaa, the story of Lazarus, of Mary Magdalen, of Our Lord's Passion, the singers imitating to perfection the personages the Evangelist writes about. I cannot praise the Recitative Music enough; one must hear it to judge of its merit.

During the first half of the seventeenth century two strands of oratorio developed in Rome, the *oratorio volgare* and the *oratorio latino*. The principal distinction between the two was in text rather than music. The *oratorio volgare* used an Italian, that is, vernacular text, which would have been widely understood by audiences. The settings were poetic and in this respect shared features with operas, madrigals and cantatas. The *oratorio latino* on the other hand used narrative and dramatic texts predominantly in prose, a feature which it shared with the motet, and the Latin language would have been understood only by an educated audience.

Among the early composers who made an important contribution to the *oratorio volgare* were Domenico Mazzocchi (1592–1665) and his brother Virgilio (1597–1646), Pietro Della Valle (1586–1652) – whose use in a letter written in 1640 of the word 'oratorio' to denote a musical composition is the earliest documented instance – Luigi Rossi and Marco Marazzoli (*c.*1602–62). Latin oratorios in Rome were chiefly associated with the Oratorio del Santissimo Crocifisso. Its flourishing musical tradition is mirrored in the list of composers who at one time or another fostered it – Palestrina, Marenzio, Anerio, Landi, Virgilio Mazzocchi, Carissimi, Stradella and Alessandro Scarlatti. The Crocifisso remained the most important centre for Latin oratorio performance throughout the second half of the seventeenth and into the early eighteenth century.

Carissimi and Jephte

The greatest Italian composer of oratorio during the mid-seventeenth century was Giacomo Carissimi (1605–74). Carissimi was born near Rome and became, first, a singer at the cathedral at Tivoli, then organist there between 1624 and 1627. During the following two years he was *Maestro di cappella* at S. Rufino at Assisi, but by the end of 1629 he had taken up a post as a teacher at the Collegio Germanico in Rome; at the same time he was appointed *Maestro di cappella* at Sant'Apollinare, the church of the Collegio, a position which he held until his death. The Collegio Germanico had been founded in the previous century by the Jesuits to train Germans for the priesthood. It had a fine reputation for music, as we learn from Bernardino Castorio, rector of the Collegio during the first three decades of the century, who wrote in 1611 that 'the excellence of the music there was the sole reason for its being one of the most frequented churches in Rome', and 'the best music of the city was to be found at the Collegio, that it was listed in books as one of the marvels of Rome, and that all the foreign visitors wanted to hear it'. Carissimi's post, however, did not prevent him from activities outside the Collegio, and in 1656 Queen Christina of Sweden, who had renounced the Swedish throne, embraced Catholicism and arrived in Rome the previous year, appointed him her *Maestro di cappella del concerto di camera*. Carissimi also is known to have worked at the Oratorio del Santissimo Crocifisso, though he declined appointments which might have taken him further afield.

Although Carissimi wrote masses, motets and one hundred and fifty surviving cantatas, it is for his Latin oratorios that he is chiefly renowned. Little of his music has survived in autograph, which means that precise dating is impossible in a great many instances; nor, except for the

Historia de Abraham et Isaac which was performed at the Collegio Germanico in 1656, do we know where his Latin oratorios were performed, though it is likely that they were intended for the Crocifisso. One of Carissimi's best known masterpieces in this form is *Jephte*. The text as with all his Latin oratorios is anonymous, and like the majority of them is based on the Old Testament. Jephtha promises God that he will sacrifice the first living thing he sees on his return home if he wins the battle against the Ammonites. His army of Israelites is victorious but his joy is short-lived, for it is his own daughter whom he first encounters on his return. Carissimi's feeling for drama is immediately and forcefully apparent in this work. The story is told principally by the *historicus*, or narrator, but also in concertato style, a favourite textural effect of contrasting and combining solo elements with larger forces, by the characters themselves and the chorus. The score is rich in dissonant harmonies to represent Jephtha's plight and in strikingly contrasted 'affects', ranging from the fierce, warrior-like bass solo, 'Fuggite, cedite', to the deeply expressive lament of Jephtha's daughter, 'Plorate, plorate colles'.

One of those present at a performance of *Jepthe* in Rome during the late 1640s was the German theologian and music theorist Athanasius Kircher (1601–80). Kircher gives us a valuable impression both of the composer and the work in his influential musical compendium, *Musurgia universalis*, published in Rome in 1650. He praises Carissimi as 'a very excellent and famous composer ... [who] through his genius and the felicity of his compositions, surpasses all others in moving the minds of listeners to whatever affection he wishes. His compositions are truly imbued with the essence and life of the spirit.' Of *Jephte* he writes,

> In a musical style called recitative, Carissimi gives expression to the bewildered father with singular genius and piercing tones. Jephte is suddenly transported from joy to sadness and lamentation as his daughter unexpectedly runs towards him, because the irrevocable decree of the vow must fall on her for this fateful greeting. Carissimi achieves this transition to the opposite affection beautifully with a change of key. To this he later adds a lament for six voices by the daughter's virgin companions, in which they intensely bewail her misfortune. This is composed with such skill you would swear that you hear the sobs and moans of the weeping girl.

In England, more than a century after Carissimi's death, Dr Burney remarked in his *General History of Music* (1789) that: 'No composer of the last century was more the delight of his contemporaries or more respected by posterity than Giacomo Carissimi.' Carissimi will be considered further as a composer of cantatas.

Later oratorios. Stradella

Operatic elements further penetrated the oratorio during the later decades of the seventeenth century. An important reform was instigated by the Roman oratorio librettist Archangelo Spagna (c.1632–1720), who remarks in the preface to his *Oratorii overo Melodrammi sacri*, published in 1706, that by abandoning the narrator he is furthering his aim to achieve *un perfetto melodramma spirituale*. As the relationship between opera and oratorio strengthened, so oratorio began to thrive in centres other than Rome. In Florence it flourished under the patronage of Prince Ferdinando de Medici (1663–1713); in Venice, receptive to opera-related entertainment, oratorios were performed at the four charitable orphanages. The most important composer of oratorio working in Venice during the latter part of the seventeenth century was Giovanni Legrenzi (1626–90), who was *Maestro di coro* at the orphanage of the Mendicanti, *Maestro* of the Oratorio at Sta Maria della Fava and eventually *Maestro di cappella* at S. Marco. His role in the development of the sonata was an important one, and his name will appear again later in the chapter.

The outstanding oratorio composer of the late seventeenth century was, like Carissimi, a representative of the Roman school. Alessandro Stradella (1644–82) was born in Rome, and as a boy sang in various Roman churches. By the age of twenty he had received a commission for a cantata from Queen Christina of Sweden, who appointed him *servitore di camera*, and he also enjoyed the patronage of other leading Roman families. His personality was colourful; after an attempt to embezzle money from the Roman Catholic Church in 1669 he was persuaded to leave Rome, but returned after a brief absence. In 1677 he fell out with a senior representative of the Catholic Church and was obliged to leave Rome once more. Stradella seems first to have travelled to Venice, where after a brief stay he left with one of his pupils who was also the mistress of his employer, Alvise Contarini. Contarini pursued the couple to Turin, intent on retrieving the girl and killing Stradella. He failed in this and a second attempt on Stradella's life, and Stradella, by now alone, moved to Genoa where he carried on an intrigue with a girl from a wealthy family. This time an assassination attempt by a soldier was successful.

Stradella made important contributions to several musical forms, such as opera and instrumental music, but the work for which he is chiefly renowed is his *oratorio volgare*, *San Giovanni Battista*, performed in

Rome at the oratory of the church of S. Giovanni dei Fiorentini in 1675. The libretto, by a Sicilian priest Girardo Ansaldi, dispenses with a *testo* or narrator, providing Stradella with a straightforward story which he set with considerable dramatic force. The work is striking both for the subtlety with which Stradella portrays the central relationship of the drama, between Herod and John the Baptist, and for the example which it provides of division between concertino and concerto grosso textures in the orchestra. This is one of the earliest known instances of such writing before Corelli (who was very probably a violinist in the ensemble at the first performance, as he was in Handel's *La Resurrezione*). Stradella's dramatic gifts – he was a successful opera composer, also – are seldom more affectingly displayed than in Herodiade's *Sode Dive*, with its yearning suspensions and the final duet in which the contrasting emotions of foreboding and joy are expressed by Herod and his daughter. Stradella emphasizes the characters' depth of incomprehension, both of their own and each other's feelings, by ending the oratorio on the dominant and with a question, 'And tell me, why? And tell me why?'

'Composers of renown did not fail to regard themselves as fortunate and happy when compositions of Stradella fell into their hands,' wrote Francesco Maria Veracini in his treatise *Il trionfo della pratica musicale* (*c.*1765), 'their intention being not only to study them but even to take from them phrases or imitations.'

The cantata

The most important form of vocal music in the Baroque period, other than opera and oratorio, was the cantata. We have discussed in previous chapters the development of songs, or monodies, for solo voice with continuo accompaniment which took place during the first three or four decades of the seventeenth century. Alongside this development can be seen the gradual decline in popularity of the older type of polyphonic song, so that Pietro Della Valle, in his discourse *Della musica dell'età nostra* (1640), was able to observe that, by then, madrigals were seldom sung, 'nor is there occasion to sing them, since people prefer to hear singing freely by heart with instruments in the hand rather than to watch four or five companions singing with book in hand at a table like schoolboys'. In fact, composers continued to bring out polyphonic madrigals well into the seventeenth century, the eight unaccompanied examples in four and five parts by Alessandro Scarlatti (undated) being among the last.

The earliest known occurrence of the term 'cantata' is its use (*cantada*) by Alessandro Grandi (c.1575–1630) in a reprinted edition of his *Cantade et arie* (1620) to describe three pieces in the form of strophic-variation solos over a regularly moving ostinato bass. A more familiar example of this type of composition is Monteverdi's *Ohimè ch'io cado* which appeared both in his posthumous ninth book and in a collection of *Ariose vaghezze*, c.1624, by Carlo Milanuzzi. One of the first composers to use the designation 'cantata' extensively was the Italian composer, singer and teacher Giovanni Sances (c.1600–79). In his two-part collection *Cantade ...libro secondo* (1633), Sances applies the term both to strophic pieces – that is to say, pieces in which all stanzas of the text are sung to the same music – and to pieces that are through-composed, i.e. in which new music is given to each stanza. Sances's collection contains a rich variety of pieces drawing upon both old and newer techniques, but significantly for the early development of the cantata, it included extended compositions in which recitative and arioso or aria-like writing follow one another according to the requirements of the text.

Although the collections both of Grandi and Sances were published in Venice, the early growth of the cantata took place largely in Rome. Rome offered a fertile environment for the cultivation of all kinds of chamber music. Many of its leading families, such as the Barberini, Pamphili, Colonna, Ruspoli and Ottoboni, were generous, enthusiastic and informed patrons of the arts who encouraged and supported composers as well as painters and sculptors. There the cantata gradually developed from monody with strophic variation and crystallized into a clearly defined pattern of alternating recitatives and arias for one or two solo voices with continuo accompaniment. In this it somewhat resembled a scene from an opera, so going some way to satisfy the Roman demand for lavish entertainment, which was expensive to mount and for which opportunity was limited.

One of the earliest and most successful composers of cantatas in Rome was Luigi Rossi, who as we have already seen was a gifted opera composer. His patrons belonged to the Borghese and Barberini families, and it was through the latter that Rossi was invited to Paris to compose and stage his opera *Orfeo* in 1646. Rossi's cantatas range from simple strophic ariettas, or *ariette corte*, to works comprising sections of recitative, arioso and aria. An attractive example of the short arietta is the song 'Quando spiega la notte', in which the three twelve-line stanzas are unified both by a common bass line and an affecting refrain; but it is perhaps in the 'lament' in opera and cantata that Rossi reveals his considerable expressive and melodic gifts most vividly. The 'Lamento della Regina di Zverzia', mourning the death of Gustavus II Adolphus who fell in battle in 1632, is a fine example, skilfully combining recitative, arioso and aria.

Whereas the greater number of Rossi's cantatas are simple strophic ariettas, many of those by his slightly younger contemporary, Carissimi, take the form of arias in several sections, or *arie di più parti*. In Carissimi's cantatas of this type the sections are both fewer and longer than those of Rossi. Here too the composer blends the element of recitative, arioso and aria with subtlety. Carissimi's cantatas, like Rossi's, are notable for their lyrical melodies, but also for their strong sense of tonality, revealed in clear-cut modulations. These qualities are even more pronounced in the cantatas of Cesti, who is chiefly remembered for his opera *Il pomo d'oro* (1667). Cesti's cantatas are mainly for solo voice and continuo, usually following the pattern of alternating recitative and aria; but he also achieves variety in uninterrupted sequences of stylistically diverse and melodically inventive arias. We should not leave the mid-century Italian chamber cantata without briefly mentioning those of the Venetian singer Barbara Strozzi (1619–64). Her assured style, bold harmonies and colourful interpretation of text can be found in works such as *Appresso a i molli argenti* (1659).

Among the greatest Italian composers of cantatas and closely related forms during the later years of the century were Stradella, Pasquini, Steffani, Legrenzi, and, above all, Alessandro Scarlatti. In the hands of these composers the chamber cantata form became more clearly defined. Stradella's cantatas are varied in their requirements, ranging from what was becoming an established pattern of two alternating recitatives and arias to elaborate compositions with an important instrumental element, such as we find in his operas and oratorios.

In contrast to the main body of vocal chamber works of his contemporaries, Steffani preferred the duet. He was no less an influential figure than Stradella in the development of late Baroque vocal style, revealing in his duets an acute sensibility to nuances of texts which he set in a variety of forms; they were influential for many composers of a younger generation, and were highly praised by Johann Mattheson in his treatise *Der vollkommene Capellmeister* (1739):

The Italian style of duet now lacks much of the good qualities of piety and clarity ... because of its fugal, artificial and interwoven nature. However, [Steffani's] duets ... are a special delight to musically educated ears, in the chamber as well as in the church (and formerly, in Steffani's time, also in the theatre), provided that accomplished and reliable singers can be found for them; ... in this kind of duet ...

Steffani incomparably surpassed all other composers known to me and deserves to be taken as a model to this day; for such things do not easily grow old.

Alessandro Scarlatti: life, cantatas, serenatas

The Italian chamber cantata reached a peak in the works of Alessandro Scarlatti (1660–1725). Scarlatti was born at Palermo, in Sicily, and was sent to Rome in 1672. By the end of the decade he had completed an oratorio and an opera, but despite early successes and generous patronage from the Pamphili and Ottoboni families, he left for Naples, where he was appointed *Maestro di cappella* to the Viceroy. He remained in Naples for eighteen years, composing operas, cantatas, serenatas and oratorios, mainly for the Viceroy and his household but also for the public. In 1702 Scarlatti left for Florence, and, after a period of some eighteen months, returned to Rome, where he became assistant music director at S. Maria Maggiore and once again entered the service of Cardinal Ottoboni. In 1706 Scarlatti was admitted to the Accademia dell'Arcadia established by Queen Christina of Sweden, earlier a patron of the composer. The esteem in which he was held in Rome did not, however, keep him there, and in 1708 he returned to his former position at Naples. Scarlatti remained in Naples during the following decade, composing in the increasingly popular comic opera and intermezzo forms as well as writing keyboard and instrumental music. By 1718 Scarlatti was back in Rome, where his patrons financed his last operas. His stay, however, was short, and by 1722 he had returned to Naples where he died in 1725.

Scarlatti's cantatas number about six hundred, most of which are for solo voice and continuo. More than any other composer, he standardized the pattern of recitative-aria-recitative-aria which remained established in Italy until the end of the Baroque period. His cantatas, however, do not invariably fall into this pattern, and, notably in some early compositions, a rich variety of movement sequences occurs, such as those where verses of a text are separated by intervening sections of recitative, aria and arioso. An example of this is to be found in the cantata *No, non ti voglio Cupido* for two voices and continuo. Towards the end of the seventeenth century Scarlatti moved towards the alternating pattern of secco recitative and da capo aria. The formal scheme of a da capo movement, so called because of the indication 'da capo' at the end of the B section, is in its simplest terms, ABA. Sometimes the repeat section did not return to the opening bars but instead to a point within it; when this occurred the letters DS (*dal segno*), as opposed to DC, were used, and in these instances performers would return 'to the sign'.

The texts of mid to late Baroque Italian secular cantatas are varied both in structure and in subject, though most have the theme of lovers in a pastoral landscape. The stories are most frequently taken from mythology, and their texts determine the musical expression, which illustrates certain basic 'affections' such as triumph, love, joy, sorrow, pain, anger, hatred, and so forth. The poetry was predominantly lyrical in character and expressly designed for musical treatment. Scarlatti excelled in his settings of these 'Arcadian' texts, and was both skilled and imaginative in his treatment of the larger form of the serenata.

Serenatas were predominantly occasional pieces, commissioned by a patron, and occupying territory somewhere between the chamber cantata and the opera. A notably fine example by Scarlatti is his *Venere e Adone: Il giardino di amore* (*c.*1700–5) for solo soprano and alto voices with instrumental ensemble. In such pieces the orchestra usually plays an important role, and in this work there are several features of interest, notably the division into concertino and concerto grosso and the use of pizzicato, never ordered by Corelli. In the closing duet Scarlatti achieves a radiant fusion of vocal and instrumental techniques where the voices provide a concertino punctuated by the instruments in alternating bursts of sound. *Il giardino di amore* reveals Scarlatti as a gifted melodist, and accomplished in his treatment of the interrelationship between vocal and instrumental elements. Scarlatti's cantatas and serenatas are sophisticated compositions, mainly written for performance by professional or gifted amateur singers for the enjoyment of the cultivated audiences who gathered at the weekly *conversazioni* organized by Cardinal Ottoboni, the Marchese Francesco Maria Ruspoli and Cardinal Pamphili at their respective palaces.

The sonata

It was in the second half of the century that the sonata finally shook off the characteristic of the older canzona. The canzona was multi-sectional with contrapuntal roots, and its sections were generally short. As the sonata developed, it gradually reduced the number of voice-parts – a process which eventually resulted in the trio and solo sonata. As tonal gradually supplanted modal thinking in the minds of composers, and with the new possibilities afforded by key relationships, sections expanded in length to become movements. During the 1660s a basic four-movement pattern of *slow-fast-slow-fast* began to emerge, in which the customary imitative writing of the opening section of the canzona was often retained in the second movement of the sonata. At about the same time instrumental sonatas began to fall into two discernible categories, the *sonata da chiesa* (church sonata) and the *sonata da camera* (chamber sonata). The *sonata da chiesa* excluded movements which were overtly classified as dances – though dance measures occur in a great many pieces in this category – and were generally of serious intent; the *sonata da camera*, on the other hand, contained movements bearing the names of dances and often falling into the pattern of a dance suite; their opening movement, however, is usually a prelude and seldom a piece in dance measure. The customary instrumentation for mid- to late seventeenth-century Italian sonatas is two violins with basso continuo. This was the standard trio-sonata texture throughout the Baroque period, though it should be stressed that four rather than three players are required: two violinists, a cellist and a keyboard player to 'realize' the figured bass. Likewise a solo sonata, unless specifically stated to be without a bass part, requires three players.

Among the composers whose music reflects the many significant developments leading to the formation of the late Baroque style were Giovanni Legrenzi (1626–90), Maurizio Cazzati (c.1620–77) and Giovanni Battista Vitali (1632–92). In Legrenzi's instrumental music we find an interesting blend of the older ensemble canzona style with forward-looking characteristics such as strong tonal affirmation and clarity of design. Legrenzi was a skilled contrapuntalist whose *Suonate da chiesa, e da camera* (Opus 4, 1656) and the sonatas of Opus 8 (1663) and Opus 10, *La Cetra* (1673), deserve to be more widely known. Cazzati was less gifted than Legrenzi as a composer but made an important contribution to the development of violin playing with imaginative slow movements and the publication of *Sonate a 2 istrementi* in 1670, while *Maestro di cappella* at S. Petronio in Bologna (between 1657 and 1671). Cazzati's most talented pupil, Vitali, was like Legrenzi an able contrapuntalist. In 1689 he published his *Artificii musicali* consisting of a veritable compendium of contrapuntal forms. As well as being associated with S. Petronio, Vitali was also a member of the Accademia dei Filarmonici. This institution played an important part in musical activities in Bologna by providing an opportunity for learned discussion and the performance of new music by its members; at the same time schools of trumpet and cello playing did much to create the textural and structural possibilities which were to be developed so imaginatively in the next century.

Corelli. The sonatas and concerti grossi

During the last two decades of the seventeenth century the focus of instrumental music shifted from northern Italy to Rome. Here the techniques of two composers, Stradella (p. 87) and Corelli (p.72), were beginning to exert influence both in Italy and abroad. Arcangelo Corelli (1653–1713) was born in Fusignano, near Ravenna. In 1666 he went to study at Bologna, and four years later was admitted to the Accademia dei Filarmonici there. By the mid-1670s, however, Corelli was living in Rome, where he acquired a reputation as one of the city's foremost violinists. His first important patron in Rome was Queen Christina of Sweden, to whom he dedicated his earliest published collection, the twelve church *Sonate a tre*, Opus 1 (1681). In the artistically avant-garde climate prevailing in Rome at this time it is hardly suprising to find wealthy patrons indulging in rivalry; Cardinal Pamphili became Corelli's next patron, though the composer remained on cordial terms with the exiled Swedish queen. In 1684 Corelli began to play for the musical gatherings or academies organized by Pamphili at his Palazzo al Corso; in the following year he published his *Sonate da camera a tre* (Opus 2) which he dedicated to his new patron. In 1687 Corelli became music director in the Pamphili household, but when Pamphili left Rome for Bologna in 1690 the composer was taken up by Cardinal Ottoboni. A friendly rapport developed between the two men, and Corelli lived in the Ottoboni palace, the Cancellaria, almost until the end of his life. He dedicated his *Sonate a tre* (Opus 4) to Ottoboni in 1694. Corelli's contribution to the solo violin repertory consists of a single set of twelve sonatas, six each of the 'church' and 'chamber' idiom, published in 1700 as his Opus 5. It gained immense popularity and was reprinted many times throughout the century.

The period of employment with Ottoboni offered Corelli a secure and musically stimulating environment. His influence as a composer and performer was widespread, and his compositional style was disseminated as a model throughout Europe. During these years Corelli continued to compose not only sonatas but also concertos; he directed operatic performances both for Ottoboni and outside the Cancellaria, and in 1706 was admitted to the Accademia degli Arcadi, one of the most exclusive of the many academies of this time. (Alessandro Scarlatti and Bernardo Pasquini were also elected members in that year.) Corelli virtually retired from public life after 1708, spending his last years revising his hitherto unpublished concertos.

Corelli was no more the inventor of the concerto than he was of the violin sonata, but in both he was the creator of a style which served as a model to later generations of composers. The concerto grosso form, of which Corelli provided twelve masterly examples, dates from at least as early as the 1670s and is a Roman concept. One of its pioneers was Stradella, who has provided us with a single surviving example of a purely instrumental piece in which he adopts the concerto grosso principle, characterized by the use of a small group of instruments or 'concertino' against the full ensemble, or 'ripieni'. Although Corelli's *Concerti grossi*, Opus 6, were not published until 1714, the year following his death, we know that he had been writing concertos much earlier in his Roman period. The German composer Georg Muffat indicates his impressions of Corelli's concertos and their manner of performance in the foreword to his *Ausserlesene Instrumental-Music* (1701), a set of twelve concertos based on Corelli's models, where he writes:

I present to you, sympathetic reader, this first collection of my instrumental concertos, blending the serious and the gay, entitled 'of a more select harmony' because they contain (in the ballet airs) not only the liveliness and grace drawn intact from the Lullian well, but also certain profound and unusual affects of the Italian manner, various capricious and artful conceits, and alternations of many sorts, interspersed with special diligence between the great choir [concerto grosso] and the trio [concertino] of soloists ... The idea of this ingenious mixture first occurred to me some time ago in Rome, where I learned the Italian manner on the harpsichord from the world-famous Signor Bernardo [Pasquini] and where I heard, with great pleasure and astonishment, several concertos of this sort, composed by the gifted Signor Arcangelo Corelli, and beautifully performed with the utmost accuracy by a great number of instrumental players. Having observed the considerable variety in these, I composed several of the present concertos, which were tried over at the house of the aforesaid Signor Arcangelo Corelli (to whom I am deeply indebted for many useful observations touching this style, most graciously communicated to me ...)

Later in the same foreword Muffat remarks that such works may be played either on single strings, or as concerti grossi with the intended contrast between concertino and the full ensemble; this is borne out by Corelli's statement on the title page of his own concertos, where he describes the concerto grosso as optional.

Vincenzo Martinelli, writing to the Duke of Buckingham in 1758, reflects contemporary opinion on the natural qualities of Corelli's style:

If we came to enquire whence comes this magical power of Corelli's compositions, we shall very quickly find that their secret inheres in their marvellously imitating the most dulcet and pleasing characteristics of the human voice, and their contriving to [be expressive], each according to its range, and with regard to the most exact rules of art. The degrees of power of the human voice are as manifold as the diverse ages of man.

What Corelli achieved, above all, was a codification and refinement of classical Baroque language of the seventeenth century through what has been termed 'the distillation of the figures of thought' (Roger North) – those multifarious affects pervading the language of Italian music in the years approaching 1700. The result was, paradoxically, a conservative style, untypical of his Italian contemporaries; neither the academic style of Bologna nor Venetian virtuosity is directly exploited. Corelli's music is characterized by clear tonal formulae, symmetry and resourcefulness of melodic line, and a consolidation and control not previously attempted.

Torelli's concertos

Before we leave the development of the early and mid-Baroque concerto we must return to the Bologna of Corelli's student years. Giuseppe Torelli (1658–1709) was born in Verona but moved to Bologna in the early 1680s, and in 1684 became like Corelli a member of the Accademia dei Filarmonici. Years of travel took Torelli to Germany and Austria, but by 1701 he was once more in Bologna, where towards the end of his life he prepared his finest concertos for publication. These were printed shortly after his death in 1709 as *Concerti grossi con una pastorale per il Ss Natale* (Opus 8). Torelli's Opus 8 contains twelve concertos, of which six have a concertino of two violins only, as distinct from Corelli's concertino of two violins and cello, and six a concertino that consists of a single violin; in his adoption of the three-movement form of the Italian opera overture (fast-slow-fast), and in his carefully organized alternating sections of solo with *tutti*, Torelli takes a decisive step towards the concerto form of the late Baroque.

Torelli's music may not be consistently inspirational, but the increasing contrast between solo instruments and orchestral *tutti*, as well as clear-cut formal patterns, were to be reflected in the way eighteenth-century composers pursued extended movements, carrying forward principles developed initially by the Venetians and by Vivaldi in particular. But first we should consider how opera became consolidated into a genre no less characteristic of the late Baroque.

7
Eighteenth-century Italy: opera and instrumental music

BY THE END OF THE SEVENTEENTH CENTURY Italian opera had acquired some universally recognized features, such as the three-movement pattern of the overture or sinfonia, and the alternating sequence of recitative and aria, discussed in Chapter 3. We have seen, too, that certain themes drawn from history, legend and myth were especially favoured by librettists. Even so, we should beware of over-generalization when dealing with forms and conventions, since important distinctions appear between operas from place to place and, indeed, in a single place over a period of years. Generally speaking, however, the basic ingredients remain fairly constant; by the late seventeenth century most arias were cast in da capo form with increasing importance being given to orchestral accompaniment as opposed to the traditional accompaniment of continuo. Emphasis was placed on arias with beautiful melodies, sometimes at the expense of drama, while comic elements, which had been a feature of music in seventeenth-century opera, were greatly reduced if not entirely excluded. The three unities – time, place and action – were generally observed, and the respective functions of recitative to carry forward the action and of aria to reflect thought and feelings were strictly adhered to.

The two focal points of opera in Italy during the first half of the eighteenth century were Venice in the north and Naples in the south. Rome, too, was an active centre, but tensions between ecclesiastical patronage of the arts on the one hand, and lay patronage on the other, eventually led to a temporary papal restriction of 'public' opera in 1697. Thereafter there was no shortage of private commissions, but since these were given to almost all outstanding opera composers of the day, a specifically Roman tradition had ceased to exist by the end of the first decade of the eighteenth century. Florence, too, though less spectacularly involved in operatic production than during the previous century, continued to perform operas at its two regular theatres, the Pergola and the Cocomero, both of which belonged to Florentine academies, and to supply operas to provincial opera houses.

The early eighteenth century was a period of reform or, more precisely, rationalization in opera. Prompted by the various complexities and extravagances of seventeenth-century opera, librettists sought a basis for their texts in the rules governing the classical literary genres, themselves subject to reform during the latter years of the century. Among the most significant of the early reform poets were Apostolo Zeno (1668–1750) and Francesco Silvani (c.1660–before 1750), both of whom influenced Venetian operatic tradition in the early eighteenth century with a trend towards classical tragedy and an emphasis upon historical truth. Zeno's principal concern was the quality of the text. Subjects were given a new seriousness as the comic element and dramatic irrelevances were excluded. Furthermore Zeno did much to simplify and condense the complicated action of contemporary 'opera seria' or heroic opera; however it would seem he himself viewed his reforms with a degree of scepticism, since in a letter to Giuseppe Gravisi (1735) he concludes that all but a few of his libretti were 'failures'.

Metastasio and opera seria

The movement towards elevating opera seria, the most important musical genre of the time, was continued by Zeno's successor as Habsburg court poet at Vienna, Pietro Metastasio (1698–1782), the greatest Italian dramatist of the period. Metastasio's rationalization of the opera libretto finally dispensed with the excesses and distractions which characterized seventeenth-century opera. His aim was to instruct his readers and audiences through pleasurable entertainment, observing that 'pleasures that do not succeed in making impositions on the mind are of short duration'. With outstanding lyricism of language and literary clarity he injected new vigour into existing conventions, and introduced a greater degree of psychological truth than had been required for the legendary tales popular in the previous century. Metastasio was notably skilful in the structure of his plots, and brilliantly effective in the way in which he distributed the arias for each singer, ensuring the greatest variety in style between one aria and the next. The 'exit' aria at the end of major scenes, where the singer leaves the stage sometimes signalling a change of scene, is standard in his texts. Many smaller scenes, however, run into one another without an aria and without opportunity for visual scene change. Usually there were five or so principal singers and two lesser ones; their arias, according to the degree of importance of the characters to whom they were allotted, dominated the performance, and in this sense opera was a vehicle for the great singers of the day. Metastasio also incorporated choruses, sometimes allowing them to function dramatically.

Metastasio had no serious rival as a librettist and his texts, for which he always envisaged a musical setting, were used by almost all composers of Italian *opera seria* at the time. His first full-length libretto, *Didone abbandonata*, was set by Domenico Sarri (1679–1744) for Naples in 1723, by Albinoni for Venice in 1725, and by Leonardo Vinci (1696–1730) for Rome in 1726. Vinci was an outstandingly successful opera composer and an important representative of Neapolitan opera tradition. In the historian Burney's words, he was the first opera composer who

> without degrading his art rendered it the friend, though not the slave to poetry, by simplifying and polishing melody, and drawing attention to the voice part by disentangling it from fugue, complications and laboured contrivance.

His music, along with that of Hasse and Leonardo Leo, was especially admired by Handel, and his last Metastasian opera, *Artaserse*, composed for Rome in 1730, acquired a European reputation perhaps second to none.

The libretto of *Artaserse* was to prove one of the poet's most popular. Hasse set it for Venice, again in 1730, and four years later Handel produced it in London as the *pasticcio*, *Arbace*. Among the many composers who used it subsequently was Thomas Arne, who made his own English translation of it in 1762. Other widely favoured libretti by Metastasio were *L'Olimpiade*, set by Caldara (1733), Vivaldi (1734), Pergolesi (1735) and Leonardo Leo (1737), and *Alessandro nell'Indie* which the poet wrote for Vinci who produced it in Rome in 1730. Thereafter it was set by Vinci's great rival, Nicola Porpora (1686–1768), and in later, altered versions by Handel (*Poro*, 1731), Hasse (*Cleofide*, 1731) and Telemann, who reworked Handel's version for Hamburg (1732).

We can see from these varied productions that no notion of impropriety attached to adjusting Metastasio's texts; indeed, the poet himself made significant alterations to three of his earliest libretti. The usual manner of adjustment was by cutting recitative and altering aria texts, though care was almost invariably taken to avoid changing the poet's original emphasis, meaning and interpretation of a story.

Not every composer of Italian *opera seria*, however, was wholly committed to Metastasian texts. Handel, who used Metastasio's libretti for his own operas on only three occasions – for *Siroe* (1728), *Poro* (1731) and *Ezio* (1732) – often preferred texts containing those very elements which the 'reformists' sought to expurgate, the supernatural, the comic and the spectacular, treating them with a dramatic insight far surpassing that of his rivals. The situation in London, however, was unlike that in Italy, for whereas Italian audiences would have immediately grasped characterization from a full understanding of the text, the average Englishman would have had to rely far more upon the music for guidance. Vivaldi similarly seems to have been little attracted by Metastasio's libretti or newer literary styles, preferring old-fashioned texts. Except in *L'Olimpiade* and *Catone in Utica* (1737), of which the music of Act I is lost, and *Siroe* (1727), all of whose music is lost, he preferred texts which contained more, though on the whole shorter arias than Metastasio's, which grew ever longer.

Metastasio and Hasse

After Vinci's death in 1730, followed by that of Caldara in 1736, Metastasio's closest relationship was with Hasse, whose influence is important for the stylistic changes in early eighteenth-century opera and church music. Johann Adolf Hasse (1699–1783) was born near Hamburg, and at the age of twenty was appointed to a post at the Brunswick court where his earliest opera, *Antioco* (1721), was performed. In the same year he left Germany for Italy, visiting Bologna, Venice, Florence and Rome before settling for six or seven years in Naples. There he was granted permanent employment at the Cappella Reale, and composed several operas and serenatas, as well as becoming a pupil of Alessandro Scarlatti. In 1730 Hasse spent time in Venice, and it was here that he set his first Metastasian text, *Artaserse*, in an arrangement by the Venetian librettist Sebastiano Biancardi, known as Domenico Lalli. In June of that year Hasse strengthened his Italian associations by his marriage to Faustina Bordoni, one of the greatest sopranos of the time, with an international reputation. Singers of this calibre, above all castrati, played an important part in shaping *opera seria*. Meanwhile Hasse had been appointed *Kapellmeister* at Dresden, and in the following year he visited Dresden and Vienna. In Dresden Faustina made her debut singing one of her husband's cantatas, but the focal event of their visit was the première of Hasse's first Dresden opera, *Cleofide*, set to an adapted Metastasian text. It is likely that this was the opera reputedly attended by Bach and his eldest son, Wilhelm Friedemann, since on the day following the performance Bach gave an organ recital in the Dresden Sophienkirche.

In October 1731 Hasse and Faustina left Dresden for Italy, where the composer provided operas for Turin, Rome, Naples and Venice. In 1733 Hasse's Dresden patron, Friedrich August I, died, but since no music was required at court during official mourning Hasse remained abroad, dividing his time between Venice and Vienna. Some of his sacred music for the Venetian orphanage of the 'Incurabili', for which he continued to supply music intermittently until 1760, probably belongs to this period. Early in 1734 Hasse returned to Dresden, but he provided no new opera for the court, and, by the end of the year he and Faustina were back in Italy where they remained for the next three years. Hasse produced no less than five operas for Dresden during a stay which lasted between February 1737 and September 1738. After a short visit to Italy he was back in Dresden in early 1740 when he conducted his *Cleonice* with Pergolesi's intermezzo, *La Serva Padrona*. The 1740s were significant years for Hasse for they marked not only a deepening friendship with Metastasio but also the composer's greater understanding of his poetry. In this he was assisted by Francesco Algarotti and perhaps also by Frederick the Great, a noted and largely discerning patron of the arts and a gifted amateur flautist and composer. Hasse's repeated visits to Italy, Austria and Germany were to last until 1772, when he and Faustina settled in retirement in Venice. Faustina died in November 1781 and 'il caro Sassone', as the Italians fondly called Hasse, a little over two years later.

Hasse, along with Handel, was the most successful German opera composer of the first half of the eighteenth century. His stage works were performed in virtually all the operatic capitals of Europe. Burney summarized Hasse's talents well:

> Equally a friend to poetry and the voice, he discovers as much judgement as genius, in expressing words, as well as accompanying those sweet and tender melodies, which he gives to the singer. Always regarding the voice, as the first object of attention in a theatre, he never suffocates it by the learned jargon of a multiplicity of instruments and subjects; but is as careful of preserving its importance as a painter, of throwing the strongest light upon the capital figure of his piece.

Melody, in other words, was the most important element in Hasse's operas, and for these he provided clear, lightly textured and graceful accompaniments. He chose keys carefully according to their colours, and attempted to bring naturalness to the drama by introducing greater structural flexibility to recitatives and arias. In this way the action could progress more swiftly and realistically.

Comic opera and intermezzo: Pergolesi and Goldoni

Alongside and, in part, as a reaction to *opera seria* a tradition of comic opera grew up during the eighteenth century. Audiences, who were increasingly made up of ordinary members of society, did not always share the informed taste of aristocrats, noblemen or connoisseurs and sought less sophisticated forms of musical entertainment. Comic scenes, once an ingredient of Italian serious opera, had more or less disappeared from the currently fashionable texts of Zeno, Metastasio and their followers. Instead, comedy was channelled into intermezzi, which were short pieces, frequently including elements of parody or satire, usually with two or three characters, performed between the acts of a full-length *opera seria*. Among the earliest was Albinoni's *Vespetta e Pimpinone* (1708) which predated the oft-alleged prototype by Pergolesi, *La Serva Padrona*, by a quarter of a century. *La Serva Padrona*, on the other hand, is a masterpiece of the form by a composer who played a significant role in the development of eighteenth-century comic opera. *La Serva Padrona* was commissioned as a companion piece to Pergolesi's own *opera seria, Il prigionier superbo* (1733), and was first performed in Naples where various types of *commedia per musica* were popular. The librettist Gennaro Federico provided Pergolesi with a lively plot and credibly drawn characters from everyday life, while the composer, for his part, produced a score of immense vitality and charm.

Almost at the time the intermezzo appeared, another form of comic opera emerged, the *opera buffa*. Unlike the intermezzo the *opera buffa* was a full-length entertainment with a cast of perhaps six or more characters, all of whom had singing roles, similar in size to that of a typical *opera seria*. One of the earliest eighteenth-century comic operas was produced in Naples in 1709; it was a three-act comedy, *Patrò Calienno della Costa*, with music by Antonio Orefice and a libretto in dialect, something of a speciality in Neapolitan *buffa* entertainment at the time. Its success led to regular seasons of *opere buffe* in Naples, and among the many composers who contributed to the form over the following two decades were Vinci, Leo and, above all, Pergolesi.

Giovanni Battista Pergolesi (1710–36) studied in Naples under Vinci and Francesco Durante, and received his first opera commission in 1731. In the following year he was appointed *Maestro di cappella* to the equerry of the Viceroy of Naples, and his first comic opera, *Lo frate 'nnamorato*, in Neapolitan dialect, was performed in the autumn. The librettist was Federico who in the next year, 1733, provided him with the text of *La Serva Padrona*, discussed above. During the remaining three years of a very short life Pergolesi composed *opere serie*, intermezzi, a further comic opera and a variety of settings of sacred texts. The most celebrated of these are the *Stabat mater*, probably the most frequently printed single work in the eighteenth century, and two settings of the *Salve regina* for solo soprano and strings. The *Stabat mater* is scored for two solo voices, soprano and mezzo-soprano, with strings. It was commissioned about 1735 by the brotherhood of the Cavalieri della Vergine dei dolori at Naples which had previously commissioned a similar piece from Alessandro Scarlatti. The two settings are similarly scored, and both subdivide the text into short arias and duets. Pergolesi draws on a variety of styles, inclining towards the idiom of contemporary Italian opera but achieving an affecting simplicity with a strong element of pathos. This work and the C minor *Salve regina* were among Pergolesi's last compositions.

It was in the librettist Carlo Goldoni (1707–93) that Italian comic opera acquired a dramatist with gifts comparable to those of Metastasio. Goldoni was a Venetian rather than a Neapolitan, but by the time composers like Baldassare Galuppi (1706–85) were setting his comic libretti during the 1750s, *opera buffa* productions had spread far beyond Naples to towns and cities almost throughout Italy. Goldoni's fine characterization enabled composers to respond with music reflecting many subtle shades of feeling. Galuppi's talent, above all, perhaps, complemented the satire, wit and lightness of Goldoni's texts, as witness the masterly *Il filosofo di campagna* (1754).

Albinoni. The Venetian concerto

At approximately the same time as *opera seria* was progressing towards a peak in sophistication the Italian Baroque concerto reached stylistic maturity. Although there were gifted composers of concertos resident in many Italian cities, the focal point for the concerto during the first half of the eighteenth century was Venice. There a group of composers, notably Albinoni, Alessandro and Benedetto Marcello, and above all, Vivaldi, made distinctive and often brilliant contributions to the form. Tomaso Albinoni (1671–1751) termed himself a 'dilettante' early in his career, for he depended for a living neither on the success of his compositions nor on his prowess as a performer. We possess few facts about his early training as a musician, but by 1704, when his first opera was staged in Venice and his first trio sonatas were published, it had become evident that Albinoni was a composer of considerable and varied talent. His operas, amounting to at least fifty, include settings of texts by Zeno, Metastasio, Silvani and other leading librettists of the time, while a smaller number of chamber cantatas together with concertos and sonatas testify to fine craftsmanship and pleasing melodic gifts. Albinoni's earliest concertos were published in 1700 as his Opus 2, and a further set of twelve, Opus 5, followed in 1707. As in the earlier publication, the string parts consist of divided violins and violas with cello and basso continuo. The three-movement pattern – which Albinoni as much as Vivaldi favoured – prevails in each concerto, and in slow movements especially there is considerable variety in formal pattern. Albinoni's leaning towards counterpoint was perhaps the aspect of his style which chiefly attracted the attention of the young J.S. Bach.

A distinctive, and indeed novel feature of Albinoni's next two sets of twelve concertos was the inclusion of works for one and two oboes. The earlier of the two, Opus 7, was published in 1715 and contains four concertos for one oboe, four more for two oboes and four for strings. The oboe concertos were among the earliest of their kind, for although oboes had played a prominent role in French court music and above all in Lully's opera orchestra since the 1670s, it was not until the turn of the century that they began to appear in Italian ensemble music. Opus 7 was followed in 1722 by Opus 9, in which Albinoni followed a similar pattern of instrumentation except that the four string concertos of the later set contain a part for solo violin. Opus 9, though showing no stylistic advance on the previous set, contains one of Albinoni's finest creations in the Concerto in D minor for oboe and strings (No. 2 of the set). Its lyrical *Adagio*, whose wistful melody and undulating contours are perfectly suited to the oboe, may be considered one of Albinoni's outstanding instrumental achievements in its pleasing melodies with simple harmonies. A further set of string concertos, Opus 10, appeared about 1735; the music is vigorous and convivial, leaning towards the *galant* idiom of the mid century (discussed in a later chapter), but this very fact tends to emphasize the now somewhat old-fashioned formal layout within the movements themselves. The music seems sometimes to long to expand in a more extended framework.

Alessandro and Benedetto Marcello

Two of Albinoni's Venetian contemporaries who also styled themselves 'dilettante' were the brothers Alessandro (1684–1750) and Benedetto Marcello (1686–1739). Alessandro was not a prolific composer by the standards of his day, but his small number of concertos are sufficiently personal to be worthy of note. His set of six concertos *La Cetra* (The _yre) was published in Augsburg around 1740 and contains a wealth of varied and individual musical expression, sometimes, as for example in he Andante larghetto of the Concerto No. 3 in B minor, quite distinct rom that of his contemporaries. The work by which he is best known, however, does not belong to any known set of his concertos but rather to a set of twelve by various composers published about 1718. It is an Oboe Concerto in D minor, notable both for its all-pervading pathos and for he fact that Bach was sufficiently fascinated to make a transcription of it or solo harpsichord (BWV 974).

Benedetto Marcello occupies a more important place in history than his elder brother both because his compositions are more diverse and by virtue of his treatise *Il teatro alla moda*. Benedetto's only published concertos were printed in 1708 and issued as the composer's Opus 1. In he predominantly four-movement pattern and in the frequent juxtaposing of fast and slow sections within a single movement, Benedetto favours he Corellian model (p. 94); but the obbligato writing, for two instruments, violin and cello, as opposed to the three-strand concertino of Corelli, is often more extended, and the lively idiomatic figurations more in character with Venetian style. In the two later concertos by Benedetto which are known to us, the Venetian idiom, and that of Vivaldi n particular (p. 155), became more apparent.

Vivaldi

Antonio Vivaldi (1678–1741), who brought the Venetian Baroque concerto to its peak of invention, was born in Venice, and after learning he violin from his father, and probably others too, he played in the orchestra of S. Marco. In 1703 he was ordained, but because of a chest ailment suffered from birth he shortly afterwards abandoned active priesthood. In the same year Vivaldi was engaged as *Maestro di violino* by the Ospedale della Pietà, one of four Venetian female orphanages; in this capacity he was responsible for teaching stringed instruments and possibly wind instruments as well. Unofficially, he may also have been expected to direct concerts and provide music. Vivaldi's superior at the Pietà at the time was Francesco Gasparini (1661–1727) who had been appointed *Maestro di coro* in 1701. Gasparini was a pupil of Corelli, and an opera composer of note. He had worked in Rome until 1700 when he came to Venice to take up his duties at the Pietà. In 1713 he applied for six months' leave of absence and in the following year returned to Rome, where he remained for the rest of his life. Gasparini's departure was an event of importance for Vivaldi's career since, although he was never formally appointed *Maestro di coro*, responsibility for providing new music for the Pietà chapel seems to have devolved upon him. In 1715 Vivaldi was praised by the governors of the Pietà for 'a complete Mass, a Vespers, an oratorio, over 30 motets and other works', and was awarded a special payment of fifty ducats; 'and may this reward also stimulate him to make further contributions, and to perfect still more the performing abilities of the girls of this our orchestra, so necessary to the musical standards and the good reputation of this our chapel,' ran the text of the award.

Vivaldi's operas, cantatas, serenatas

Although Vivaldi's association with the Pietà lasted, intermittently, almost throughout his career his sphere of creative activity extended far beyond its confines, with periods of travel and an involvement in opera so considerable that we should be justified in thinking of him almost as much a man of the theatre as an orchestral composer. In his own time, certainly, Venetians would have known Vivaldi better by his operas than by his instrumental music, which they would have had less opportunity to hear, and of which only a comparatively small quantity was available through publication. Vivaldi himself claimed to have written ninety-four operas, a figure which, if correct, evokes respect if not a degree of incredulity; but if we take into account the various capacities in which he was involved in opera production – as composer, arranger, producer, impresario and promoter – it is quite possible to envisage his involvement in such a vast number of stage works. Few if any of Vivaldi's contemporaries so multifariously busied themselves in opera production, and none, with the exception of Handel, most of whose orchestral music was a by-product of his dramatic output, exercised such an effective conjunction of talents for purely instrumental music on the one hand, and for a wide variety of vocal music on the other.

Vivaldi's active years in opera span a period of rather over a quarter of a century, between 1713 and 1739. Contemporary reports are scarce, but several do occur in the Venetian-based periodical *Pallade Veneta*. From the issue of January 1717, for example, we learn that 'the magnificent *Incoronazione di Dario* opened with great applause'; this was at the Teatro San Moisè, one of three flourishing Venetian theatres in which Vivaldi's operas were performed. With the exception of Metastasio, whose libretti in various rearrangements Vivaldi used during the last phase of his opera production, the composer seems to have avoided the great librettists of his day. He never collaborated directly with Zeno,

Silvani, Piovene or Metastasio, for instance, and in the opinion of Reinhard Strohm (*Essays on Handel and Italian Opera*) 'excelled in setting libretti which nearly no-one else ever chose'. However, he probably collaborated with the young Goldoni in 1735 at the outset of what was to be a brilliant career for the dramatist. Vivaldi asked him to adapt the text of Zeno's *Griselda* for an opera performed at the Venetian Teatro San Samuele in the spring of 1735. Goldoni himself wrote that 'I went on to murder Zeno's drama as much as, and in whatever way, [Vivaldi] wanted. The opera was performed and met with success.' Vivaldi seems seldom to have chosen the most famous singers of the time, though the soprano Cuzzoni (on one occasion) and the alto castrato Giovanni Carestini, both of whom sang for Handel in London, appeared in his productions. Beyond Venice, Vivaldi's operas were performed in Mantua, where the composer worked between 1718 and 1720, Milan, Ferrara, Florence, Reggio, Rome, Vicenza, Verona, Vienna, and in Prague which he visited in 1730–31.

Few Italian opera composers overlooked the secular chamber cantata and Vivaldi – one might say true to form – composed a fair number. Most are for female voice (most commonly soprano) with continuo accompaniment, but nine – five for soprano and four for alto – have instrumental parts. Of greater interest, though, are Vivaldi's serenatas, whose form falls between an opera and a cantata. Usually scored for from two to four voices, they were mostly occasional pieces performed to mark important events such as royal birthdays, the arrival of distinguished visitors or a military victory. Three serenatas by Vivaldi are known to us; two, *La Sena festeggiante* (RV 693) and the *Serenata a tre* (RV 690), are for three voices and instruments, while the third, *Gloria Himeneo* (RV 687), is for two voices and instruments. The most extended and perhaps the most interesting of these is *La Sena festeggiante* (The Seine 'en fête') which Vivaldi composed during the 1720s in honour of the French royal house of Bourbon. The libretto by Domenico Lalli, whom Vivaldi frequently set, is conventionally obsequious in its praise of Louis XV, but the music is of an altogether higher order. Much of the vocal interest lies in 'La Senna', a bass role with a notably wide range covering more than two octaves; but the two soprano roles contain some affectingly beautiful music both in aria and duet form. Two overtures, introducing Parts I and II of the work, give further distinction to this well-sustained work. The first, a three-movement Italian opera sinfonia, has an Andante molto middle section striking in its chromaticism, while the second, a French *Ouverture* both in name and character, contains a well-constructed fugue. The arias and duets in *La Sena festeggiante* and in the *Serenata a tre*, a captivating Arcadian allegory for two sopranos and a tenor, are a reminder that Vivaldi was able to write sympathetically and dramatically for the voice in a manner quite different from that of his instrumental idiom. Tartini once suggested that Vivaldi did not distinguish between the human throat and the neck of a violin when writing for the voice, but against that we should set the verdict of the Hamburg composer and critic Mattheson who observed that 'Vivaldi, albeit no singer, has had the sense to keep violin-leaps out of his vocal compositions so completely that his arias have become a thorn in the flesh to many an experienced vocal composer [who sought to emulate them]'.

Vivaldi's sacred music

Vivaldi's sacred vocal music is both diverse in character and varied in design. It embraces settings of liturgical and non-liturgical texts among which are psalms, responses, motets for solo voice with instruments, hymns, antiphons and a single surviving oratorio, *Juditha triumphans* (RV 644). To what extent the settings of liturgical texts may have formed part of Vespers cycles is not possible to determine, but that some were intended to do so is almost beyond question.

As we have seen, Vivaldi's duties as *Maestro di coro* at the Pietà were unofficial and unexpectedly thrust upon him, but seldom in his sacred vocal music is there indication of lack of skill or commitment. Indeed, in the greater part of it Vivaldi succeeds as brilliantly as he does in the purely instrumental sphere. His settings of liturgically related texts fall into three distinct patterns. The most frequently occurring of them is an alternating scheme of movements for solo voices, choir and orchestra of which two *Glorias* in D major (RV 588/589), a *Magnificat* in G minor (RV 610), a response *Domine ad adiuvandum me* (RV 593), and three psalm settings with double choir and orchestra, *Dixit Dominus* (RV 594), *Beatus vir* (RV 597), and *Laudate pueri* (RV602), are outstandingly successful examples. The second pattern, similar to the first except that a single voice is employed throughout, often in a notably virtuoso manner, occurs in the psalms *Nisi Dominus* (RV 608) for alto, and *Laudate pueri* (RV 601) for soprano and orchestra, and the *Stabat Mater* (RV 621) for alto and strings. The third pattern is somewhat different in that Vivaldi contains the music within a single movement. Examples of this are provided by a smaller setting of *Beatus vir* (RV 598) for soloists, choir and orchestra, and by a *Lauda Jerusalem* (RV 609) for two sopranos, two choirs and two orchestras. The French musicologist and biographer of Vivaldi, Marc Pincherle, saw in the composer's larger setting of *Beatus vir* the fusion of three styles – the operatic, the instrumental and the sacred; there is much truth in his observation, which could be extended to many other works in this category. In the duet for two basses in *Beatus vir* we are certainly in the proximity of the opera house, while many of the movements for solo voice adopt ritornello patterns similar to those of the concerto. Elsewhere, extended movements such as the fugues which conclude the *Dixit Dominus*, already cited, and the *Beatus vir* (RV 597) adhere to more conventional stylistic traits in Italian sacred music. Vivaldi's skill in preserving composite unity within each of these works, together with many instances of colourful textual interpretation ensures a high level of interest for which he is not sufficiently credited.

Vivaldi's sacred music set to non-liturgical texts is smaller in quantity and includes motets, *introduzioni* and a single surviving oratorio. There is little to distinguish between the motets and the *introduzioni*, which serve as elaborate preludes to more extended sacred vocal compositions such as the *Gloria* (RV 588) – the 'introduction' to which, exceptionally, forms an integral part of it.

Quantz, in his *Versuch einer Anweisung die Flöte traversiere zu spielen* (Essay of a Method for Playing the Tranverse Flute, 1752), provides us with a useful definition of the Italian motet in the early eighteenth century in saying, 'this name is applied at the present time to a sacred Latin solo cantata that consists of two arias and two recitatives and closes with an "Alleluia", and is ordinarily sung by one of the best singers during the Mass after the "Credo"'. Vivaldi's motets usually have only a single recitative with two arias and a closing Alleluia, while the *introduzioni* further dispense with the Alleluia. All of them are scored for a soprano or alto voice with strings and continuo.

Far and away the most ambitious sacred work by Vivaldi is the 'sacrum militare oratorium', *Juditha triumphans*. The Latin inscription on the title page translates: 'Judith Triumphant, Conqueror of the Barbaric Holofernes: A Sacred Military Oratorio Performed in Times of War by the Chorus of Virgin Singers, to be sung in the Church of the Pietà, Venice, 1716'. The libretto, by Giacomo Cassetti, is based on chapters in the Apocrypha, but has additional allegorical significance relating to the war with Turkey in which Venice had been engaged for several years. The work requires five female solo voices, a four-part chorus, the male content of which was presumably mustered from outside the Pietà, and an orchestra which, as Michael Talbot aptly remarks in his biography of the composer, 'puts virtually the whole of the Pietà's arsenal of instruments on display': recorders, oboes, clarinets, chalumeau, trumpets and drums, mandolin, theorbos, viola d'amore, 'viole all'inglese', strings and continuo. Despite this rich assembly of instruments, *Juditha* is dramatically disappointing. There is little in the way of interaction between the characters, hardly any variation in tension and an overall lack of dramatic purpose. Among the many striking numbers in *Juditha* are Holofernes' aria, 'Agitata infido flatu', where Vivaldi admirably captures the textual imagery with restless figures and chromaticisms; Judith's aria, 'Veni, veni, me sequere', with its affecting obbligato for chalumeau (an early member of the clarinet family) above palpitating string figures, in which she hints to her faithful servant, Abra, the dreadful fate she is preparing for Holofernes; and the short but splendidly martial choruses.

Vivaldi's concertos

Gifted and successful though Vivaldi unquestionably was as a composer for the voice, it was as an instrumental composer that he made his most original and far-reaching contribution. In his work the Venetian Baroque concerto reached a summit of invention and organization (p. 155). He achieved greater variety in slow movements than his predecessors, established ritornello structures, and was notably imaginative in his pictorial writing. His contemporary the English historian Burney described him as 'the most popular composer for the violin, as well as player on that instrument', adding that 'his pieces called Stravaganze ... among flashy players ... occupied the highest place of favour. His Cuckoo Concerto, during my youth, was the wonder and delight of all frequenters of country concerts ... If acute and rapid tones are evils, Vivaldi has much of the sin to answer for ...'.

After early chamber music publications, Vivaldi published nine collections of concertos between 1711 and 1729, in the course of which we can discern clear, if uneven development both in his skill as a composer and in the form of the concerto. His first set, *L'estro armonico* (Harmonic Caprice or Inspiration), Opus 3, appeared in 1711 and quickly became known in northern European countries both through his Amsterdam publisher Estienne Roger and by means of performances by travelling virtuosi. The young Bach, at Weimar, had probably seen most if not all of the set, since he arranged five of the twelve concertos for solo keyboard. *L'estro armonico* is the most varied of Vivaldi's published sets of concertos, containing concertos for one, two and four violins arranged in four symmetrical groups. Five of the concertos call for divided violas and an obligato cello, while the assorted effects of solo and concertino violin writing in each of these works sometimes pay tribute to earlier models,

The first violin part of Vivaldi's 'Winter' concerto from *The Four Seasons*, Opus 8, No. 4 (1725) sometimes demonstrate Vivaldi's strengthening personal idiom and ability to experiment. Several concertos of the set are outstandingly effective, but one might single out Concertos No. 8 in A minor (two violins), No. 10 in B minor (four violins and cello) and No. 11 in D minor (two violins and cello) for their happy blend of fertile invention, fine craftsmanship and lyricism.

Vivaldi followed *L'estro armonico* with several further published sets of concertos, outstanding among them *La stravaganza*, Opus 4 (*c.*1714), *Il cimento dell'armonia e dell'inventione*, Opus 8 (1725), and *La cetra*, Opus 9 (1727). Most of the concertos in these sets are for solo violin and string orchestra; Opus 8 includes *The Four Seasons*, which enjoyed wide currency both in and beyond Italy in Vivaldi's lifetime, as well as two concertos for a solo oboe. Vivaldi's mature style is handsomely on display in *La cetra*, which unusually in the music of this composer, includes two concertos (Nos 6 and 12) requiring 'scordatura', or the retuning of the open strings of the solo violin.

Plentiful though Vivaldi's published concertos were, they are nevertheless greatly outnumbered by those which remained in manuscript until the present century. Furthermore, while in all but one or two instances the published concertos are representative of his finest work, they do not so well reflect Vivaldi's flair for colourful instrumental groupings as the unpublished pieces. As well as solo concertos for a wide variety of wind instruments – pairs of trumpets and horns, flute, oboe, recorder and bassoon – there are others in which these instruments, in various combinations, join with the strings to create rich and often subtle textures. The most familiar example of Vivaldi's unique sense of colour is contained in the Concerto in C major (RV 558), the work the composer performed at the Pietà in 1740 in honour of a visit to Venice of the Prince Elector of Saxony. Its scoring consists of chalumeaux, mandolins, theorbos, concertante violins and cello, strings and continuo, perhaps with additional recorders and trumpets. Vivaldi's feeling for colour reveals itself not only in his wide choice of instruments but also in his string-writing. Twenty-seven concertos for cello and strings, six for viola d'amore (an instrument with six bowed strings with sympathetic strings under the fingerboard), another for viola d'amore and lute (RV 540), and several violin concertos with titles evoking a particular affect – *L'amoroso* (RV 271), *Il riposo* (RV 270), *Il sospetto* (RV 199), *L'inquietudine* (RV 234) and so on – provide evidence of the composer's interest in string sonority and tonal colour as well as his ability to move the listener.

Some contemporaries. Tartini

Among Vivaldi's gifted Italian contemporaries in the sphere of sacred vocal music was Domenico Zipoli (1699–1726). Born in Tuscany, Zipoli was recruited by the Jesuits to prosletyze in South America, where his music was much admired and widely disseminated. Though he is remembered chiefly for his attractive solo organ and harpsichord collection *Sonate d'intavolatura* (1716), his psalm and antiphon settings, many of which have only recently come to light, reveal skilled craftsmanship and a refreshing, expressive vitality.

Vivaldi's dominant role in the development of the Baroque concerto should not obscure the important contributions to the form of many of his contemporaries. Francesco Bonporti (1672–1749) in the north and Francesco Durante (1684–1755) in Naples (better known for his vocal chamber duets), were skilful craftsmen, Bonporti, especially, revealing lyrically expressive powers in his slow movements. Pietro Antonio Locatelli (1695–1764) published five sets of concertos between 1721 and 1762. The earliest of them are indebted to Corelli but progressively, and above all in his Opus 3, *L'arte del violino*, Locatelli explored much wider possibilities in solo violin technique, requiring great virtuosity from the performer.

The most gifted and original of Vivaldi's younger contemporaries was Tartini who, while consolidating the form of the mature Italian Baroque concerto, made distinctive contributions of his own. Giuseppe Tartini (1692–1770) was born at Pirano, near Venice, and in 1728 founded a school of violinists in Padua which became known as the Scuola della Nazioni, 'The School of Nations', because it attracted students from all over Europe. Its aim was not merely to heighten virtuosity but, more significantly, to explore the expressive possibilities in string playing. Through his own playing, teaching and compositions Tartini made important contributions to both these facets of musicianship. Celebrated though he was, and is, for fiery passagework and brilliant virtuosic gestures, Tartini's outstanding gifts as an expressive composer are far more remarkable. These are readily apparent in the slow movements of his sonatas and violin concertos. More and more they became the focal point of a composition, and to a greater extent, perhaps, than with either Vivaldi or Locatelli, the guiding principle is the imitation of the human voice. So much is this the case that among Tartini's autograph manuscripts we find poetic mottoes, sometimes in secret code, mainly drawn from Metastasio's opera libretti, setting the scene or 'affect', so to speak, of a given movement. Poets such as Tasso also provided Tartini with sources of musical inspiration. One example is afforded by an alternative slow movement (Tartini in his concertos sometimes included two, one of which he usually regarded as definitive) to the Concerto in A major (D 96). Here, the Largo andante, a notably affecting piece, is prefaced by the lines *A rivi a fonti a fiume/corrette amare lagrime/sin tanto che consumi/l'acerbo mio dolor* (Like streams, springs, rivers,/flow bitter tears/until my cruel grief is spent).

Although Tartini spent most of his life in Padua his musical style was Venetian. He favoured the three-movement pattern established by Albinoni and Vivaldi in their concertos though he did not invariably follow it. Tartini's most lyrical writing is contained in his slow movements, but fine examples of his cantabile style permeated both solo and *tutti* elements of faster movements, too.

Tartini composed a small number of sacred vocal pieces, but by far the greater amount of his music is contained in his legacy for the violin. It consists of 190 sonatas and 130 concertos as well as one concerto each for cello and viola or viola da gamba. (Two well-known flute concertos, however, are of doubtful authenticity.)

Domenico Scarlatti: life, harpsichord sonatas

There remains to be considered the work of a single composer whose inspired contribution to the solo keyboard repertory sets him apart from all other Italian composers of the late Baroque. Domenico Scarlatti was born in Naples on 26 October 1685. He was the sixth child of Alessandro Scarlatti, who had been appointed *Maestro di cappella* to the Naples court in the previous year. We know little of Domenico's early life, but that he showed precocious talent we can hardly doubt, since in 1701, at the age of fifteen, he was appointed *Organista e compositore di musica* at the royal court. Apart from a period of five months or so in 1702 spent with his father in Rome and Florence, Scarlatti remained in Naples until 1704. Meanwhile, his father had returned to Rome in 1703 to become *vice-Maestro di cappella* at Sta Maria Maggiore. Alessandro's absence from Naples gave his son an opportunity to provide music for the opera. Domenico's first operas were probably *L'Ottavia ristituita al trono* and *Il Giustino*, both performed during the 1703–4 season; but it was Gaetano Veneziano and not Domenico Scarlatti who was appointed *Maestro di cappella* in 1704. Domenico joined his father in Rome, and then in 1705, at Alessandro's instigation, set out for Florence and Venice. In a letter Alessandro commends his son to Ferdinando de Medici:

I have forcibly removed him from Naples for, though there was scope for his talent, it was not the kind of talent for such a place. I am removing him from Rome as well, because Rome has no shelter for music, which lives here like a beggar. This son of mine is an eagle whose wings are grown; he must not remain idle in the nest, and I must not hinder his flight. Since the virtuoso Nicolino [the castrato Nicolo Grimaldi] of Naples is passing through here on his way to Venice, I thought fit to send Domenico with him, escorted only by his own ability . . .

Ferdinando was evidently favourably impressed by the young Scarlatti, giving him a letter of introduction to a Venetian nobleman, Alvise Morosini.

Domenico Scarlatti probably spent a little over two years in Venice, encountering both Gasparini who was *Maestro di coro* at the Ospedale della Pietà, and Handel, who was in Venice between November 1707 and February 1708. Early in 1708 Domenico returned to Rome where at first, in the absence of regular employment, he assisted his father at Sta Maria Maggiore as well as fulfilling various commissions. In the following year he entered the service of the exiled Polish queen, Maria Casimira. His first commission for her was an oratorio, *La conversione di Clodoveo* (1709) whose music is lost. During the next three years he provided her with several operas including *Tetide in Sciro* (*c*.1712), of which only ten arias have survived. As his reputation as an opera composer grew, further opportunities presented themselves, and between 1715 and 1718 he provided operas for the public theatres in Rome. While serving Maria Casimira, Scarlatti also became assistant *Maestro* of the Cappella Giulia in the Vatican. On her departure in 1714 he was appointed *Maestro* of the Cappella Giulia, and also to the Portuguese ambassador.

In 1719 Scarlatti resigned from both positions and left Rome for Palermo for reasons which are not clear. It is possible that about this time he visited England – his opera *Narciso*, first performed in Rome in 1714 with the title *Amor d'un ombra e gelosia d'un aura*, was staged in London in 1720 – but the composer's presence cannot be verified. Scarlatti probably remained in Palermo until 1724 at the latest, by which time he had accepted an offer from the Portuguese court at Lisbon as *Mestre de capela*. Most of what he wrote during the mid- to late 1720s has been lost and we know little of his activities at this time. In addition to his duties as court composer at Lisbon Scarlatti taught music to the King's daughter, Maria Barbara, and to his younger brother, Don Antonio. He also made several visits to Italy, including one in 1725 when he saw his father in

Naples shortly before he died, and another to Rome in 1728 where he married Maria Catarina Gentili.

In 1729 Maria Barbara married Crown Prince Fernando of Spain, leaving Lisbon for Seville. She took Scarlatti with her, and as *Maestro di musica* he continued to serve her for the remainder of his life. In 1733 the court moved from Seville to Madrid, but shortly afterwards the palace was destroyed by fire and the royal household occupied various residences in and around Castile.

We know tantalisingly little of how Scarlatti occupied his time over the succeeding years. After 1737 a friendship developed between Scarlatti and the Italian castrato Farinelli. Farinelli had turned his back on an international career seemingly in order to entertain the King, Philip V, with a repertory of Italian airs reputedly confined to five in number. In 1739 Scarlatti's wife died but within three years he had married again, this time espousing Anastasia Maxarti Ximenes from Cadiz. When Fernando VI succeeded to the throne in 1746, music at court became greatly enlivened by the appointment of Farinelli as director of the royal operas. He was given resources which enabled him to engage the finest Italian singers and to secure first-rate librettos from poets such as Metastasio, with whom he was on friendly terms. Scarlatti meanwhile continued in his role of composer and harpsichordist, numbering among his pupils the gifted Antonio Soler (1729–83). Scarlatti died on 23 July 1757, and his employer, Maria Barbara, a little more than a year later. She had bequeathed instruments and manuscripts, including Scarlatti's keyboard sonatas, to Farinelli, who shortly afterwards returned with them to Italy.

Scarlatti's first published music was issued in London in 1738 and consisted of thirty harpsichord solos, the *Essercizi per gravicembalo*. In the following year the English organist and composer Thomas Roseingrave (1688–1766), who had met Scarlatti in Italy some twenty years earlier and probably had a hand in recommending his opera, *Narciso*, to the Royal Academy, brought out a pirated edition of the same pieces. Roseingrave's two-volume publication contained in addition a second version of one of the *Essercizi* and twelve further sonatas by Scarlatti, a fugue by his father Alessandro and a piece by Roseingrave himself. The two main sources of Scarlatti's harpsichord sonatas, however, were copied in Spain between 1742 and 1757.

We know little about the sonatas' chronology and can only speculate as to exactly how and by whom they were performed. There is strong, though by no means conclusive evidence advanced by Ralph Kirkpatrick that the composer intended the sonatas to be performed in pairs, and occasionally in groups of three. In both the principal sources they are grouped according to key, and since different sources offer different pairings, it would seem likely that Scarlatti, who probably supervised much of the copying, was indicating a general performance-procedure rather than precisely planned juxtapositions.

The sonatas are not cast in the two-, three-, or four-movement patterns which characterize typical Baroque and early Classical examples but almost invariably as single-movement 'lessons' (*Essercizi*). A single movement, however, may be subdivided into sections, as we find for instance in the Sonata in F minor/major (Kk 204a) and the Sonata in C major (Kk 513). The movements are for the most part binary in form, moving from tonic to dominant, or from minor to major, by a rich variety of bold, often unusual cadences; but we should beware of over-simplifying what appears at first glance to be mere formula, for that formula is treated to an almost infinite number of variations. No Scarlatti sonata, as Kirkpatrick wisely observed, should be regarded as 'typical'. Indeed, in the means by which he superimposes one harmony upon another without conventional regard for the dictates of the bass fundament, Scarlatti shows notable daring; such an example occurs in a modulation from F minor to D major in the Sonata in G major (Kk 124).

Other features contributing towards a distinctive style in the sonatas include triplet patterns, cascading arpeggios, florid runs, daring hand-crossing, imitative passages, syncopations, dissonances, chromaticism (Kk 547), percussive effects and a rich rhythmic variety. By such means Scarlatti achieved affects ranging from the pensive, even elegiac (Sonata in B minor, Kk 87) to the exuberant (Sonata in D major, Kk 492). Sometimes, too, he captures local colour and evokes ceremony with drone basses (Sonata in C major, Kk 513), simulated trumpet fanfares (Sonata in D major, Kk 491), or repeated notes and chords (Sonata in E major, Kk 380). In much of this repertory it is the Spanish and Portuguese influence on Scarlatti's melodies and rhythms which contribute distinctively to the composer's keyboard style.

Iberian musical characteristics may not figure largely in the main-stream of Baroque culture, but such peculiarly distinct national traits provide the variegated colours which seem to glow so radiantly in this period. The contribution of Hispanic music is not dissimilar to that of English music in this respect.

8

Seventeenth-century England: music of court and Commonwealth

THE MUSIC OF ENGLAND during the period of the early Stuarts, the Commonwealth and the Restoration of the Monarchy was receptive to developments taking place on the Continent, although she was perhaps the latest of the larger nations to adopt foreign styles. In music as in the visual arts, the most important stimuli came from abroad, with examples from Italy and France playing decisive roles against a background of stubborn preservation of indigenous qualities.

Madrigal and lute-song

During the reign of James I (1603–25) the madrigal and the lute-song were the most widely cultivated forms of secular vocal music. The madrigal reached England during the 1580s, some half century after the earliest Italian manuscripts containing madrigals had appeared; Thomas Morley (1557/8–1602), John Wilbye (1574–1638)) and Thomas Weelkes (1576–1623) were influential masters of the genre. By the early 1600s this form of domestic chamber music was yielding ground to the lute-song, which was much more of a native English product though, like the consort-song repertoire, it had French antecedents. The great master of the lute-song was John Dowland (1563–1626), whose *First Booke of Songes or Ayres* (1597) ran to five editions in little over fifteen years. Although Dowland and other composers published many of their solo songs with lute in alternative part-song versions, a practice that was widely cultivated in France, the solo element remained the primary one. Dowland published three further collections of lute-songs in 1600, 1603 and 1612. Two other important early seventeenth-century lute-song anthologies are Morley's *First Booke of Ayres* (1600) and Dowland's son Robert's *A Musicall Banquet* (1610) which contains three songs by his father as well as several

Italian monodies. These monodies, contrary to the Italian examples of the day, were not provided with a figured continuo bass but with an accompaniment for lute and viol. The earliest known English publication with figured bass was by Martin Peersòn (c.1572–1650), whose *Mottects or Grave Chamber Musicke* was published in 1630. Another progressive composer was Walter Porter (c.1588–1659) who claimed Monteverdi as a 'good Friend and Maestro'. Porter's individual and expressive *Madrigales and Ayres of two, three, foure, and five Voyces, with the continued Base, with Toccatos, Sinfonias, and Ritornellos to them. After the manner of Consort Musique*, were published in 1632.

The masque

A closer link with the 'new music' of the early Italian Baroque at this time can be found in the masque songs and dialogues of Nicholas Lanier (1588–1666). Describing *Lovers Made Men* (1617), the author Ben Jonson (1572–1637) tells us that 'the whole masque was sung after the Italian manner, *stylo recitativo*, by Master Nicholas Lanier, who ordered and made both the scene and the music'. Since that music has not survived we must treat Jonson's claim with caution, and turn rather to Lanier's *Hero and Leander*, set in recitative somewhat in the manner of an Italian 'lament', for evidence of his skill in handling the recitative style. Roger North in his *Musicall Gramarian* (1728) describes Lanier as 'a nice observer of the Italian musick ... and more especially of that, which was the most valuable amongst them, I mean the vocall'.

The masque was the most important form of theatre entertainment with music in England during the first half of the seventeenth century. Its antecedents go back to the time of Queen Elizabeth I and even earlier, but it was during the reigns of the first two Stuart monarchs, James I and Charles I (1603–49), that the masque reached a peak of sophisticated entertainment.

Tudor and Stuart masques were usually court entertainments whose elaborate stage-designs, dances, mime and allegorical treatment of subject show an affinity with the French *ballet de cour* as it was developed by Lully (Chapter 5). In England the masque and the play with music were the forerunners of opera, though compared with opera, which emphasized the music throughout, the masque gave greater importance to the varied components mentioned above. One of the reasons the masque, both courtly and private, achieved distinction during the first three decades of the century was that it attracted several of the greatest dramatists of the age. Notable among them was Ben Jonson, one of

England's foremost playwrights during the reign of Elizabeth I (1558–1603). From 1605 Jonson became increasingly occupied in producing masques for the court. His talent for combining fine poetry with classical erudition resulted in entertainments of high literary distinction, particularly attractive to the English audience with its predilection for the spoken word. John Milton alludes in the poem *L'Allegro* (1622) to Jonson's (and the masque's) popularity:

> *Then to the well-trod stage anon*
> *If Jonson's learned sock* [comedy] *be on.*

Jonson's collaborator in many masques was the great architect and designer, Inigo Jones (1573–1652). Jones had travelled on the Continent as a young man where he had studied the principles of Classical form and also may have seen something of the elaborate stage machinery then being evolved by the Italians. Following his first visit to Italy (*c.*1601) he began to design his own machinery, experimenting with various forms of mobile sets in an attempt to achieve visual homogeneity and continuity. The earliest collaboration between Jonson and Inigo Jones was the *Masque of Blackness* (1605). Seven more masques were produced in as many years, and it was not until 1631 that playwright and architect parted company. An important musical collaborator, especially in the earlier masques of Ben Jonson, was Alfonso Ferrabosco (*c.*1578–1628). Little music for the masques of this period has survived and no complete score is known, but the scores of Ferrabosco's extant songs show him to have been an expressive melodist. Other composers associated with Jacobean masque include Robert Johnson (*c.*1583–1633), John Coprario (*c.*1570–1626) and, most notably, the poet Thomas Campion (1567–1620) who also made a significant literary contribution to the form. The masque reflected a growing English interest in the fusion of arts while at the same time enabling each art-form to maintain a distance. The contribution of music remained incidental, however, since theatre was the prime attraction, whereas in Continental opera a more equal partnership was sought.

Later masques: Henry and William Lawes

Although Jonson had no successor of comparable stature the masque continued to flourish during the reign of Charles I (1625–49). The most important composers associated with the Caroline court masque were the brothers Henry Lawes (1596–1662) and William Lawes (1602–45), and Nicholas Lanier who as we have seen had collaborated with Ben

A MASKE
PRESENTED

At Ludlow Caftle,

1 6 3 4 :

On cMichaelmaffe night, before the

RIGHT HONORABLE,

IOHN *Earle of Bridgewater , Vicount* BRACKLY,
Lord 'Prefident of WALES , And one of
His MAIESTIES moft honorable
Privie Counfell.

Ehen quid volui mifero mihi ! floribus auftrum
Perditus ——— *By John Milton*

LONDON,

Title page of John Milton's
masque *Comus*, performed at
Ludlow Castle in 1634

Printed for HVMPHREY ROBINSON,
at the figne of the *Three Pidgeons* in
Pauls Church-yard. 1 6 3 7.

Jonson during the previous reign. Most of the surviving music for masques of this period is contained in an autograph manuscript of William Lawes, while many of the instrumental dances are collected in two published anthologies by John Playford (1623–86), a crucial disseminator of printed music up to the Restoration (the *Court Ayres*, 1655, and *Courtly Masquing Ayres*, 1662). Among the most elaborate masques of the period was the *Triumph of Peace* (1634) by James Shirley (1596–1666) with music by William Lawes and Simon Ives (1600–62).

Henry Lawes was the most celebrated song-writer of the English mid-Baroque. At an early age he was involved in composing music for masques, and by the early 1630s had established a friendship with Milton. Musician and poet collaborated in two masques which had been commissioned from Lawes by the Egerton family who employed him as music teacher to their daughters. The text of the earlier masque was Milton's poem *Arcades*, and it was performed about 1629; that of the second was *Comus*, and it was performed for the inauguration of the Earl of Bridgwater as Lord President of Wales at Ludlow Castle in 1634.

Comus differed from a typical Stuart masque in three important ways. Firstly, the element of pageantry and dancing was reduced in order to bring the poetry to the fore; secondly, an outdoor setting replaced the more usual banqueting hall; and, thirdly, spoken dialogue was expanded beyond customary proportions – indeed, it forms the greater part of *Comus*. Lawes himself took the role of an attendant spirit, Thyrsis, to whom Milton gives the following lines in tribute to the composer:

> Thyrsis? Whose artful strains have oft delayed
> The huddling brook to hear his madrigal,
> and sweetened every muskrose of the dale. . . .

This was the first of two occasions on which Milton praised Lawes in his poetry, and many other Cavalier poets were to do likewise. Unhappily the songs which Lawes wrote for *Arcades* have been lost, but those from *Comus* have survived, providing interesting examples of the continuo song in England at this time.

The declamatory songs of Henry Lawes have been harshly assessed by some writers who have found them lacking in pathos and flexibility. Performance, however, has shown that in Lawes's subtle blend of recitative and air there is that very flexibility of rhythm that is so often denied; even when he writes strophic declamatory songs Lawes is skilful in his accommodation of the text – shaping 'Notes to the Words and Sense', as he himself remarked – while songs such as *A Complaint against Cupid* or the *Hymns to the Holy Trinity* show him sensible to pathos. Lawes set to music the songs of several Cavalier poets, that 'mob of gentlemen that writ with ease', as Pope later disdainfully referred to them, notably Thomas Carew (*c*.1595–*c*.1639), Robert Herrick (1591–1674), William Cartwright (1611–43) and Edmund Waller (1606–87). Many of them he collected in an autograph songbook, later making selections for three books of *Ayres and Dialogues*, published in 1653, 1655 and 1658. Further songs appeared in collections published by John Playford after Lawes's death but with the composer's 'free consent'.

Like his elder brother Henry, William Lawes became one of the musicians at the court of Charles I. Both were appointed 'musicians in ordinary for the lutes and voices', Henry in 1631 and William in 1635. Unlike Henry, however, William Lawes composed instrumental music as well as a wealth of songs in a variety of styles for the Caroline court masques. Among the most successful masques with which he was associated were James Shirley's *The Triumph of Peace* in which he collaborated with Simon Ives, and two masques by Sir William Davenant (1606–68): *The Triumphs of the Prince d'Amour* (1635), in which he collaborated with his brother Henry, and *Britannia triumphans* (1638), whose clear tonal organization, effective contrasts between declamatory air and popular song, chorus and instrumental symphonies make it one of the most advanced and musically interesting of all surviving court masques. Lawes's death in 1645, fighting for the royalist cause at the Siege of Chester, prompted elegies and tributes from many of his friends.

Commonwealth entertainment

Although during the eleven years of the Commonwealth (1649–60) spoken plays were banned, theatre entertainment which incorporated a musical element thrived. In the absence of a monarch it was hardly to be expected that masques, which were chiefly expensive court entertainments, should continue to flourish; yet the Commonwealth did not entirely put an end to them, and one notable masque was performed in honour of the Portuguese ambassador in March 1653. This was Shirley's *Cupid and Death*, with music by Matthew Locke (*c.*1622–77) and Christopher Gibbons (1616–76). The work was revived in 1659, and this version, in Locke's autograph, the only complete score of a seventeenth-century English masque that we know of, is of particular interest for what it tells us of their content. *Cupid and Death* consists of five entries, or acts, each containing a suite of dances, choruses, and a varied pattern of solo song, recitative or duet; the comic element, in the form of 'antimasque', for which composers might use a mixture of popular and newly composed material, is interspersed throughout the entertainment.

During the 1650s playwrights and composers were beginning to experiment with new forms of staged musical entertainment. One of these was Sir William Davenant's *The Siege of Rhodes*, produced in 1656 at Rutland House, Aldersgate Street, London, before a paying audience (p. 154). The music was provided collectively by five composers: Henry Lawes, Charles Coleman (d.1664), Henry Cooke (*c.*1616–1672), George Hudson (*c.*1615/1620–72) and Locke, but nothing of it has survived. *The Siege of Rhodes* marked a development in such entertainments in two important respects. First, the piece, 'sung in Recitative Musick', was apparently continuous throughout – a feature which has perhaps misleadingly led to its being regarded as the first English opera, and which prompted Davenant to describe it as a variety of entertainment 'unpractis'd here, though, of great reputation amongst other Nations'. Second, in keeping with the Commonwealth political climate it was intended as public entertainment rather than as court spectacle. Davenant spent most of the period of the Civil War in Paris, where he would probably have become acquainted with both Italian opera and the fashionable *tragédies à machines*, performed at the Théâtre du Marais.

English instrumental music

Before we discuss the music of the Restoration we must briefly examine some other important aspects of music-making during the early Stuart period. In the first half of the seventeenth century instrumental ensemble music took second place to vocal music: 'There is not any Musicke of Instruments whatsoever, comparable to that which is made of the voyces of Men,' observed William Byrd (1543–1623) in his preface to *Psalmes, Sonets and Songs* (1588). Ensemble music written exclusively for instruments was uncommon, but pieces for voices and instruments which could be performed equally well by one or the other were popular, hence the designation of Robert Jones's *The First Set of Madrigals* (1607) as 'for Viols and Voices, or for Voices alone; or as you please'; and there were many more besides, keeping the madrigal within the consort song tradition and therefore marketable. Not every household would have been in possession of a 'chest' or family of viols, but a group of mixed instruments or voices could more easily be mustered. Performances depended largely upon resources, and composers generally recognized this. When Antony Holborne (fl.1584–1602) issued his *Pavans, Galliards, Almains and Other Short Airs* in 1599 he described them as suitable 'for Viols, Violins or other Musicall Winde Instruments'.

Some of the best known solo instrumental repertory of the early seventeenth century is contained in the *Fitzwilliam Virginal Book*. As Thurston Dart remarked in *The Interpretation of Music*, virginals music could be played on any instrument that happened to be handy, though of course some pieces are better suited to one instrument than to another. The *Fitzwilliam Virginal Book* is generally associated with the reign of Elizabeth I and many of the pieces do belong to the late sixteenth century, yet this extensive and immensely varied compilation was probably made between 1609 and 1619. It was the work of a Catholic, Francis Tregian, who was eventually imprisoned for recusancy. The composers most generously represented are Byrd, John Bull (*c.*1562–1628), Peter Philips (*c.*1560–1628), Gibbons and Giles Farnaby (*c.*1563–1640). The virginalists were especially skilled in variation techniques, and in the hands of composers like Byrd and Philips, these were often complex, abstract and technically brilliant. This style was to have great influence in the development of continental keyboard styles of the Amsterdam composer Sweelinck and his contemporaries.

The style of instrumental writing during the first three decades of the seventeenth century was still essentially polyphonic, since it was not until the 1630s that basso continuo became established in England. The most popular ensemble form was that of the 'fantasia' or 'fancy' which was usually in a single section and written in imitative counterpoint. Canzonas, which were sectional, allowing for greater stylistic variety, were less favoured in England at this time, a mellifluous continuity being preferred. Among the most accomplished fantasias of the early English Baroque are nine *Fantasias a 3* by Orlando Gibbons (1583–1625) which were published in about 1620 and others by Thomas Lupo (d.1628). Five pieces in Gibbons's collection, for two violins and a bass, qualify him for consideration as one of the earliest composers in England to approach the texture of the trio sonata.

Consorts of viols or members of the violin family were the most favoured types of instrumental ensemble, and as with the rise of the sonata in Italy, so too in England was the violin the catalyst for innovation. One of the first English composers to explore the expressive potential of the violin was Coprario in his 'courtly' fantasia suites in which the instrument became an equal protagonist with the bass viol in varied and idiomatic writing. Other composers quickly recognized the effectiveness of the violin in a small ensemble, where it was not necessarily treated as an equal partner in the contrapuntal texture but was exploited for its distinctive tonal character.

Two composers who took string instrumental music further along the road to independence were William Lawes (p. 154), earlier discussed as a composer for masques, and John Jenkins (1592–1678), both of whom wrote outstanding pieces for viols and violins, laying the path for Purcell. Jenkins's concept of 'fantasia' belonged to an older school, but he nevertheless successfully combined contrapuntal skill with the simpler idiom of the dance styles of both pre- and post-Commonwealth, as well as modern Italianate features. None of Lawes's music was published during his lifetime and only a very small quantity was printed later in the century, mainly under his brother's supervision. The pieces for viol consort in four, five and six parts probably date from the 1620s. The writing is idiomatic, sometimes extravagant, introspective and often passionate, much of the five-part consort music revealing Lawes at his best as perhaps the most individually expressive composer of his time. The 'setts' – the term sonata was not yet used in England at this date – or fantasy-suites follow a pattern established by Coprario with lively, idiomatic violin-writing foreshadowing that of the early Italian Baroque violin sonata. Lawes wrote two sets of eight sonatas, one set for violin, bass viol and organ, and the other for two violins, bass viol and organ. The dance element is strong in these works, each of which has a fantasia followed by two dances, alman and galliard, in duple and triple time respectively. As with the consort music, Lawes's sonatas are deeply felt and powerfully expressed, as witness the affecting four-part Sonata No. 1 in G minor with its darkly-coloured fantasia and striking dissonances and chromaticism at the close of the galliard.

Christopher Simpson (c.1605–69) extended the consort in another direction with virtuoso works for violins and viols; his greatest contribution however was his treatise *The Division-violist*, published in 1659 and in a revised version again in 1665. A second theoretical work, *A Compendium of Practical Musick* (1667), was described by Purcell as 'the most Ingenious Book I e'er met with upon this subject'. The discussion of tonal pitch, tempo, intervals, counterpoint, and all the rudiments of music secured for Simpson a place as one of the most important writers on music in mid-seventeenth-century England. He was highly regarded by his contemporaries, and was described by Locke as 'a person whose memory is precious among good and knowing Men, for his exemplary life and excellent skill'.

The consort music of Jenkins like that of William Lawes stems from the style of the Renaissance composers working at the end of the previous century. In many of his fantasia-suites, scored for a variety of stringed instrumental combinations, Jenkins placed emphasis on virtuosity, reaching great heights of display in the 'divisions' or forms of variation which frequently occur. Roger North (c.1651–1734), an entertaining writer and a valuable source of information on musical matters during the Restoration and later, described Jenkins, whom he had known, as 'a great reformer of musick in his time, for he got the better of the old Fancys, and introduced a pleasing air in everything he composed ...'. Indeed, it is this classical restraint and internal balance which was much admired. When Charles II was restored to the throne in 1660, Jenkins, now an old man, was appointed theorbo player in the King's Musick, but according to North, seldom appeared at court. It was a period of thriving patronage, and Jenkins was associated with more than one family. 'Nothing advanced music more in this age than the patronage of the nobility and men of fortunes,' wrote North, 'for they became encouragers of it by great liberallitys, and countenance to the professors' (*The Musicall Grammarian*, 1728).

A composer of instrumental chamber music on an inspirational level comparable with Simpson, Jenkins and William Lawes is Matthew Locke (c.1622–77). Locke wrote most of his music for strings during the

Commonwealth, assembling it first into seven collections and then, in the late 1660s, bringing it all together in a single autograph volume. Locke gave formal definition to the stylized dance suite, as we see, for example, in the *Little Consort of Three Parts* (1656) for violins with a basso continuo. His predilection for adventurous, often dissonant harmony, and his ability to hit upon striking melodic ideas give a pleasingly distinctive if at times experimental quality to his instrumental pieces.

Sacred music: the early Baroque anthem

Following the Protestant-Catholic strife of the sixteenth century the greatest early seventeenth-century composer of church music in England was Thomas Tomkins (1572–1656). Most of his anthems and services were collected and published after his death under the title *Musica Deo sacra* (1668). An outstanding contribution was also made by Orlando Gibbons whose Services, anthems and organ music are often striking in their expressive imitative polyphony. Several of his verse anthems are treated in a distinctive and elaborate fashion, with written-out parts for viol consort and alternative accompaniment for organ. Among the finest of these are *This is the record of John* and *See, see, the word is incarnate*. A significant body of church music was also provided by Weelkes (p. 118), Richard Dering (c.1580–1630), who published two volumes of Latin motets with continuo in 1617 and 1618, and Thomas Ravenscroft (c.1582–c.1635). Ravenscroft's psalter *The Whole Booke of Psalms* (1621) contains 105 settings, not only by Ravenscroft himself but also by Tomkins and many of the leading church composers, both of the Jacobean period and earlier.

During the Civil War and the Commonwealth (1649–60), Anglican church music ceased to flourish, though compositions continued to be written for private use. Oliver Cromwell attempted to remodel the Church of England on extreme Protestant lines in adopting the precepts of Puritanism. Little room remained for the ornamental aspects of divine worship, and music and choirs were suppressed. With the Restoration of the Monarchy came a revival of English church music, and for the remaining years of the seventeenth century the Baroque anthem was developed by several gifted composers. The fundamental difference between the Restoration anthem and its pre-Commonwealth antecedents was the shift away from polyphony towards a more declamatory style, with voices, solo and in chorus, often with string ensemble, over a basso continuo.

Music at the Restoration court

During the reign of Charles II the musical centre of the court was the newly revived Chapel Royal. As early as 1628 a 'King's band' had been established under Charles I; at the Restoration Charles II appointed violinists to the royal household, and in 1661 these became the King's band of 'Twenty-four violins' – the term 'violin' embracing the four main members of the violin family. Between 1646 and 1654 Charles and his mother had lived at Louis XIV's court in Paris where they had acquired a taste for both Italian and French music. On his return to England, Charles largely took the French court music as his model, emulating the '24 Violons du Roi' with his own newly assembled Twenty-four violins. He sent the elder John Banister (c.1625–79), one of the Twenty-four, to Paris to encounter French styles first hand; on his return Banister formed a select band of twelve string players from the Twenty-four, in imitation of Lully's *Petits Violons*, or *La petite Bande*, which had been formed in 1648. In his *Memoires of Musick* Roger North notes Continental influences:

> during the first years of Charles II all musick affected by the beau-mond run into the French way; and the rather, because at that time the master of the Court musick in France, whose name was Babtista [Lully], (an Itallian frenchifyed), had influenced the French style by infusing a great portion of the Italian harmony into it, whereby the Ayre was exceedingly improved.

Little or none of the court music written under Charles II and James II requires players over and above what could be provided by the Twenty-four, and it was these, usually in groups of five or six, who from 1662 provided the instrumental accompaniments to the more elaborate anthems for Sunday and feast day services, especially when the King was present.

In choosing Henry Cooke (c.1615–72) to be Master of the Children of the Chapel Royal, Charles II acted shrewdly. Captain Henry Cooke, as he was known, had fought for the royalist cause in the Civil War, and after the Restoration had become first a bass then a composer in the King's Private Musick. Cooke was a gifted teacher, a fine singer – the diarist Samuel Pepys (27 July 1661) assures us that he had 'the best manner of singing in the world' – and was energetic in his pursuit of talented singers and musicians. Among the choristers whom he engaged for the Chapel Royal were several who were later to emerge as the finest composers of their generation; they included Pelham Humfrey, John Blow, William Turner and Henry Purcell, the last three of whom provided music at the coronation of James II in 1685. Henry Lawes, Locke and William Child also contributed fine examples of the English anthem repertoire during the middle or later decades of the seventeenth century.

Pelham Humfrey, John Blow and the verse anthem

Among the first and most talented composers to develop the new type of verse anthem was Pelham Humfrey (1647–74). Humfrey was precociously gifted, and while still a choirboy in the Chapel Royal had begun to compose anthems for the services there. At the end of 1664 he embarked upon travels to France and Italy in order to study Continental styles in composition, and returned to England in the autumn of 1667, having been appointed a royal lutenist and a Gentleman of the Chapel Royal. Within a month, one of his anthems had been performed in the Chapel Royal, prompting an entry in Pepys's Diary which clearly shows by his disapproval his leaning towards the older full anthem, or anthem mainly excluding solo voices:

> and so I to the Chapel ... and heard a fine Anthemne, made by Pellam (who is come over) in France, of which there was great expectation; and endeed is a very good piece of Musique, but still I cannot call the Anthem anything but Instrumentall music with the Voice, for nothing is made of the words at all.

Nevertheless, Humfrey's expressive handling of the English language is evident in such anthems as *O Lord My God* and *By the Waters of Babylon* where vividly pictorial word-painting creates strongly contrasting and at the same time subtle effects. Much of Humfrey's sacred vocal writing has a marked Italian bias, and consolidates earlier Italian leanings of fellow English composers such as Locke. As in his consort music, so too in his sacred writing Locke reveals himself an inventive and experimental composer. His early training at Exeter Cathedral gave him a firm grounding in vocal and instrumental writing, apparent later in his skilful integration of voices and instruments. One can observe this skill in his many beautiful verse anthems, and perhaps above all in the elaborately constructed *Be thou exalted Lord*, performed for Charles II as 'A Song of Thanksgiving for His Majesty's Victory Over the Dutch on St. James His Day 1666'. Humfrey's instrumental writing, by contrast, is influenced by French forms established by Lully, incurring the displeasure of Pepys's fellow-diarist John Evelyn, who protests in an entry for 21 December 1662 that:

> instead of the ancient grave and solem wind musique accompanying

the Organ was introduced a Consort of 24 Violins betweene every pause, after the French fantastical light way, better suiting a Tavern or Play-house than a Church.

In 1672, on the death of Captain Cooke, Humfrey became the new Master of the Children of the Chapel Royal; this important office carried with it not only the training of the boys' voices but also the instruction of the lute and of bowed string instruments.

When Humfrey died in 1674 he was succeeded as Master of the Children of the Chapel Royal by his slightly younger contemporary and former fellow-chorister, John Blow (1649–1708). Blow had re-entered the King's service in 1669 as musician for the virginals, and had already served his probationary year as organist at Westminster Abbey. He had also become a Gentleman of the Chapel Royal in 1674. Further appointments followed. In 1676 Blow became one of the three organists of the Chapel Royal, and in 1700, the first holder of the newly created post of Composer of the Chapel Royal. The effectiveness of Blow's style in his choral works is well illustrated by his extended verse anthem *God spake sometime in visions*, composed for the Coronation of James II in 1685. In this work for eight-part choir, smaller vocal ensembles and strings, Blow goes some way towards bringing together the full anthem tradition with that of the verse anthem. Here as so often, his robust exploration of harmonies and modulations in both the vocal and instrumental parts is an invigorating and distinctive feature. Blow's contribution to opera will be considered later in the chapter.

Purcell: life, sacred music, odes

The dramatic use of solo voices in the English anthem as defined and developed by Humfrey and Blow was carried to new expressive heights in the sacred vocal music of their pupil, Henry Purcell (1659–95). Purcell, justly described in an obituary notice as 'one of the most Celebrated Masters of the Science of Musick in the Kingdom and scarce Inferiour to any in Europe' (p. 153), was engaged throughout his short life in the service of the Church and court. He was a chorister in the Chapel Royal, but in 1673, after his voice had broken, he was appointed to an unpaid post as assistant repairer and tuner of instruments belonging to Charles II, and between 1674 and 1678 had an additional responsibility for the tuning of the organ at Westminster Abbey. In 1677 Purcell succeeded Locke as Composer-in-Ordinary for the King's violins, and in 1679 he replaced Blow as organist of Westminster – a position which Blow assumed once again after Purcell's death in 1695. Purcell married either in 1680 or 1681, and in the following year became one of the organists of the Chapel Royal; duties as a singer in the choir, then composed of eight countertenors, eight tenors and sixteen basses, went hand-in-hand with the appointment. In 1683 Purcell was made keeper of the King's instruments, and in 1685 he became harpsichord player in James II's private music. The Roman Catholic James II customarily attended his own chapel in Whitehall which was opened in 1686, but services in the Chapel Royal were apparently held none the less, for Purcell continued to compose church music during James's short reign.

Purcell's sacred compositions include English anthems and services – the two main musical categories of Anglican worship – as well as miscellaneous chants, hymns, sacred songs and Latin psalm settings. The anthems, like those of his Restoration contemporaries, fall into two main types: the full anthem, predominantly contrapuntal, sometimes with solo or ensemble vocal sections alternating with the whole choir; and the verse anthem whose structure is dependent on basso continuo, already discussed in connection with Humfrey and Blow. Purcell's full anthems, which mostly belong to the early part of his life, reveal an accomplished technique and colourful musical language as well as a lively and imaginative response to the texts. Among many fine examples are the eight-part O Lord God of Hosts and the five-part Remember not, Lord, our offences, whose searing dissonances and intensity of expression, recalling the style of his French contemporary, Charpentier, bear witness to Italian influence. Purcell's verse anthems, especially the early ones, keep closely to the pattern set by Humfrey, but they are characterized by a vocal exuberance missing in the work of his elder contemporary. Purcell's fire is ignited in such anthems as My beloved spake, while a virtuoso element – reflecting the rise of vocal brilliance in Italy – appears in the solo bass writing of They that go down to the sea in ships. Purcell's skill in composing anthems is at its height in his My heart is inditing. This work, written for the Coronation of James II in 1685, and scored for strings, eight-part choir and groups of solo voices, unites elements of full and verse anthem techniques such as polyphony, antiphony and instrumental ritornello in a way both masterly and affecting.

As a court composer Purcell was expected not only to provide music for the Chapel Royal, but also to compose odes and welcome songs for special occasions such as royal birthdays and marriages. The earlier occasional pieces are interesting above all, perhaps, for what they show us of Purcell's developing style. The finest of them date from the 1690s, and include the ode, Hail, bright Cecilia (1692), the last of six birthday odes for Queen Mary (1689–94), 'Come ye sons of art away' (1694) and the 'Funeral Music for Queen Mary' (1695). Purcell's last music for St Cecilia's Day (1692) is also his most sumptuous. It is scored for soprano, two altos, tenor and bass soloists, with a six-part chorus and an ensemble of two treble recorders, a bass recorder, oboes, trumpets, timpani and strings. Among its noteworthy movements are the inspired and affecting fugal chorus, 'Soul of the World', the da capo bass aria on a ground, 'Wondrous machine', and the declamatory high-tenor aria, 'Tis Nature's voice', which at its first performance, according to *The Gentleman's Journal*, 'was sung with incredible Graces by Mr Purcell himself'. The birthday ode 'Come ye sons of art away' is a piece of indifferent verse, but Purcell's music enables us at once and throughout to overlook its literary deficiency. Its many captivating movements include an overture in the French style, a florid duet for two countertenors, 'Sound the trumpet', a resonant bass aria, 'These are the sacred charms', and one for soprano with oboe obbligato, 'Bid the virtues'.

Purcell's greatest gifts as a composer for voices are revealed in the music which he wrote for the stage, especially the 'semi-operas' performed during the last five or six years of his life.

English semi-opera

Earlier in the chapter we left theatre music with Davenant's production of *The Siege of Rhodes* in 1656. Upon his restoration to the throne Charles II authorized the establishment of two theatre companies in London. One of these, the Duke's Company, was run by Davenant, to whom the King granted an hereditary monopoly. From 1671 its home became the Dorset Garden Theatre in Salisbury Court. The other was the King's Company run by the actor Thomas Killigrew; the King granted him a patent in the same year and the Company established itself in the Drury Lane Theatre. In 1682 the two troupes united under a single patent, and, becoming known as the United Company, made use of both theatres until the end of the century.

Although Restoration England continued to take an interest in theatre music from abroad, English musical staged entertainments developed along hybrid lines of their own. Isolated examples of English opera were occasionally to appear, but the favoured form was the 'semi-opera', a term apparently invented by the contemporary writer Roger North, who said that it 'consisted of half Musick, and half Drama' and added his view that

there is a fatall objection to all these ambigue enterteinements: they break unity, and distract the audience. Some come for the play and hate the musick, others come onely for the musick, and the drama is pennance to them, and scarce any are well reconciled to both. Mr Betterton (whose talent was speaking and not singing) was pleased to say, that 2 good dishes were better than one, which is a fond mistake, for few care to see 2 at a time of equall choice.

North's observations are not without validity, but it would be wrong to assume from his remarks that semi-opera, in which song and speech are mixed, was necessarily of a lower order than some of the operas being performed in France and Italy at the same period, or that the English settled for semi-opera through ignorance of alternative forms of staged musical entertainment. London, after all, had witnessed a performance of the opera *Ariane, ou le Mariage de Baccus*, with a text by Pierre Perrin and music by Robert Cambert (*c.*1627–77) and Louis Grabu (fl.1665–94) in March 1674. Again, in 1685 Grabu collaborated with the poet Dryden on an operatic venture *Albion and Albanius* which was, in essence, an English version of a French *tragédie en musique*. In February of the following year, Londoners had an opportunity of seeing a true *tragédie en musique* by the creator of the form, Lully; this was his *Cadmus et Hermione*, given by a French company. None of these productions was successful, for English taste, formed by a strong theatre tradition, preferred an entertainment where speech reigned supreme. Music, dancing and elaborate spectacle were regarded mainly as diverting interpolations.

The 1670s witnessed a profusion of semi-operas among which several produced by the Duke's Company were particularly successful. Of these, *Psyche* (1675), adapted by Shadwell from the Molière-Lully *comédie-ballet* of the same name, with music by Locke, is in many ways the most interesting since, as Curtis Price has remarked in *Henry Purcell and the London Stage*, it is the 'first English musical extravaganza without a tap-root in the Stuart masque or the early Restoration play with music', and comes 'closer to the *dramma per musica* than any of Purcell's theatre works except *Dido and Aeneas*'. On the other hand, when Locke published his vocal music for *Psyche* in 1675 under the title *The English Opera*, he explained his intention in his preface:

after much consideration, industry and pains for splendid scenes and machines to illustrate the grand design, with art are composed in such kinds of music as the subject requires: and accordingly performed ... And therefore [*Psyche*] may justly wear the title [opera], though all the tragedy be not in music: for [I] the author prudently considered, that though Italy was, and is, the great Academy of the world for that science and way of entertainment, England is not, and therefore mixed it with interlocutions, as more proper to our genius.

There is no record of a semi-opera between the *Circe* of Charles Davenant (1677) with songs by John Banister – although Purcell wrote the music for one scene, in a revival – and the première of Purcell's *The Prophetess*, alternatively called *Dioclesian*, in 1690. This text derived from the joint efforts of John Fletcher (1579–1625) and Philip Massinger (1583–1640), but was adjusted 'after the manner of an opera' by the actor-manager Thomas Betterton (*c*.1635–1710) whom Charles II had earlier sent to Paris to study French musical drama – Betterton had, in fact, seen the Molière-Lully *Psyche* while in France. *Dioclesian* was the first of Purcell's large-scale works for the professional stage. It was a resounding success, and established his reputation as a dramatic composer. The score, made up of 'first' and 'second music' played before the performance, an overture or 'curtain tune', 'act tunes' played between the acts, and a masque containing a rich variety of songs and dances, is enchanting, and prompted Dryden publicly to acknowledge Purcell's genius as a composer.

Purcell followed *Dioclesian* with *King Arthur, or the British Worthy*, performed in 1691 at the Queen's Theatre, Dorset Garden. Unlike his other semi-operas, this was specifically designed as such rather than stemming from adaptations. The text was by Dryden, who had written it some years earlier for a performance which had never taken place. The patriotic story is a mixture of fantasy and historical legend. Purcell's music maintains a high level of invention and humour and is sometimes strikingly original, as for instance in the Act III 'Frost Scene'. Here extended passages of *tremolando* figures with arresting harmonic progressions evoke the frozen wastes inhabited by the Cold Genius. Four years earlier Lully had introduced a similar effect in the fourth act of his *tragédie lyrique, Isis* (1677), but his writing lacks the musical interest of Purcell's harmonic invention. Among the work's many engaging pieces are an extended song with chorus on a ground bass, 'How happy the Lover', the celebrated soprano air 'Fairest Isle', and a noble chaconne.

In 1692 Purcell's longest dramatic work was performed at Dorset Garden. This was an adaptation, once ascribed to Elkanah Settle (1648–1724), of Shakespeare's *A Midsummer Night's Dream*. The semi-opera was called *The Fairy Queen*, and although the music is not inferior to that of *King Arthur* the work lacks comparable unity. Among many delights to be found in Purcell's score, running to some sixty numbers in all, are colourful dances such as that for the Green Men, French in idiom but with characteristic Purcellian chromaticisms; Italianate da capo arias, sometimes with obbligato parts; affecting choruses like that sung over the sleeping Titania at the end of Act II, and a rich variety of vocal ensembles.

The two remaining semi-operas in which Purcell was involved date from 1695, the year in which he died. His last major stage work was *The Indian Queen* with a text by Dryden and his brother-in-law Sir Robert Howard. Unlike the earlier semi-operas, this was cast as a tragedy in which music played an integral part, to the point where, as Curtis Price has remarked, the 'composer has, in truth, contributed as much to the drama as the poet'. The score of *The Indian Queen* is shorter than either *King Arthur* or *The Fairy Queen* but Purcell's music is hardly less varied and evocative. Almost all of it was newly composed, though the 'symphony' which opens Act II was borrowed from the ode 'Come ye sons of art away'. Among the many captivating numbers in *The Indian Queen* is the popular soprano air, 'I attempt from love's sickness to fly'. The concluding masque to the work, however, was composed by Purcell's brother, Daniel Purcell (d.1717).

Purcell's contribution to the 1695 revival of the Dryden-Davenant version of Shakespeare's *The Tempest* is smaller than was once thought, though the Act IV song 'Dear pretty youth' is certainly by him. The 'Dance of Winds' in Act II, however, is borrrowed from Lully's *Cadmus et Hermione* which had been performed in London in 1686; and it is unlikely that Purcell was the composer of the remainder of the score, fine though it is, and notable for the lyrical da capo air, 'Halcyon days'. It seems likely that the music is largely the work of John Weldon (1676–1736), one of Purcell's pupils.

Opera: Purcell's Dido and Aeneas, Blow's Venus and Adonis

Purcell's and England's only true seventeenth-century operatic venture, *Dido and Aeneas*, was not written for the professional stage but probably for Josias Priest's School for Young Ladies at Chelsea (then a village near London). Priest was a dancing-master who first collaborated with Purcell in arranging the dances in *Dido* and subsequently for *Dioclesian, King Arthur* and *The Fairy Queen. Dido and Aeneas* was performed at Priest's boarding school in 1689. The librettist, Nahum Tate (1652–1715), based his text on the famous love story in the fourth book of Virgil's epic poem, *Aeneid*. As poetry it is undistinguished but it provided Purcell with what he required – a descriptive story with musically promising situations. Short though the work is – its overture and three acts take only an hour or so to perform – Purcell's music expresses a wide range of emotions, ranging from Dido's pathetic 'Ah! Belinda' (Act I) and deeply affecting monologue with lament (Act III), to the spirited sailors' chorus and dance and strikingly imaginative music for the witches. Small weaknesses in the work, such as the somewhat perfunctory and conventional handling of the role of Aeneas, fade into insignificance beside the expressive quality of the recitative, the atmospheric instrumental contributions where Locke's influence is apparent, and the freshness of Purcell's invention. From start to finish this masterly score holds our attention with a strength of character exerted only by works of the greatest genius.

Dido and Aeneas, however, was not without precedent. A significant precursor to Purcell's opera was Blow's Venus and Adonis. Although termed a 'Masque' this work, sung throughout, is as much an opera as Purcell's. Musically, Venus and Adonis is of considerable interest. Blow had never written such a work before, and although he was probably influenced by the musically self-contained masques of Locke, the absence of an existing operatic convention in England enabled him to create an original masterpiece incorporating features of French musical drama such as the overture and dance music, and to a somewhat lesser extent those of the Italian chamber cantata. Within the framework of a prologue and three acts Blow introduces a wealth of ideas; there is an engaging spelling-lesson for little Cupids in the Act II, for instance, and dances which reveal Blow's harmonic individuality. The fervent emotional responses of the two lovers in Act III, however, are the most remarkable feature of the opera; here, as Adonis slowly dies, he and Venus engage in a passionate dialogue far removed from the artificiality of their surroundings. The author of the charming libretto – in part a gently mischievous satire on courtly conduct – is unknown, but the opera was probably composed in 1681 for the entertainment of Charles II, and performed before the court in Oxford in the summer of that year.

Purcell's instrumental music

We have seen how, in his church music, odes and dramatic works, Purcell drew upon French and Italian styles as well as those of his native England. In his purely instrumental compositions this is no less the case, though the emphasis is more on English and Italian influences and less on French. Two distinct categories are discernible in Purcell's instrumental music: one in which the writing is for viol consort without continuo, and another in which the composer writes for the more progressive texture of violins with bass viol and continuo in 'just imitation of the most fam'd Italian masters'. To the first category belong thirteen *Fantasias* and two *In Nomines* for viol consorts of varying strengths. The pieces, which date from around 1680, reveal Purcell's gift for polyphony, as well as seeming to be, in Jack Westrup's words, 'passionate revelations of the composer's most secret thoughts'. This subtle and elusive music is the highest development of a tradition forged by earlier composers of the English Baroque, notably Gibbons and Locke.

Purcell's twenty-two trio sonatas are contained in two collections, the twelve *Sonnata's of III Parts*, published in 1683, and *Ten Sonatas in Four Parts*, published in 1697, two years after the composer's death. In the preface to this later set the composer's widow remarks upon its 'having already found many Friends'. It contains not only what has become Purcell's best-known trio sonata, called for its excellence the *Golden Sonata*, but also his most extended piece of chamber music, a *Chacony* built over a five-bar ground bass. It has been argued that the Italianate style of these works was inspired by Corelli's early examples.

Compared with Purcell's abundant instrumental chamber music the quantity of solo keyboard pieces seems meagre – though very recently several have turned up in the composer's few surviving autograph manuscripts; but they are attractive and full of character. As well as eight short suites there are many isolated pieces of which the 'grounds' are especially rewarding. The quantity of solo songs, on the other hand, is enormous; taken together they amount to a veritable compendium of styles in which we can find songs built on ground basses, da capo airs with florid Italianate writing, and rondeaux.

It will be apparent that the development of music in England during the seventeenth century was somewhat fragmented and inconsistent. Nobody, perhaps, has summed it up better than Purcell, in the dedication of *Dioclesian* to the Duke of Somerset in 1690:

> Musick is yet but in its Nonage; a forward Child, which gives hope of what it may be hereafter in England, when the Masters of it shall find more Encouragement. 'Tis now learning Italian, which is its best Master, and a little of the French Air to give it somewhat more of Gayety and Fashion. Thus, being further from the Sun we are of later Growth than our Neighbour Countries, and must be content to shake off our Barbarity by degrees.

Yet in all genres, England created a unique, idiosyncratic Baroque musical culture, a poignant and expressive language, notwithstanding, or even because of, its hybrid and parochial traits.

9
Eighteenth-century England: musical diversity in the age of Handel

W E HAVE SEEN IN THE PREVIOUS CHAPTER that Italy and, to a more limited extent France, played crucial roles in the formation of English musical styles during the seventeenth century. The taste in England during the first half of the eighteenth century was largely for Italian music, and was reflected above all in a growing interest in Italian opera. The period was one of comparative stability; political power remained with the aristocracy and wealthy landowners, but cultured society was no longer confined exclusively to those of privileged birth. It included to a growing extent bankers, merchants and a new breed of politicians who were able to buy themselves into Parliament. Clubs and coffee-houses became centres for elegant and informed conversation, at least among those fortunate enough to belong to a class which entitled them to a good education. The spirit of the time was neatly summarized by Lord Chesterfield: 'We are refined', he wrote, 'and plain manners, plain dress and plain diction would as little do in life, as acorns, herbage, and the water of the neighbouring well, would do at table.' Little wonder, then, that an extravagant entertainment such as Italian opera should become fashionable.

From the beginning of the eighteenth century the focus of musical life in London was no longer the court but theatres, concert-rooms, private houses and pleasure gardens. Theatres were built in profusion, sometimes opening and closing within a very short space of time. The most important theatre for Italian opera was the Queen's or, after 1714, the King's Theatre in the Haymarket (the name changed according to the gender of the reigning monarch), built in 1705 by the playwright and architect Sir John Vanbrugh. As we shall see, Handel directed there the première of *Rinaldo*, his first opera for London, as well as all subsequent premières of his operas until 1734. Theatres at Lincoln's Inn Fields, Drury Lane, and, from 1732, Covent Garden also played an active role in the promotion of musical entertainment. Lincoln's Inn Fields Theatre provided a home for many shades and varieties of playhouse entertainment such as pantomime, masque and ballad opera. It was here, in 1728, that one of the greatest theatre triumphs of the century, *The Beggar's Opera*, was first staged. The Drury Lane Theatre, on the other hand, mainly presented straight plays, but during the 1720s also staged masques. Other theatres of the time included the Little Theatre in the Haymarket and a theatre at Goodman's Fields.

Eighteenth-century England witnessed a growth in almost all aspects of musical life and music-making. Societies were founded, festivals inaugurated and concert rooms opened both in London and in many of England's larger towns and cities. Amateur and professional musicians were active not only in the promotion of the music of their own day but also in the discovery of their musical heritage. In 1710 an Academy of Ancient Music was founded, and in 1726 an Academy of Vocal Music, which met fortnightly in 'an attempt to restore ancient church music'. Charitable institutions, too, played an important role in fostering English musical life. The 'Three Choirs Festival' was inaugurated about 1715 in aid of charity; and in London the 'Foundling Hospital' of Thomas Coram, founded in 1739, had musical connections: from 1749 Handel gave an annual performance of his music in its chapel in support of the foundation and in 1750 he presented it with an organ.

In short, English musical life flourished in the eighteenth century. As well as the great figure of Handel and several lesser arrivals from the Continent, England could boast of indigenous talent in composers like Boyce, Arne, Avison, Maurice Greene and John Stanley. Notable, too, was the emergence of the music journalist and of two fine English music historians, Sir John Hawkins and Dr Charles Burney. Music printing thrived, and was dominated in the first half of the century by John Walsh, father and son: Walsh became Handel's regular publisher from about 1734. Printed music of all kinds was increasingly in demand for clubs, societies and private subscribers. Printing standards varied and so, too, did ethical ones: piracy thrived and copyright was largely ignored. Song-sheets were printed profusely during this period, ranging in quality from the merely functional to works of art such as those from the presses of the distinctive and gifted map-maker George Bickham. His collection of songs, *The Musical Entertainer*, issued between 1737 and 1739, is a particularly fine example of his detailed illustrative work.

The growth of opera

Interest in Italian opera was such that two theatres embarked on a competitive course of presenting it to the public. The Drury Lane Theatre was first off the mark, in 1705, with *Arsinoe, Queen of Cyprus*. The music was compiled by Thomas Clayton, one-time violinist in the court orchestra of William and Mary. Spoken drama, not in itself part of the opera which followed as an afterpiece, was included in the performances of *Arsinoe*, this being the well-established custom of the previous century. Clayton described his work as 'An opera, after the Italian manner; All sung', and explains his use of English for the libretto in its preface:

> The Design of this Entertainment being to introduce the Italian Manner of Musick on the English Stage, which has not before been attempted; I was oblig'd to have an Italian Opera translated: In which the Words, however mean in several Places, suited much better with that manner of Musick, than others more Poetical would do.

Later in the same year, the Queen's Theatre in the Haymarket, newly opened by Sir John Vanbrugh and the dramatist William Congreve, responded with *The Loves of Ergasto* with music by a German composer Jakob Greber. Unlike *Arsinoe* this opera was reputedly sung in Italian and employed an Italian cast, described by one witness as 'the worst that e're came from thence'. The Queen's Theatre, having suffered an inauspicious beginning, must, however, have been heartened by Drury Lane's production of *Rosamond*. Notwithstanding the literary distinction of its librettist, Joseph Addison, the music composed, or perhaps partly compiled by Clayton was of lamentable quality, and the production in 1707 was one of the great operatic failures of the century.

The next and last all-sung opera at Drury Lane, in 1707, was *Thomyris, Queen of Scythia*, a *pasticcio* with music arranged mainly from Giovanni Bononcini and Alessandro Scarlatti and with recitatives by Pepusch. The performances were notable for the first appearance on the London stage of an Italian 'castrato' singer, Valentino who, while the remainder of the cast sang in English, sang his arias in Italian. Soprano and alto castratos had appeared in operas from the beginning of the seventeenth century but reached the height of their popularity during the mid to late Baroque period. They were mostly Italian, and several acquired international reputations and considerable wealth – above all, perhaps, in England during the period of Handel's operas. The best of them had voices of considerable strength and purity, and for these qualities were much in demand as great vocal instrumentalists.

During the next two or three years, the Queen's Theatre experimented with bilingual operas in Italian and English. The most successful of these was *Pyrrhus and Demetrius* which ran to twenty-three performances in the 1708 season. The music largely derived from Alessandro Scarlatti's successful opera *Pirro e Demetrio*, while the libretto was translated from Italian by Owen Swiney (d.1754), a colourful Irishman who occupied an influential position as opera impresario and manager successively of the Drury Lane and the Queen's Theatre. The experiment of bilingual opera was shortlived, for, as Addison later contemptuously remarked, 'the Audience got tired of understanding half the Opera; and therefore to ease themselves intirely of the Fatigue of Thinking, have so ordered it at present, that the whole Opera is performed in an unknown Tongue'. The following two operas at the Queen's Theatre showed a bias towards performance in Italian. The anonymous *Almahide* (1710) had minor characters singing in English while *Hydaspes* (1710) was sung entirely in Italian with music by Francesco Mancini (1672–1737).

Hydaspes was a success and, for the time being, at least, assured the future of Italian opera in London. The public had been delighted both by the excellence of the singing, above all by that of the castrato Nicolo Grimaldi, known as Nicolini, and by his fight with a lion on stage. Addison's only complaint was that the lion could not be persuaded to perform his part in an encore. Among those who assumed this role, according to Addison, were a candle-snuffer, a tailor and a country gentleman. This was the point which Italian opera had reached in London when Handel arrived there in the autumn of 1710.

Handel: early life

George Frideric Handel was born in the German town of Halle in Saxony on the 23 February 1685. His interest in music began at an early age, and while at school he studied under the Halle composer and organist, Zachow. In 1702 Handel matriculated at the University of Halle and shortly afterwards was appointed organist at the Calvinist Cathedral. He remained at the University little more than a year before leaving Halle for Hamburg. Hamburg, as we have seen in an earlier chapter, was one of the most important commercial centres in Europe, and its wealthy merchants contributed generously to cultural activities. Outstanding among them was the opera company controlled at this time by Reinhard Keiser. Handel joined the opera as a rank-and-file violinist in 1703 and at about the same time became friendly with the Hamburg theorist and composer Johann Mattheson. In the following year the two men quarrelled over how to perform the continuo accompaniment of Mattheson's opera *Cleopatra*; such was the animosity between them that a duel ensued, but friendship was eventually restored. Handel's first two operas, *Almira* in which Mattheson sang the leading tenor role, and *Nero*, were produced in the early months of 1705. *Almira*, the only one to survive, shows the influence of both Keiser and Mattheson, and employs a bilingual text in German and Italian following a custom frequently adopted by Keiser and the Hamburg opera composers.

Handel in Italy

In 1706 Handel travelled to Italy where a stay of some four years played a vital role in the formation of his mature style. Throughout the seventeenth and eighteenth centuries, Italian culture was a prerequisite for an artist's education; Italy was the home, not only of the principal vocal forms of the Baroque period – opera, oratorio and cantata – but also of the instrumental forms, sinfonia, sonata and concerto. Handel's visit probably began in Florence where his first Italian opera, *Rodrigo*, was produced in 1707. Before that, however, he had moved on to Rome where he composed his first oratorio, *Il trionfo del Tempo e del Disinganno*. While in Rome, Handel enjoyed the patronage of several wealthy noblemen, above all that of the Marchese Francesco Maria Ruspoli, who employed the young composer at three periods between 1707 and 1709. Handel wrote numerous works for Ruspoli including the oratorio *La Resurrezione* (1708), Latin motets, and a great many chamber cantatas. Some of these, like *Aminta e Fillide* and *Armida abbandonata*, are extended pieces with melody instruments, but the majority are for solo voice and continuo accompaniment. It was at Rome, too, that Handel composed his Latin psalms, *Dixit Dominus*, *Laudate Pueri* and *Nisi Dominus*. These were almost certainly part of a complete Carmelite Vespers setting for the feast of the Madonna del Carmine on 16 July 1707.

In the months when Handel was not in Rome he occupied his time principally in Florence, Venice and Naples. In the summer of 1708 he wrote the serenata *Aci, Galatea e Polifemo* for a ducal wedding at Naples, and in December of that year gained popular success with his opera *Agrippina*, written for Venice, Italy's leading operatic centre. While in Italy Handel probably met most of the leading composers of the day, including Alessandro Scarlatti, Caldara, Corelli, Albinoni and Vivaldi. The significance of Handel's Italian period has been perceptively summarized by the Handel scholar Winton Dean:

> The most important lesson he learnt there, chiefly from the operas and cantatas of Alessandro Scarlatti, was the command of a rich, free and varied melodic style, long-breathed but rhythmically flexible, which

distinguished all his later music. With it he won absolute mastery of the technique of writing for the voice. The warm climate of Italian lyricism melted the stiffness and angularity of his German heritage, and at the same time refreshed his counterpoint ...

Rinaldo: Handel's first London opera

When Handel left Italy in February 1710 (p. 156) he would seem to have determined on regular employment as a court *Kapellmeister* in his native Germany. In June of that year he accepted a post at the Hanover court, but at once obtained leave of absence for a year to visit London. What he found there was, as we have seen, a city where Italian opera had begun to flourish, though to quote Handel's later biographer, John Mainwaring:

all that regards the drama, or plan, including also the machinery, scenes, and decorations, was foolish and absurd almost beyond imagination ... The arrival of Handel put an end to this reign of nonsense.

The Queen's Theatre had a regular opera company and a permanent orchestra, enthusiastically supported by the aristocracy. What it needed now was a composer of Handel's 'uncommon abilities', which according to Mainwaring, 'had been conveyed to England before his arrival, and through various channels,' for 'some persons here had seen him in Italy, and others during his residence at Hanover ... Many of the nobility were impatient for an Opera of his composing.' Almost on his arrival, therefore, Aaron Hill, the new theatre manager at the Queen's Theatre, commissioned an opera from him. This was *Rinaldo*, which opened on 24 February 1711 and was the first Italian opera written specifically for the London stage. The libretto was based on a famous episode in Tasso's *La Gerusalemme Liberata* (Jerusalem Delivered), an epic poem much favoured in Baroque opera. It was the first of five 'magic' operas by Handel, in which the supernatural element plays an essential part. *Rinaldo* was a sensational success but it was not without its critics. Among the most vociferous were those entertaining satirists of *The Spectator*, Addison and Steele. Their criticism was not unprejudiced for Addison's own opera, *Rosamond*, had been a resounding failure, while Steele as a playwright had a vested interest in spoken drama; but their remarks add colour to the picture of Italian opera in London at the time. Addison found the extravagances in *Rinaldo* outweighed any sterling merit, while Steele objected to the absurdities of the production:

As to the Mechanism and Scenary ... at the 'Hay-Market' the Undertakers forgetting to change their Side Scenes, we were presented with a Prospect of the Ocean in the midst of a delightful Grove; and th' the Gentlemen on the Stage had very much contributed to the Beauty of the Grove, by walking up and down between the Trees, I must own I was not a little astonished to see a well-dressed young Fellow, in a full-bottom'd Wigg, appear in the midst of the Sea, and without any visible Concern taking Snuff.

Notwithstanding a minority of adverse criticism, *Rinaldo*, with the castrato Nicolini in the title role, was a triumph for Handel, and the opera was performed fifteen times between February and June of 1711.

In *Rinaldo* Handel was already putting into practice his almost inveterate custom of borrowing music both from his own earlier works and from the work of other composers. Several numbers are drawn from his Italian secular cantatas and others from his operas *Almira* and *Agrippina*. Among them is Rinaldo's affecting aria 'Cara sposa' (Act I, Sc. 7) which, according to Sir John Hawkins, Handel 'would frequently say was one of the best he ever made'. No other opera of Handel's was performed during his lifetime as often as *Rinaldo*. Serious opera in English, meanwhile, was in a decline that would continue until the production of Arne's *Artaxerxes* in 1762, though Handel's *Semele* (1744) with its text by Congreve, neither opera nor oratorio, offered an inspired and interesting hybrid form.

Handel's first visit to England lasted about eight months, at the end of which he returned to Hanover and to his duties as court *Kapellmeister*. That he intended to return to London, however, is strongly implied by the fact that almost at once he began to learn English. In the autumn of 1712 Handel received permission from the Elector to make a second journey, but as Mainwaring relates, 'on condition that he engaged to return within a reasonable time'. Late in 1712 Handel was back in London once more, this time to settle, and eventually to become a naturalized Englishman. Over the next eight years or so he led a varied musical life. Between 1713 and 1716 he enjoyed the patronage of Lord Burlington, and during this period also wrote four operas: *Il Pastor Fido*, *Teseo*, *Silla* and *Amadigi di Gaula*. *Rinaldo* was revived several times, but in spite of its continuing success with the public Handel's fortunes were mixed. Aaron Hill had been succeeded by Owen Swiney in 1712 as manager of the Queen's Theatre, and as a contemporary report relates, Swiney 'Barkes & runs away & leaves ye Singers unpaid ye Scenes & Habits also unpaid for'. Swiney was succeeded by the Swiss, J.J. Heidegger, who was to work closely with Handel in the production of the majority of his operas. Between 1717 and 1720 no operas were staged at the Queen's Theatre and Handel entered the service of the Earl of Carnarvon, later first Duke of Chandos, as resident composer. He had already been commissioned by Queen Anne to compose occasional church music, among which was the Te Deum celebrating the Treaty of Utrecht (1713), and the ceremonial 'Ode for Queen Anne's Birthday' (1713). Now, for the Earl of Carnarvon, who kept his own modest band of singers and instrumentalists under the direction of Johann Christoph Pepusch (1667–1752), Handel provided eleven Chandos anthems, a Te Deum and two English masques, *Acis and Galatea* (1718), and the first version of *Esther* (1718).

Handel's Academy operas

An event of great significance to Handel occurred in the winter of 1718– 19 with a move to establish Italian opera in London on a more secure financial basis than hitherto. Leading members of the nobility, under the patronage of George I, who had succeeded Queen Anne in 1714, proposed a 'Royal Academy of Music'. With such an institution Handel could look forward to a salary, sound theatre management, an established orchestra and first-rate singers. Handel himself set out in search of the finest singers in Europe during the summer of 1719. Shortly after his return later in the year the Academy directors appointed him 'Master of the Orchestra with a Salary'. His first Academy opera, *Radamisto* (1720), was rapturously received, but for a short time subsequently operas by Giovanni Bononcini (1670–1747), whom the Academy also had approached, offered serious rivalry.

Handel's greatest heroic operas belong to the period of the Royal Academy, reaching a peak in *Giulio Cesare in Egitto* (1724), *Tamerlano* (1724) and *Rodelinda* (1725). By this time he had a wealth of fine singing talent at his disposal which he placed at the service of some of his most profound utterances. The resident soprano Francesca Cuzzoni (Cleopatra) and the castrato Senesino (Caesar) were outstandingly successful in *Giulio Cesare*, and Handel's rich and colourfully depictive orchestral and melodic gifts did not fail to win over audiences. Among a profusion of memorable arias in *Giulio Cesare*, Caesar's 'Va tacito e nascosto', with its 'stalking' repeated quavers and horn obbligato, evocative of the chase, in which he likens Ptolemy's suspected treachery to a hunter tracking his prey with measured tread, and Cleopatra's two great laments, 'Se pietà' with its independent bassoons, and 'Piangerò' stand out for their glorious melodies and for the deep compassion with which Handel draws the characters. The Royal Academy survived until 1728 despite directorial debate and fierce squabbling among some of the musicians, notably between Cuzzoni and the soprano Faustina Bordoni who had been invited to join the company in 1725.

Opera seria *challenged*

In the year the Royal Academy closed its doors English musical theatre challenged Italian *opera seria* with *The Beggar's Opera*, produced at Lincoln's Inn Fields Theatre on 29 January 1728. The work was a blend of English comedy with opera in which the librettist, John Gay (1685–1732), inserted a great many popular tunes from England, Scotland, Ireland and France into spoken dialogue. Few aspects of respectable life escaped Gay's sharp satire – government, politics, class, even Italian opera were scrutinized and ridiculed. The music, too, had political overtones; the overture, by Johann Christoph Pepusch who also provided the thorough-basses for the songs, contains a melody known as 'Walpole, or The Happy Clown' (Robert Walpole was the Prime Minister of the time). *The Beggar's Opera* ran for sixty-two nights, proving to be an immensely popular novelty.

Handel's second Academy

Neither the success of *The Beggar's Opera* nor the collapse of the Royal Academy deflected Handel from the continuance of his operatic career. In 1729 he rented the King's Theatre from the former directors of the Royal Academy and in partnership with Heidegger began a second opera Academy on a subscription basis. The opening season was indifferently received but the following three were more successful, the failure of *Ezio* (1732) being more than balanced by the warm reception given to *Poro* (1731) and *Orlando* (1733). Trouble was in store for Handel's second Academy, however, in the form of a rival establishment calling itself the Opera of the Nobility, which was 'got up against the dominion of Mr Handel'. Almost all Handel's finest singers left him for the opposition, including Senesino, whose conduct was scheming and may have been less than honourable. Handel retaliated by entering into an agreement with the manager John Rich, whose new theatre at Covent Garden had been opened in 1732. Handel produced six new operas in three seasons, using English as well as Italian singers and even including a ballet troupe led by the celebrated French *danseuse*, Marie Sallé. Among his finest achievements of this period were *Ariodante* (1735) and *Alcina* (1735), his last great operatic triumph.

During the mid-1730s both opera companies were in decline, and in
1737 both folded. Handel was by now active in the spheres of oratorio
and English ode, but his health broke and he left for Aix-la-Chapelle in
search of a cure. When he returned, cured, Heidegger engaged him for
two more opera seasons; neither really succeeded, for public taste for
Italian *opera seria* seemed to have waned, at least for the time being.
Fashion now inclined towards English burlesque, of which *The Dragon
of Wantley*, a satire on Italian opera by John Frederick Lampe, was a
notable example. *Pasticcio*, a form consisting of music borrowed from
existing works by various composers, was also popular; but an attempt to
establish Italian comic opera in London was largely unsuccessful.

Handel and English oratorio

Whereas by the 1660s oratorio, whose foundations lay in Italy, was firmly
established in many Italian cities, English oratorio was unknown before
the arrival of Handel. It was Handel's creation and, in its synthesis of
English, French, Italian and German elements, often appears strikingly
different from its European counterparts. Handel's English oratorios
usually consist of a drama in three acts, based on or at least related to a
sacred subject; in some, however, such as *Israel in Egypt* and *Messiah*,
Handel used non-dramatic libretti. The music embraces the style of
Italian opera and English sacred choral music, but was performed as a
concert, usually in a theatre but also in concert halls, and occasionally in
the music rooms of taverns, where a concert tradition had grown up in
London during the previous century. Between the acts the orchestra often
performed concertos, and this gave rise to another of Handel's
innovations, the organ concerto, in which he himself would normally
play the solos.

In the extensive and dramatic use of the chorus, by his use of stage
directions and by the division of his oratorios into acts – features which
distinguish Handelian English oratorio from its Italian counterpart –
Handel reveals himself, as ever, a man of the theatre. Performance of
Handel's first English oratorio took place privately in the early spring of
1732 at the Crown and Anchor Tavern in the Strand. The work was
Esther, which he had initially written in 1718 for his patron James
Brydges, Earl of Carnarvon, but had now substantially revised. The
enterprise was successful and Handel's pupil, Princess Anne, asked him
to stage the work at the King's Theatre in the Haymarket. However,
while the arrangements for this were under way a pirated performance of
Esther was advertised. Handel responded by enlarging his score and

announcing that he had done so. A further problem arose when the Bishop of London prohibited members of the Chapel Royal from donning costumes and enacting a sacred subject in the theatre. Handel was obliged to accede, adding to his announcement: 'N.B. There will be no Action on the Stage, but the House will be fitted up in a decent manner for the Audience. The Musick to be disposed after the Manner of the Coronation Service.' In this manner the performances of *Esther* took place in the King's Theatre in May 1732, when they were enthusiastically received.

Handel's rivals were quick to recognize an opportunity for profit. Hardly had the performances of *Esther* finished when an opera company which functioned at the New Theatre, also in the Haymarket, staged Handel's masque *Acis and Galatea*. Once again, Handel responded to the piracy by expanding the 1718 score with music from other works of his own; this version was performed at the King's Theatre in June 1732, sung in a mixture of English and Italian. Although it was popular and several times revived in this form, Handel eventually returned to the musically more satisfying English version of 1718.

The variety in Handel's oratorios is considerable, yet of course there are ingredients common to all of them; many of these, furthermore, such as recitative, aria and overture, are similar to those in eighteenth-century Italian opera, but whereas in Handel's operas the chorus played a very small part, or was totally absent, it assumed a large and dramatically significant role in the oratorios produced between the late 1730s and the early 1750s. His subjects were drawn largely from the Old Testament though there were notable exceptions: one of them was *Semele* (1744), described by Charles Jennens (1700–73) as 'no Oratorio, but a bawdy Opera ... An English Opera, but called by "fools" an Oratorio, and performed as such at Covent Garden'. Jennens, in fact, was right; *Semele*, though produced 'after the Manner of an Oratorio', is essentially an English opera with a libretto by William Congreve, and stylistically close to its Italian counterparts. Jennens was an important figure in English musical life at the time; he provided Handel with texts for three great oratorios, *Saul* (1739), *Messiah* (1742), and *Belshazzar* (1745), as well as adapting Milton and adding his own serviceable *Il Moderato* for Handel's English ode *L'Allegro, il Penseroso ed il Moderato* (1740).

Handel followed up the success of *Esther* with further seasons of oratorio which usually occurred during Lent. Performances were generally held in London's theatres, but one first performance, that of *Athalia* in 1733, took place in the Sheldonian Theatre at Oxford, where Handel had been invited by the University Vice-Chancellor to provide music for a degree-giving ceremony. In 1739 Handel performed *Saul* at the King's Theatre. It was his most lavishly scored oratorio yet, and a work hardly less dramatic than his operas. The orchestral requirements included three trombones, a carillon, and a pair of extra large kettledrums which had to be borrowed from the Tower of London. These were said to have been used at the Battle of Malplaquet in 1709, and sounded an octave lower than standard kettledrums of the time; they are heard in the famous Act III 'Dead March' as well as in an Act I chorus. Handel must have liked the sound they made for he used them again in subsequent oratorios.

Saul was greeted enthusiastically, but not so his next oratorio, *Israel in Egypt* (1739), which, with its imposing succession of choruses, was considered by some to be unsuitable for a theatre, and by others to lack a sufficient element of contrast.

Handel's Janus-like stance towards opera and oratorio was finally resolved in the direction of oratorio by an invitation to Dublin which he took up in 1741, and by an idea of Jennens'. Jennens had made a 'Scripture Collection', as he called it, and in a letter to his friend Edward Holdsworth, wrote: 'I hope he [Handel] will lay out his whole Genius & Skill upon it, that the Composition may excell all his former Compositions, as the Subject excells every other Subject'. The subject was that of Handel's most celebrated oratorio, *Messiah*. The text, though essentially non-dramatic, nevertheless gave Handel scope to write music which embraces a wide spectrum of affects. Jennens justly saw the work as 'a fine entertainment', for although the subject is sacred there is nothing peculiarly so in the style of Handel's music.

Messiah, which Handel had written in little over three weeks in the late summer of 1741, was first performed at Neal's Music Hall in Dublin on 13 April 1742. It was rapturously received, and fully realized the high expectation which Jennens had of it. *Messiah* was given its first London performance in the following year but the reception was very different. The Methodists and others viewed its performance in a theatre as blasphemous. Handel tried to avert condemnation by advertising the work, not as *Messiah*, but as 'A new Sacred Oratorio'. Even so, it failed, and only began to impress English audiences in the following decade.

Handel followed *Messiah* with a steady succession of oratorios during the next ten years, outstanding among them being *Samson* (1743), *Semele* (1744), *Belshazzar* (1745), *Solomon* (1749), *Theodora* (1750) and *Jephtha* (1752). *Semele*, as we have seen, was not really an oratorio and is a Classical drama rather than a biblical one. *Hercules*, based on a stage play, is not biblical either, and was termed by Handel a 'musical drama'.

The dramatic sense in each of these works is vivid, powerful, resourceful and original. The handling of the chorus, 'the great lesson which he had learned from England' (Dent), is masterly, and the pictures Handel paints in the mind of the listener are profound and often minute in detail. Such an instance is the five-part 'Nightingale Chorus' at the end of the first Act of *Solomon* in which Handel draws an enchanting vignette of nature. Of a very different hue is the thrilling picture 'of clanking arms and neighing steeds' conveyed through a colossal eight-part chorus in Act III.

The success which Handel enjoyed with the greater number of his oratorios encouraged English composers to try their hand at the Handelian form. Maurice Greene (1696–1755) was one of the first off the mark with *The Song of Deborah and Barak* (1732). The work, though short in comparison with Handel's oratorios, contains some fine music and is not lacking in drama. Greene followed it with a handful of similar works among which was *Jephtha* (1737). Other oratorios by English composers include Boyce's *Solomon* (1742) and Arne's *The Death of Abel* (1744) which was first performed at Drury Lane. This marked the beginning of a period when Drury Lane mounted its own oratorio seasons in rivalry with Covent Garden, where Handel's oratorios were still being performed on a regular basis.

Masques and pastorals

The towering musical personality of Handel, who made the London of the 1720s and 1730s one of the leading opera centres of Europe, makes it easy to overlook activities which were taking place in the theatres and playhouses other than those where Handel himself worked. While as we have seen, Italian opera was the chief form of entertainment at the King's Theatre, other theatres offered a wider variety of drama – spoken, sung or incorporating both speech and music. There were masques, pantomimes, ballad operas, pastorals and dialogue operas in profusion. The Drury Lane Theatre, for instance, under its manager Colley Cibber, attempted to combat Italian opera with English masque. After the Restoration, masques were generally all sung, and during the eighteenth century usually fulfilled the role of 'after-piece' following a spoken drama. Cibber appointed as musical director the German-born Pepusch, who scored a success with his *Venus and Adonis* (1715). Cibber himself provided the libretto, describing the work as 'an Attempt to give the Town a little good Musick in a Language they understand'. The success was short-lived, however, and by the 1720s we find both Drury Lane and Lincoln's Inn Fields involved in another form of 'afterpiece' entertainment: English pantomime. Eighteenth-century pantomime contained airs, recitatives, ensembles and choruses interspersed with short instrumental pieces which accompanied the 'mime' element in the show. Characters such as Columbine, Pantaloon and Harlequin from the Italian *Commedia dell'arte* were popular, and between 1723 and 1728 the two theatres produced between them nearly six hundred pantomime performances of well over a dozen works. Among the great successes were *The Necromancer or Harlequin Dr Faustus* (1723) and *Apollo and Daphne or the Burgomaster trick'd* (1726).

Much of the most imaginative theatre music in London between the 1730s and early 1760s was composed by Thomas Arne (1710–78), Maurice Greene (1696–1755) and William Boyce (1711–79). The favoured forms were those of masque and pastoral, between which there was little distinction. Among Greene's most successful pastorals was *Florimel, or Love's Revenge* (1734). Arne scored notable triumphs with his masque *Comus* (1738), in whose songs Burney found 'a light, airy, original and pleasing melody, wholly different from that of Purcell or Handel', and *Thomas and Sally* (1760), an all-sung afterpiece with an engaging libretto by Isaac Bickerstaffe. Boyce's greatest success was *The Chaplet* (1749), popular in playhouses both in London and other parts of England.

English instrumental music. Handel's orchestral music

The chief forms of instrumental music during the first half of the eighteenth century were the keyboard suite, the sonata for one melody instrument and basso continuo, and the trio sonata for two melody instruments and continuo. The most widely cultivated orchestral forms were those of the suite, concerto grosso, and from mid-century, the solo concerto. To these we must add the many orchestral movements contained within opera and oratorio, especially those of Handel. As in these dramatic forms so, too, in the production of non-vocal music Handel was the dominant figure in England during this period.

It is not possible to date Handel's solo keyboard music with certainty and some of it was doubtless written before he came to England. Similar problems of dating occur with his solo and trio sonatas, of which four sets were published during his lifetime. Although comparatively small in quantity the music is graceful and inventive, and in the hands of sensitive players, full of vitality and charm.

Apart from the non-vocal music contained in the operas and oratorios, Handel's orchestral compositions fall into three categories: occasional music, concerti grossi and solo concertos. Much of it, even so, was used in one form or another in his stage works or as interval music. The earlier of two magnificent occasional pieces is the *Water Music*, which, however, was probably composed for more than one outdoor event. The popular story that Handel wrote and performed his *Water Music* in order to appease his former employer, the Elector of Hanover, when he arrived in London as George I, may be only partly true. We have neither Handel's autograph nor his conducting score to assist us in performance details, but it is certain that some of the music was heard on 17 July 1717 when a royal barge party sailed up-river from Whitehall to Chelsea. A report of the colourful occasion was printed in the *Daily Courant*:

> a City Company's Barge was employ'd for the Musick, wherein were 50 Instruments of all sorts, who play'd all the Way from Lambeth ... the finest Symphonies, compos'd express for this Occasion, by Mr. Handel; which his Majesty liked so well, that he caus'd it to be plaid over three times in going and returning. ...

Such river parties were popular in London during the eighteenth century, as the many reports and contemporary copperplate engravings testify.

Our knowledge of the performance of Handel's *Music for the Royal Fireworks* in 1749 is fuller for the occasion is well documented. What prompted such a lavishly scored work was the signing of the Treaty of Aix-la-Chapelle, concluding the War of the Austrian Succession, on 7 October 1748. To mark the event elaborate plans were laid for a magnificent firework display in the following year. Handel was to compose music for the occasion as well as a Peace Anthem for the Chapel Royal in St James's Palace. A successful public rehearsal in Vauxhall's Spring Gardens took place on 21 April, drawing an audience of over twelve thousand and causing a three-hour jam of carriages; but the display proper, a week later in Green Park, was according to Horace Walpole less impressive:

> the illumination was mean, and lighted so slowly that scarce anybody had patience to wait the finishing; and then what contributed to the awkwardness of the whole, was the right pavilion catching fire, and being burned down in the middle of the show.

Handel's instrumentation for the *Royal Fireworks* music is imposing – 9 trumpets, 9 horns, 3 pairs of kettledrums, 24 oboes, 12 bassoons and a double bassoon – and before he had completed the score, he had further decided upon strings as well, making the sumptuous overture and five shorter movements among his most resplendent orchestral creations.

Henry Purcell, England's greatest Baroque
composer and, in the words of his obituarist
(1695), 'scarce Inferiour to any in Europe'

Below: The practice of celebrating the Feast day
of the patron saint of music, St Cecilia, became
established in the 1680s, and in 1692 Purcell
contributed his most sumptuous ode, Hail,
bright Cecilia. The solo 'Tis Nature's voice' was
sung (it was reported) 'with incredible Graces
by Mr. Purcell himself'

Above: William Lawes, among the foremost composers of Charles I's court, who died fighting under the loyalist banner at the Siege of Chester (1645)

Left: Costume design for The Masque of Blackness *(1605), the earliest collaboration between the architect Inigo Jones and the playwright Ben Jonson*

Below: Backdrop for Sir William Davenant's public entertainment The Siege of Rhodes *(1645)*

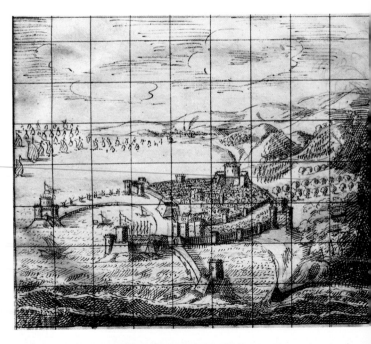

Above: Performance of a Venetian intermezzo, after Longhi. The lighter operatic pieces performed between the parts of an heroic opera, or opera seria, grew into a tradition of comic opera in the early eighteenth century, alongside opera seria, and in part in reaction to it

Left: Antonio Vivaldi, the greatest master of the Italian Baroque concerto. The sketch by Pier Leoni Ghezzi (1723) represents the only authenticated likeness of the composer

Below: Vivaldi's manuscript of the Concerto in G minor, La notte, the second of three musically descriptive pieces published as the composer's Opus 10 (c. 1728)

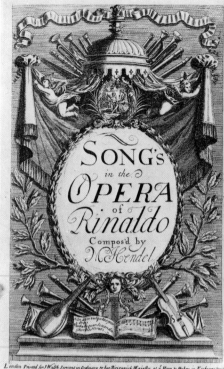

An early portrait of Handel, painted c. 1710, when the composer was in his mid-twenties

Handel's first London opera, Rinaldo (1711), was a triumph for the composer. John Walsh the elder published the songs in the same year

Autograph page ('I know that my Redeemer liveth') of Handel's most celebrated oratorio, Messiah (1741), described by the librettist Jennens as 'a fine entertainment'

William Boyce, perhaps the greatest of Handel's younger English contemporaries. A composer chiefly of odes, he is famous for eight colourful symphonies (1760)

François Couperin, portrait frontispiece to L'Art de toucher le clavecin (1716). This most brilliant of French composers for the harpsichord had an enduring interest in blending French and Italian musical styles

Part of the Passacaille from the 8th Ordre (Book 2), one of Couperin's noblest and most celebrated pieces

France's greatest dramatic composer Jean-Philippe Rameau, about 1725. Below: Sketch of Rameau with Voltaire, who was on occasion his librettist. It refers to the famous argument known as the 'Querelle des Bouffons' in which Voltaire sided with Rameau (and the French musical tradition) against supporters of Italian music, who included Rousseau and the Encyclopédistes

The manuscript of one of Rameau's last and most virtuosic pieces, La Dauphine (1747)

Late Baroque opulence: the setting of a musical celebration held in Rome at the house of French ambassador to mark the birth of the Dauphin (1729). The music was by Leonardo Vinci, who set a text by Metastasio

Georg Philipp Telemann, contemporary and friend of both Bach and Handel, whose long creative life linked an older generation with composers writing in a lighter, simpler, early Classical vein

Left: Performance of a cantata in a south German church; frontispiece of Musikalisches Lexicon *by J.G. Walther, Leipzig, 1732*

J.S. Bach in 1746

A student concert or Serenade by the Leipzig collegium musicum, *the society founded by Telemann and directed by Bach after 1729*

The final autograph page of Bach's Art of Fugue. *We cannot know precisely when and why this fugue was left unfinished, but the comment in C.P.E. Bach's handwriting after the final bars tells us that, 'while working on it . . . the author died'*

Handel's concertos

Handel's first set of concertos was published in London in 1734 as the composer's Opus 3, but it was apparently issued without close consultation with Handel himself, for the fourth of the six concertos was almost certainly not by him. When a second edition was issued later in the same year the work was replaced by another, while the fifth concerto was extended by the addition of three further movements. Much of the music in Handel's Opus 3 had been composed many years earlier for a variety of purposes, but it loses nothing in its concerto context, revealing Handel as a resourceful composer in his handling of spirited fugues and beguiling dances. No two concertos of the set are identically scored, and the imaginative use of woodwind instruments is an attractive feature of the set.

Handel's next set of published concertos were of a different kind and to a great extent his own invention. They were written for solo organ with strings and woodwind, and were published in 1738 as the composer's Opus 4. For Handel their role was primarily functional, since they were intended for performance in theatres between the acts of his oratorios and odes. He played the organ himself on these occasions. From the first they seem to have had a wide appeal, for a second set appeared in 1740, and in 1761, two years after his death, a third was issued as his Opus 7. All but one of Handel's organ concertos (Opus 7, No. 1 in B flat) are written for an instrument without pedals, because instruments with a pedal-board were a rarity in the England of Handel's day.

In the early autumn of 1739 Handel embarked on what was to be his finest set of concertos, and by the end of October he had completed it. In the following year his London publisher, John Walsh, printed the set by subscription as *Twelve Grand Concertos* (Opus 6), or in other words, concerti grossi. In so far as they derive from the Corellian model, with which Handel was thoroughly conversant from his earlier years in Italy, Handel's Opus 6 concertos were old-fashioned for the late 1730s. In England, however, Corelli had long been admired and this was still the taste of the time. Although Handel's technique is often similar to Corelli's – his concertino group consists of two violins and cello rather than a quartet, for example – in few other senses are these works backward-looking. Handel's terms of reference are impressively wide, embracing features of the French overture and dance suite and of both Roman and Venetian concerto styles; but it is, above all, the level of musical inspiration that assures them a place alongside Bach's *Brandenburg Concertos*, creating a peak among Baroque works in this form.

Handel's younger contemporaries

Such is the stature of Handel's music that the achievements of a small group of indigenous English composers are apt to be underrated. Yet the instrumental music of men such as Boyce (p. 157), Arne, Avison, Stanley and others is also well constructed, often inventive, and seldom without a distinctive trait of character. Boyce was a champion of Handel's music, which he promoted with zeal, but in his trio sonatas, his handful of concertos, and above all in his 8 *Symphonys in 8 Parts*, Opus 2 (1760), his own robust style is strikingly apparent. Burney held Boyce's trio sonatas in high esteem, remarking that they were 'longer and more generally purchased, performed and admired, than any production of the kind in the kingdom, except those of Corelli'. Arne, though like Boyce chiefly a composer for the voice, wrote *Six Favourite concertos* for keyboard and orchestra which were posthumously printed about 1787. In stylistic versatility they range from Handelian grandeur to a reflective, sometimes melancholy manner.

The most active composer of concertos among the English-born musicians was Charles Avison (1709–70). Some fifty or so were published during his lifetime, and in many of these Avison inclined towards the example of his teacher, Geminiani, both in his preferred four-movement scheme and in his use of a concertino group of two violins, viola and cello. Among Avison's concertos are twelve arrangements for string orchestra of harpsichord sonatas by his great contemporary, Domenico Scarlatti. Their fancifully explicit tempo markings provoked a note of censure from the novelist Laurence Sterne, who ridiculed them in his novel *Tristram Shandy* (Book 3, Chapter 5); but these works generally show a boldness of invention and a lively feeling for orchestration lacking in some of the works in others of his sets.

No less accomplished than the concertos of Avison are two sets of six by the blind composer John Stanley (1712–80). The earlier of them was a set of six concerti grossi for strings, published in 1742 as the composer's Opus 2. Perhaps reflecting the success of the example set by Handel, they were arranged shortly afterwards for organ and strings, with the organ taking over the concertino role. They are in the Corellian tradition, but owe something to Handel whom Stanley both admired and imitated. It is perhaps the Concerto in A minor, the fifth in the set, which affords us the finest example of Stanley's considerable gifts as a composer.

England, as we have already seen, was a welcoming host to foreign musicians: 'he who in the present time wants to make a profit out of music takes himself to England', observed the German theorist, critic and composer Johann Mattheson in 1713 (*Das Neu-Eröffnete Orchestre*). One such successful settler was Francesco Geminiani (1687–1762). Geminiani was born in Lucca and came to England in 1714. Apart from visits to Dublin, where he died, Geminiani remained in London, establishing there a fine reputation as a teacher – the English composer Michael Christian Festing was his pupil – composer, theorist and violin virtuoso. His earliest concertos, a set of twelve published in two parts in 1726, were arrangements of Corelli's Opus 5 sonatas for violin and basso continuo, retaining Corelli's thematic material and basic harmonic structure while extending the imaginative character of the music through richer textures and newly developed string techniques. In this as in subsequent sets, Geminiani's concertino group consists of two violins, viola and cello rather than the more usual trio of two violins and cello. Among several sets of concertos which followed, two are perhaps especially noteworthy. In 1732 he published six concerti grossi, Opus 3, which in the opinion of Burney 'established his character, and placed him at the head of all the masters then living, in this species of composition'. Perhaps Geminiani's most distinctive contribution to the concerto is found here. Geminiani revised this set, issuing them in full score, around 1755. Further evidence of his fine craftsmanship is provided by Geminiani's last set of concerti grossi, published in 1746 as his Opus 7. The six works of this set differ from his earlier concertos in an important respect: here he matches the viola of the concertino with a viola in the ripieno which otherwise consisted of two violin parts and basso continuo. Other features, such as the inclusion of solo passages for a bassoon in the sixth concerto of the set – an impressive work in its design – reveal Geminiani as both less conservative and less rigid than is sometimes claimed.

Other foreign composers who published concertos in London included two Dutchmen, Willem de Fesch (1687–?1757) and Pieter Hellendaal (1721–99). De Fesch came to live in London during the 1730s, and in 1741 published eight concertos as his Opus 10. Burney reckoned them 'dry and uninteresting'; Hellendaal's *Six Grand Concertos*, Opus 3, though uneven, possess greater character. Hellendaal was a pupil of Tartini; he came to England in 1752 and lived there for the remainder of his life. Like Geminiani's and Avison's, Hellendaal's concertino group includes a viola, though he is less consistent than Geminiani in his use of it. These concertos possess an assured style and an expressive individuality which compare favourably with much concerto writing of the time; the fourth of the set, in E flat is perhaps one of the most interesting in the effectively contrasting character of its five movements. Two further composers of concertos active in England during the first half of the eighteenth century deserve mention for their contribution to the form. Pietro Castrucci (1679–1752) came to London during the second decade of the century and led Handel's opera orchestra for over twenty years; his twelve concerti grossi, Opus 3, were published in 1736. Richard Mudge (1718–63) was a relatively minor but skilful English composer of concertos. His only known published collection, *Six concertos in seven parts* . . ., appeared in 1749. The first concerto has a part for solo trumpet, while the last, following the fashion of the time, has a solo part for keyboard.

Pleasure gardens

An overview of English music-making in the first half of the eighteenth century would be incomplete without mention of London's pleasure gardens. Marylebone Gardens, one of the earliest, opened *c*.1659 and Ranelagh Gardens, Chelsea, in 1742, when the English composer and Master of the King's Musick, Michael Festing (d.1752), became the first director of its concerts. The chief musical attractions, however, were at Vauxhall Gardens in Lambeth. These opened to the public during the Restoration when they were called Spring Gardens. By the beginning of the eighteenth century the Gardens had acquired a colourful reputation both as a place of cultural amusements and for sensual delights. In 1728 Jonathan Tyers acquired the lease and gradually raised their moral tone. They were frequented by almost all classes of English society, for the entertainment they offered ranged from fashionable music to games, pastimes and all manner of simpler pleasures.

Music, however, remained one of the most powerful attractions, with great composers including Corelli, Arne and Boyce among those represented. Although Handel never wrote specifically for Vauxhall his music would frequently have been heard there. Fittingly, one of the finest works of art to appear in the Gardens was Handel's statue by Louis François Roubiliac, unveiled in 1738. By then, Handel had been acclaimed not only as a composer of grand instrumental works but as a dramatist of European renown, whose achievements in this genre are perhaps only approached by those of Rameau in France.

10

Eighteenth-century France: from Couperin to Rameau

URING THE EARLY AND MIDDLE YEARS of Louis XIV's long reign the
court was, as La Bruyère observed, 'le centre du bon goût et de la
politesse'. Towards its close, however, court influence over artistic
matters was beginning to weaken, and the importance of Versailles as a
centre for both the commissioning and the staging of opera was greatly
diminished. This shift away from court in the promotion of the arts
continued through the eighteenth century, so that around the end of
Louis XV's reign a Scottish traveller, John Moore, was able to record that
while 'Obedient to the court in every other particular, the French
disregard the decisions pronounced at Versailles in matters of taste. It
very often happens that a dramatic piece, which has been acted before the
royal family and the court with the highest applause is afterwards
damned with every circumstance of ignominy at Paris.' (*A View of
Society and Manners in France, Switzerland and Germany*, 1779).

Following the death of Louis XIV in 1715 the court at Versailles was
dissolved, and for some eight years France was governed by his nephew,
Philippe, duc d'Orléans (1674–1723). The Regency witnessed a sharp
move away from the austerity which shadowed the declining years of the
Sun King. The Regent displayed a lively interest in the sciences, painting
and music as well as in politics; his lifestyle was flamboyant and not
without the taint of scandal. When Philippe died in 1723, the young Louis
XV re-established the court at Versailles and in 1725 married Marie
Leczinska, daughter of ex-King Stanislas of Poland.

The musical genius who would dominate eighteenth-century France
was Rameau, but in the period between the death of the great Lully in
1687 and the performance of Rameau's first opera in 1733, several
composers added significantly to the French Baroque repertory, outstanding among them Couperin (p. 157).

François Couperin (1668–1733), whose trio sonatas were briefly
mentioned in a previous chapter, was known as Couperin 'le grand' in
order to distinguish him from other members of a remarkable musical

dynasty. He was born in Paris, where he spent the greater part of his life. Like his father and uncle before him, Couperin became organist at the church of St Gervais, and in 1693, one of four *Organistes du Roi* at Versailles. As well as performing these duties he took on harpsichord pupils from among the royalty and nobility, and by the turn of the century was active both as a composer and performer. In 1717 Couperin officially replaced D'Anglebert as *Ordinaire de la musique de la Chambre du Roi pour le clavecin*, holding both this and his court organist's appointment until 1730 when he resigned them on grounds of ill health.

By 1690 or so, the blending of Italian with French styles in music was becoming widespread in France. Couperin self-effacingly, and perhaps fashion-consciously, rearranged the letters of his name to look Italian when writing his earlier trio sonatas, in which he deliberately set about uniting the two styles, blending Italian discipline and vigour with French sensibility and graceful gesture. Such an attempt at unification was all part of the search for that indefinable quality '*le bon goût*', which stemmed in part from the connoisseurs' growing interest in and demand for works of art of all kinds.

Couperin's earliest compositions are two organ masses comprising his *Pièces d'orgue*. They were the fruits of his first 'royal privilege' or patent, taken out in 1689; the masses, '*à l'usage ordinaire des paroisses*', and '*propre pour les convents de religieux et religieuses*', consist of organ music for the liturgy. Only one copy of Couperin's original publication, which appeared in his own hand but with an engraved title page, has survived. The mass *des paroisses* is the grander and more spaciously laid out of the two, and was intended for use on the principal church feast days; that for *les convents* is more intimate in character, technically easier for the performer and shorter. In both masses Couperin provides details of organ registration, though tempo, phrasing and ornamentation are left to the discretion of the performer.

Chamber instrumental music covers a wider period in Couperin's career than organ music, from the composition of his earliest trio sonatas in the 1690s to the *Pièces de violes* of 1728. Like many of his French contemporaries Couperin was fascinated by the Italian trio sonata and especially admired Corelli's use of the form; but the presence of pieces unequivocally in the style of his native France remind us that he was not merely imitating Corelli but was intent on uniting the strongest features inherent in the styles of both countries. *La superbe*, *L'astrée* and *La Sultane* provide fine examples of Couperin's essays in the trio sonata medium, while another, *La Steinquerque*, a slighter work, betrays the French Baroque predilection for pictorial imitation, in this instance an evocation of a military encounter (the great battle of Steenkerke, fought in 1692 during the Ten Years War, and won by Louis XIV's lieutenant the duc de Luxembourg).

In 1724 and 1725 Couperin paid tribute to Corelli and Lully respectively in two extended trios, *L'apothéose de Corelli* and *L'apothéose de Lully*. The earlier of these is structurally the more straightforward and takes the form of a *sonata da chiesa* – or 'Grand Sonade en Trio' as Couperin himself designated it – in seven movements. The later trio is more complex, possessing features of both the suite and the sonata, and it contains a more important programmatic element than the other, inspired by some of the declamatory and danced conventions established by Lully. The descriptive titles such as 'Lully aux Champs Elysées, concertant avec les ombres liriques' (Lully in the Elysian Fields, in concert with the lyric spirits) and careful tempo-markings act as signposts to the listener, who might otherwise hardly be aware of Couperin's meticulous, often detailed scheme. Couperin seldom specified instrumentation in his chamber works, and in the preface to *L'apothéose de Lully* he explains that while both pieces can be played by a mixed ensemble of instruments they are equally effective on two harpsichords.

Couperin's fascination with the blending of French and Italian styles is reflected in his remaining chamber works. The four *Concerts royaux* were published in his third anthology of harpsichord pieces in 1722 but had been composed earlier. Although they are written out on two staves suitable for solo harpsichord, Couperin nevertheless performed some of them, at least, with a mixed chamber ensemble at the Sunday concerts at Versailles organized by Mme de Maintenon for Louis XIV at the very end of his life. The *Concerts royaux*, like the ten concerts published in 1724 as *Les goûts réunis ou nouveaux concerts*, are essentially suites, and contain music of great charm and refinement; the *Prélude* of the second *Concert*, the *Muzette* of the third and the *Forlane* of the fourth are just three of the movements which demonstrate Couperin's delicate feeling for colour.

In *Les nations*, published in 1726, Italian and French styles are once again represented, but in the case of these four suites the styles are united more by juxtaposition than by synthesis. Each work begins with an Italianate trio sonata which serves as prelude to a longer, characteristically French dance-suite. Three sonatas of the 1690s, *La pucelle*, *La visionnaire* and *L'astrée*, now become the opening movements of *La françoise*, *L'espagnole* and *La piémontoise* respectively. The remaining work, *L'impériale*, is introduced by a sonata whose greater fluency suggests a later date of composition.

Among Couperin's very last compositions are the *Pièces de violes* published in 1728 and consisting of two suites of pieces for bass viol and continuo. The first contains an eloquent, sombre *Prélude* followed by some of the characteristic movements of the French dance suite, including an elegiac *sarabande* and a graceful, dance-like *passacaglia*. The second suite is less typically French in its layout and contains only four movements, of which the deeply affecting *Pompe funèbre* is a masterpiece in the musical-poetic *tombeau* tradition and one of the composer's most intense utterances. Perhaps Couperin had in mind his great contemporary, Marais, who had died in the year of its publication.

Couperin's sacred vocal music

Couperin's sacred vocal music deserves to be better known. He seems to have preferred the smaller forms of motet to the *grands motets* of Lully or Delalande, for instance, and while he may have composed in the larger forms as well, we have no example. Most of Couperin's sacred music is scored for solo voices with basso continuo to which concertante instruments are sometimes added. One of his most elaborate motets is the *Veni sponsa Christi* for Sainte Suzanne, scored for soprano, haute-contre and bass voices with violins in two parts and continuo. Here is music with a strong Italian bias but containing modulations which are distinctly French in character, as indeed are many of the melodic contours, which reveal Couperin's sensibility to the literary text.

It is in his three *Leçons de ténèbres* printed between 1713 and 1717 that Couperin's sacred vocal music reaches its highest level of expressive intensity. During the '*grand siècle*' – the years of Louis XIV's reign – *tenebrae* were sung on the Wednesday, Thursday and Friday evenings of Holy Week. Their texts were drawn from the Lamentations of Jeremiah but interspersed with affective, ornamental, melismatic phrases at the beginning of each verse, inspired by letters of the Hebrew alphabet. One of the earliest French composers to set *leçons de ténèbres* had been Michel Lambert (*c.*1610–96) who skilfully blended features of the Italian monodic *lamentazioni* with those of the French court air, of which he was an acknowledged master. The synthesis had wide appeal, and subsequently composers such as Charpentier, Delalande and Couperin contributed expressive examples of this peculiarly French sacred musical utterance. Couperin's surviving *leçons* were intended for the Wednesday service, but in the preface he refers to three others for Good Friday as having already been composed, and tells us that a complete set of nine *leçons* was planned. The First and Second *Leçons* are scored for a solo soprano with continuo, while the Third is written for two sopranos, allowing Couperin to extend himself polyphonically and achieve an even greater expressive fervour.

Harpsichord music

Solo harpsichord music represents Couperin's most sustained achievement. His twenty-seven *ordres* – a term which he used to denote groups of pieces in related keys, falling somewhere between a suite and an anthology – were printed in four volumes over a period of seventeen years. The pieces fall into three main structural patterns: the binary movement in which each half is repeated, the chaconne, and the rondeau.

In his didactic work *L'art de toucher le clavecin*, published in 1716 and revised in the following year, Couperin outlines aspects of teaching the harpsichord and performance, and in the preface to his second book of *Pièces de clavecin* he refers to this instruction as 'absolutely indispensable to the correct performance of my pieces'. He deals with ornamentation, fingering, the position of the body, the wrists, the touch, the character of the instrument and its capabilities. He uses pieces from his first and second harpsichord books as examples, but also includes eight preludes, mainly of an improvisatory character, which serve both as introductory pieces to the *ordres* of the first two harpsichord books and as studies for the performer. In the preface to his third harpsichord book he admonishes performers:

After taking such care to mark the ornaments suitable for my pieces . . . I am always surprised to hear of those who have performed them heedless of my instructions. This is unpardonable negligence, the more so as it is no arbitrary matter to put in any ornament that one may wish. I declare, therefore, that my pieces must be executed as I have marked them, and that they will never make an impression on those persons of real taste unless one observes to the letter all that I have marked without any additions or deletions.

The first book of *Pièces de clavecin* containing five *ordres* was published in 1713, though many of the pieces almost certainly date from earlier in Couperin's life. The second anthology appeared late in 1716 or early in 1717 and contains seven further *ordres*. The third, which included the four *Concerts royaux*, was published in 1722, and also contains seven *ordres*. The fourth book appeared in 1730 and embraces the remaining eight *ordres*, though Couperin remarks in a prefatory note that two pieces belonging to the twenty-fifth *ordre* had been lost in the three years between completion and publication.

The expressive subtlety of Couperin's solo harpsichord pieces makes them for the interpreter among the most elusive in French Baroque music. Some, like *La superbe ou La Forqueray* (No.17), *La Princesse Marie* (No. 20), *La Monflambert* (No. 25) and *Le Ménetou* (No. 7), were inspired by Couperin's pupils, friends and contemporaries; others, like *Le bavolet-flotant* (No. 9), *Le réveil-matin* (No. 4), *Les petits moulins à vents* (No. 17) and *Les abeilles* (No. 1) evoke the characteristics suggested by their titles. A few, like *Les baricades mistérieuses* (No. 6), *Les dars homicides* (No. 24) or *La reine des coeurs* (No. 21) are more enigmatic and abstract, doubtless containing an element of metaphor. It is sometimes however in the pieces which do not set out to portray that we find Couperin's noblest utterances. The B minor *Passacaille* (No. 8) and the *Allemande à deux clavecins* (No. 9), for example, are outstanding revelations of Couperin's expressive gifts as a harpsichord composer (p. 157).

The Concert spirituel

It has already been remarked that during the latter part of Louis IV's reign the artistic brilliance which had characterized the Lullian epoque began to fade from the courtly environment of Versailles and to illuminate the Paris *salons*. It was here rather than at court that the French chamber cantata flourished. As in London, Hamburg, Leipzig and other leading European cities, so in Paris a thriving public concert tradition provided a platform for a variety of musical styles, foreign and indigenous. One of the earliest Parisian concert series was given by the Abbé Mathieu, who zealously promoted Italian music; but in 1725 the composer Anne-Danican Philidor (1681–1728) established a public concert series of greater significance. This was the 'Concert spirituel', which thrived from its first concert on 18 March almost until the Revolution in 1789.

The organizers specialized in the performance of large-scale French sacred vocal and choral works but also promoted instrumental music by French and foreign composers. The concerts customarily took place at the Salles des Suisses in the Tuileries on days when the Opéra and theatres were officially closed. Their success was doubtless partly due to Philidor's foresight in contracting the services of singers and instrumentalists from the Opéra who would have been familiar to Parisian music-lovers. Encouraged by the favourable public response to the Concert spirituel Philidor launched a second series which became known as the 'Concert français'. This specialized in secular repertory, above all that of the French chamber cantata, the *cantate française*. Although short-lived – its first concert took place in December 1727 and its last in November 1733 –

the Concert français was a considerable success. Here for six years, some of the leading singers of the day satisfied a voracious appetite for French chamber cantatas that lasted through the first thirty years and more of the eighteenth century.

The French chamber cantata

Hardly any examples of the *cantate française* appear before 1700, and only in later editions of Sébastian de Brossard's *Dictionnaire de Musique* (1703) is there mention of the form. An important precursor is Charpentier's *Orphée descendant aux enfers* (H. 471). This dates from 1683 and is scored for haute-contre, tenor and bass voices, two violins, recorder, transverse flute and continuo. Like so much of his vocal music, this affecting work reveals Charpentier's gifts in blending French declamation with Italian harmonies and instrumental idioms.

Although the initial stimulus of the *cantate française* came from Italy, French composers while taking heed of *bel canto* retained the simplicity, the gentle inflexions, the ornamental subtlety and delicacy of expression which characterized their own melody, and by so doing gave the *cantate française* its distinctive quality. Their literary texts were also influenced by their Italian counterparts, almost invariably drawing upon allegorical events in Classical myth. One of the most talented writers was Jean-Baptiste Rousseau (1671–1741) who shaped the form in its earliest stages and provided texts for almost all composers of *cantates françaises*. His poems consisting of alternating recitatives and airs conclude with an aphorism, and this pattern was adopted, albeit freely rendered in some instances, by other authors of cantata texts.

Among the most gifted composers of the *cantate française* in its early stages were Jean-Baptiste Morin (1677–1745) and Nicolas Bernier (c.1665–1734). By 1723 Bernier had published seven collections of cantatas; the counterpoint and vocal writing often bear witness to his studies in Italy, while melodies and instrumental symphonies are more closely allied to the French lyric stage. *Les Forges de Lemnos* for soprano and continuo (Book I), and *Le Caffé* for soprano with flute or violin and continuo (Book III) are pleasing examples of Bernier's graceful, sometimes humorous if not harmonically adventurous style. Of greater interest for their bolder harmonic conception are the *cantates françaises* of André Campra (1660–1744) and Michel Pignolet de Montéclair (c.1667–1737) whose *tragédie lyrique, Jephté* (1732), had impressed Rameau in the year preceding his own first opera, *Hippolyte et Aricie*, and whose *Principes de musique* (1736) is an important source of French musical interpretation of the period. Both composers had experience of the theatre and were skilled in handling dramatic situations. Campra published three books of cantatas between 1708 and 1728 as well as a handful of miscellaneous works in the form. Several of his most striking cantatas are contained in the first anthology. Among them, *Daphné*, for soprano and continuo, contains three *ariettes* – a term used somewhat loosely to describe a lively air modelled on the Italian da capo aria – in which Campra successfully combines, in his own words: '*la délicatesse de la musique française*' and '*la vivacité de la musique Italienne*'. More powerfully expressive and moving is *Arion*, for soprano with flute and continuo, while *Les femmes*, for bass with two violins and continuo, brings together Italian virtuosity and French gracefulness to create an effective small-scale piece of theatre.

Montéclair published three collections of cantatas between *c.*1709 and 1728. He, like Bernier, had worked in Italy, and among his cantatas are four written there which closely adhere to their Italian models. The dramatic element in Montéclair's *cantates françaises* is stronger than in those of Campra. Swiftly changing moods, rhythms and instrumental colours abound, often giving the impression more of an operatic *scena* than a chamber cantata; indeed, Montéclair himself described his *Pyrame et Thisbé* for soprano, tenor, bass, violin, flute and continuo as 'half epic, half dramatic'. *La mort de Didon* (soprano, violin, flute and continuo), *Le retour de la Paix* (soprano, two violins and continuo) and *Pyrame et Thisbé* are among Montéclair's most ambitious works in cantata form, with vivid writing not just for the voices but for the instruments as well.

The *cantate française* reached a peak in the music of Louis-Nicolas Clérambault (1676–1749). In the words of a fellow-composer, Louis Daquin (1694–1772), 'Clérambault has found out melodies and means of expression that are his alone'. By the time he published his first cantatas in 1710 Clérambault had established a reputation as an organist. He was strongly influenced by Italian music and was notably successful, above all in his cantatas, in uniting its style with that of his native France. '*Si Clérambault module à l'Italienne, il parle à la française*' (If he modulates in the Italian manner he declaims in French), wrote a contemporary. Clérambault's five books of cantatas, published between 1710 and 1726, amount to twenty works in all; five others, including *La Muse de l'Opéra*, an elaborate piece more in the nature of a divertissement than a chamber cantata, were published separately. Two of Clérambault's masterpieces, *Orphée* for soprano, violin, flute and continuo, and *Médée* for soprano, two violins, flute and continuo, appeared in the first book, and in their operatic bias and extended length exceed the customary dimensions of a *cantate française.* Comparable in stature is *Léandre et Héro* for soprano, flutes, violins, bass viol and continuo, from the second book (1713). In all of these, Clérambault demonstrates his ability to convey pathos with the *douceur* and *delicatesse* which characterize *le goût français.* We shall find these same qualities in the chamber cantatas of Rameau.

The French sonata and concerto. Leclair, Mondonville

Just as Italy had provided the stimulus for the French cantata, so with the French sonata. Besides Couperin, other composers such as the violinist Jean Féry Rebel (*c.*1666–1747), Clérambault, Jean-Baptiste Senaillé (*c.*1687–1730) and François Duval (*c.*1673–1728) experimented with the form. Rebel like Couperin 'le grand' was the most gifted member of a musical dynasty. At the age of eight he attracted the attention of Lully, who taught him violin and composition. From then onwards he gradually rose through the ranks to become *batteur de mésure* at the Academie Royale de Musique, violinist of the Chapel Royal, one of the King's chamber composers together with his brother-in-law Delalande, and director of the Concert spirituel for the years 1734 and 1735. Rebel's twelve *Sonates à II et III parties* with figured bass, published in 1712–13 (but according to Sébastian de Brossard, written by 1695), reveal his skill in blending elements of Italian and French styles, while his solo violin sonatas with continuo were among the first of their kind in France. Rebel also possessed considerable dramatic and depictive ability. Though his one opéra, *Ulysse* (1703), was a failure he was notably successful in a genre largely of his own making: the *symphonie de danse*, of which the most celebrated examples were the *Caractères de la danse* (1715) and *Les élémens* (1737–8). The latter contains music of striking originality, above all in its introduction, 'Le cahos'.

Senaillé, who studied in Italy under Tomaso Antonio Vitali (1663–1745), was influenced by Corelli in his early violin compositions, but modelled the later ones on the more virtuosic ideas of his teacher. He was both a talented player and an effective composer for the violin, and his ability to combine Italian brilliance with French *beau chant* was acknowledged in his own lifetime. It is in the sonatas and concertos of Leclair, however, that *beau chant* and virtuosity are most strikingly united. Jean-Marie Leclair (1697–1764) was born in Lyon, and like Senaillé, studied the violin in Italy, but under Corelli's pupil, Giovanni Battista Somis (1686–1763). In the early part of his career Leclair was a professional dancer and, by way of the family trade, lacemaker, but by the 1720s he was establishing a reputation as a violinist. In 1728 he made his debut at the Concert spirituel playing his own sonatas and concertos, and in 1733 Louis XV appointed him *Ordinaire de la musique du Roi*. Leclair travelled widely, visiting Germany where he performed with the Italian violin virtuoso Locatelli, England and the Netherlands, as well as Italy. From the mid-1740s he settled in Paris, where he remained until, in the autumn of 1764, he was murdered, very possibly by his nephew.

Leclair was not a prolific composer by the standards of his day and mostly wrote for his own instrument, the violin. His only non-instrumental work was an opera, *Scylla et Glaucus* (1746), which despite a strong cast and a first-rate score was dropped from the repertoire of the Académie Royale de Musique after seventeen performances. Its unhappy ending, in which Scylla dies through an evil enchantment and her lover Glaucus is left grieving, would not have endeared the work to audiences imbued with the rational and positive ethos of the Enlightenment, but in recent times we have come to recognize the opera as comparable in stature to those of Rameau. Leclair's solo violin sonatas are contained in four collections of twelve (Opus 1, 2, 5 and 9) published between 1723 and *c*.1738. In addition to these there are two collections of six sonatas for two unaccompanied violins (Opus 3 and 12), three sets of trio sonatas (Opus 4, 12 and 13), a 'First' and a 'Second Musical Recreation easy to perform' (Opus 6 and 8), and two posthumous publications: a trio sonata (Opus 14) and a violin sonata (Opus 15). Leclair's model in these works was the Italian sonata, whose virtuosic idiom he combined with his outstanding gift for *beau chant*; this subtle blend resulted in sonatas unrivalled in France in his own lifetime and unsurpassed in the latter half of the eighteenth century.

French composers did not begin to write 'concertos' until comparatively late in the eighteenth century. Early collections by Boismortier and Michel Corrette were published during the 1720s, but, as with the sonata, it was Leclair who brought the French Baroque concerto to its finest flowering. His first set of six concertos for violin and strings was published in 1737 as his Opus 7 and was followed around 1744 by a second set of six (Opus 10), similarly scored. Though Leclair follows the formal scheme of his Venetian models, his concertos are more extended in their ideas and contain passages of virtuosity comparable to those of his Italian contemporary, Locatelli. In sonatas and concertos alike, advanced technique including multiple stops, high positions and rapid string-crossing is never employed as an end it itself but always placed at the service of musical inspiration. It is in the dance-orientated movements that Leclair's originality is perhaps most striking, and here his experience as a dancer and choreographer at the Turin Opera was invaluable. In such pieces, where dance-measures either characterize an entire move-ment or are ingeniously incorporated within others more abstract, his feeling for gesture, his melodic gift, eloquent modulations and consum-mate mastery of the language and technique of the violin, combine to create music of high distinction. It is not difficult to understand why the poet Séré de Rieux wrote in 1734: '*Leclair est le premier qui, sans imiter rien,/Créa du beau, du neuf qu'il peut dire le sien*' (Leclair is the first who, without imitation,/has created something beautiful, something new that he can call his own.)

Several of Leclair's younger contemporaries contributed significantly to the development of the French sonata. Among the most gifted of them was Jean-Joseph Cassanéa de Mondonville (1711–72). He, like Leclair, was a brilliant violinist who appeared at the Concert spirituel (from 1739) and later became its director. Mondonville was a versatile musician who was equally successful as a dramatic composer, a composer of sacred music – his *grands motets* were no less admired than those of Delalande – and as an instrumental composer. His most innovative contributions to the sonata were the *Pièces de Clavecin en Sonates avec accompagnement de Violon* (Opus 3), published in 1734, and the *Pièces de Clavecin avec Voix ou Violon* (Opus 5). The sonatas in each set contain fully written-out harpsichord solos to which, in the earlier publication, a violin, and in the later one, a violin with soprano voice may be added. No less innovatory were six violin sonatas with a treatise on playing harmonics, *Les sons harmoniques* (Opus 4), which Mondonville published in 1738.

Harpsichord, flute and bass viol

The harpsichord music of Couperin has been discussed above and that of Rameau will be considered later in the chapter. Three composers of a younger generation than Rameau represent much that is best in the final period of French solo harpsichord repertory. The eldest of them was Joseph-Nicolas-Pancrace Royer (1705–55). Royer was a prominent figure in Parisian musical life, for as well as being a successful composer for the stage – his *ballet héroique, Zaïde*, was especially popular – he became director of the Concert spirituel and leader of the Opéra orchestra. His only collection of solo harpsichord music, published in 1746, contains pieces in a variety of styles. Among the most striking are *La sensible*, a rondeau of sustained melancholy, *La Zaïde* whose wistful spirit recalls Rameau's *Les tendres plaintes*, and *Le vertigo* whose wild and virtuosic character derives from vigorously repeated chordal passages, rhythmic interruptions, tirades and mercurial passagework.

Jacques Duphly (1715–89) published four volumes of harpsichord pieces between 1744 and 1768. These contain a mixture of genre or portrait pieces and traditional dances. Announcing the publication of Duphly's third book in 1758 the *Mercure* remarked: 'His talent and merit are too well known to have need of being extolled.' There is little that is profound in Duphly's musical language but much that is gracefully expressed and evocative.

Claude-Benigne Balbastre (1727–99) was a pupil and friend of Rameau, and known principally as an organist and composer for the organ, but his single collection of pieces for solo harpsichord (1759) contains several charming portraits, among them the atmospheric *La Malesherbe* and the vigorous *La Lugeac*.

Other instruments, and notably the transverse flute, occupied an important place in French solo repertory during the first half of the eighteenth century. Jacques Hotteterre, 'le Romain' (1674–1763), published his treatise *Principes de la Flute Traversière* in 1707, and from then onwards the flute gradually usurped territory once the preserve of recorders. Among the composers who wrote most effectively for the flute at this time were Joseph Bodin de Boismortier (1689–1755), Michel Corrette (1709–95) and Jacques-Christophe Naudot (?–1762); but it was Michel Blavet (*c.*1700–68) and Leclair who raised the flute sonata to the level attained by the violin sonata. Blavet's two sets of sonatas for flute and continuo and another set for two flutes and continuo, along with a single surviving flute concerto, show him to have been a skilful and expressive composer. He and Leclair were on friendly terms, sometimes appearing together at the Concert spirituel, and it is probable that Leclair's nine sonatas (variously contained in Opus 1, 2 and 9) and the Concerto in C major, Opus 7, No. 3 – in all of which he suggests a flute as alternative to a violin – were composed with Blavet in mind.

Alongside the developing violin and flute repertory, a glorious tradition of bass viol playing which had grown up during the seventeenth century continued to flourish. Among the most notable of the early exponents were the Sieur Demachy (fl.1685–92) and Monsieur de Sainte-Colombe (fl.1691–1701), but it was the genius of Marin Marais (1656–1728), whose viol playing earned him a European reputation, that revealed the expressive range of the instrument most fully. Marais was closely associated with the French court for most of his life; he studied composition with Lully and the bass viol with Sainte-Colombe, becoming *Ordinaire de la chambre du Roi pour la viole* in 1679. He published his first collection of *Pièces de violes* in 1686, dedicating it to Lully. In the following year two important treatises on viol playing appeared: *L'art de toucher le dessus et basse de violle* by Danoville and the *Traité de la viole* of Jean Rousseau (1644–*c*.1700). Rousseau distinguishes between the melodic style of playing ('le jeu de melodie') in which the melody is presented simply, and the harmonic style ('le jeu d'harmonie') where melody and chords create a fuller texture while also allowing for greater formal complexity. Marais's handling of both styles is masterly, revealing an acute sensibility and refinement in declamation and gesture. Between 1701 and 1725 Marais published four more collections for one, two and three bass viols, cultivating a predominantly French idiom derived mainly from the dance tradition. The *tombeau* genre, earlier favoured by the lutenists and harpsichord composers, also attracted him; his *Tombeau de M. Meliton* from Book I provides but one poignant example of his broadly expressive, sorrowful declamation. Italian features, nevertheless, are also to be found in Marais's bass viol music, as for example in many of his fugal pieces and his fine set of variations on *La Folia* (Book II).

Apart from Couperin, whose *Pièces de violes* we have already discussed (p. 167), other talented composers for the bass viol in the years leading up to the mid-century include Louis de Caix d'Hervelois (*c*.1680–*c*.1760), Antoine Forqueray (*c*.1671–1745) and Marais's son, Roland-Pierre (*c*.1680–*c*.1750). The decline in popularity of the solo bass viol, which had begun by the 1730s, did not proceed without protest, nor without an attempt by some composers to retain public interest by accommodating the increasingly fashionable Italian taste of the time. The effort was of little avail, as Hubert le Blanc testified in a fanciful description of the triumph of 'Sultan Violin' (*La Défense de la Basse de Viole*, 1740), who with his two acolytes, 'Messire Clavecin' (harpsichord) and 'Sire Violincel' (cello), invades the territory of the bass viol in an attempt to gain the throne of the 'Monarchie universelle'.

Opéra-ballet

As in instrumental and vocal chamber music, so, too, in the sphere of dramatic music were composers after Lully attracted by features of the Italian style. Yet between Lully's death in 1687 and the performance of Rameau's first opera in 1733, French *tragédies en musique* underwent little change. In his organization of the opera orchestra, in his skilful deployment of it to evoke atmosphere or depict scenes, and in his profound understanding of the dance, Lully created an enduring national style admired and imitated by French composers throughout the first half of the eighteenth century. Among the gifted composers of stage music following Lully were his pupil and assistant, Pascal Collasse (1649–1709), André Cardinal Destouches (1672–1749), Campra, Marais, Henry Desmarest 1661–1742) and Montéclair. Even though there are effective scenes, and significant departures from Lullian tradition – as in Campra's *Tancrède* (1702), where the leading heroic role is sung by a baritone rather than the more usual 'haute contre' or high tenor, in *Idomenée* (1712), where the prologue is not the customary royal encomium but is closely associated with the tragedy which follows, and in Marais's *Alcyone* (1706) – Lully's powerful influence is all-embracing.

Towards the end of the seventeenth century the increasingly light mood of Parisian society demanded a decorative and intellectually less demanding form of dramatic entertainment than Lullian *tragédie en musique*. Dance and spectacle, both of which were essential ingredients of *tragédie lyrique*, now began to assume greater importance and were accommodated by *opéra-ballet*. This rethinking of the older *ballet à entrées* – a *genre tout neuf*, as the librettist Louis de Cahusac described it – typically consisted of a prologue and from three to five *entrées*, or acts. Unlike the *tragédies* of Quinault and Lully the *opéra-ballet* had no continuously developing plot; instead the *entrées* were loosely linked by a general theme, often hinted at in the title and dealing with situations and characters drawn from everyday life rather than based on classical legend. The form was concisely summarized by a mid-eighteenth-century writer, Rémond de Saint-Mard:

> Each act should include an intrigue, lively, lighthearted and, if you will, somewhat *galant* . . . two or three scenes, and these short, will do very well. The rest of the action is in ariettes, fêtes, spectacles and altogether agreeable features.

The earliest period of *opéra-ballet* was dominated by Campra, previously mentioned as a composer of cantatas (p. 172). Campra's *L'Europe galante* (1697) was one of the first works of the kind to be performed in Paris. (Collasse's *Les saisons* of 1695 was the first true *opéra-ballet*, though it did not use 'modern' characters.) Partly because of his position as *maître de musique* at Notre Dame Cathedral in Paris and partly, no doubt, because he was uncertain how it would be received, Campra did not at first reveal his authorship of *L'Europe galante*; but it was popular from the outset, and in the course of the following two decades he produced three further *opéras-ballets*, notable among which was *Les Fêtes vénitiennes* (1710). Here he introduced a comic element to an already effective combination of fantasy and divertissement. Other composers who contributed to *opéra-ballet* before Rameau include

Destouches, Mouret and Montéclair. Destouches was a pupil and friend of Campra whose music is sometimes individual in character; the three airs which he contributed anonymously to Campra's *L'Europe galante* testify to his expressive powers.

Rameau

Only with the emergence of Rameau as a dramatic composer could France once more boast a figure of comparable renown to Lully. Indeed, from a purely musical standpoint Rameau was not only vastly superior to Lully but also one of the greatest composers and theoreticians of the Baroque period. Jean-Philippe Rameau (1683–1764) was born in Dijon and was first taught music by his father. At about the age of eighteen he made his one and only brief visit to Italy. In 1702 he was back in France, where after a short period as organist in Avignon he was appointed *maître de musique* at the cathedral of Clermont Ferrand. By 1706 he was living in Paris and in that year published his earliest harpsichord pieces. From the title page we see that he was organist at the Jesuit Collège Louis-le-Grand in the rue St Jacques, and to the Fathers of Mercy in the rue de Chaume. In 1709 Rameau returned to Dijon where he succeeded his father as organist at the church of Notre Dame. Within five years he had moved again, first to Lyon, where he occupied an organist's post, then in 1715 to Clermont Cathedral, again as organist. It was probably during this period that he wrote his *Traité de l'harmonie*, the first of many theoretical works from his pen. It was published in 1722, the year in which he made his final move, returning to Paris.

Rameau regarded his theoretical writings as his most important contribution to music. For him the source of all musical consonance was the perfect major or minor triad, while the seventh interval was the source of all dissonance. Though treating music as a science he nevertheless related it to the aesthetics of composition, believing, in accordance with the wider Baroque aesthetic, that music should aim to please the ear, be expressive and thus stir the emotions. His various treatises influenced contemporary and subsequent theorists and composers including Tartini (p. 113) and, in our own century Hindemith. They also provided a lively subject for debate in Parisian intellectual circles and were mentioned in correspondence such as that between Telemann and C.H. Graun.

While Rameau was foremost an opera composer it was not until he was fifty years old that his first stage work was publicly performed. In the preceding period he involved himself in other musical activities, among them those of organist, teacher, composer and arranger of 'vaudevilles' or popular songs for the comedies staged by the two Paris fair theatres, the St Germain and St Laurent: important antecedents of the musically more sophisticated *opéra comique*. It was during the mid-1730s that he became acquainted with the wealthy *fermier-général* and musical patron Joseph Le Riche de La Pouplinière. Rameau became his director of music, encountering through him many of his future librettists, and had a house-orchestra placed under his supervision. Indeed La Pouplinière's house has been described as 'la citadelle du Ramisme'. The association between the two men lasted until 1753.

The earliest known compositions for the harpsichord by Rameau are contained in the *Premier livre de pièces de clavecin*, published in 1706. They are ten solo pieces that loosely make up a French dance suite. Two further anthologies followed: the *Pièces de clavecin* (1724) and the *Nouvelles suites de pièces de clavecin* (c.1729). Each of these contains two contrasting suites, one a conservatively cast but technically demanding dance suite, the other largely consisting of pieces with genre titles, such as we have seen in Couperin's solo harpsichord music. Compared with the modestly conceived publication of 1706, the music of the two later anthologies is more technically advanced, more ambitious in design and more varied in character. Among a wealth of inventive pieces are two virtuoso variation sets: *Les Niais de Sologne* (1724) and a *Gavotte et Doubles* (1729); *L'Egyptienne* (1729), recalling Scarlatti in its scales and arpeggios; *La Triomphante* (1729), a vigorous and harmonically satisfying rondeau; a noble *Sarabande* (1729) with some arresting harmonic progressions; *L'Enharmonique* (1724), another piece notable for its bold harmonic concept; and the subtly expressive *L'Entretien des Muses* (1724). Subsequently Rameau orchestrated several of his harpsi-chord pieces for inclusion in his operas; but he also adopted the procedure in reverse, publishing twenty-four keyboard arrangements of orchestral pieces from his *opéra-ballet*, *Les Indes Galantes* (1735), with airs and dances from the work grouped as short suites or 'concerts'.

Pièces de clavecin en concerts, Rameau's only other instrumental publication, appeared in 1741. We may recall that Mondonville had printed harpsichord pieces with violin accompaniment in the 1730s. Rameau certainly knew these, but his own *Pièces en concerts* are especially interesting in two respects: not only do three instruments, harpsichord, violin and bass viol (rather than Mondonville's two) comprise the ensemble, but the writing for the bowed instruments, notwithstanding the dominant role of the harpsichord, amounts to more than mere accompaniment. Indeed, Rameau stresses the importance of distinguishing between an accompanying role on the one hand, and one which embraces thematic development on the other. Of the eighteen pieces grouped into five suites we might single out *La Timide*, *La Livri* and *La Cupis* for their elusive, gentle, Watteau-like melancholy, and *La pantomime*, *La Rameau* and *Le Vezinet* for their spirited and graceful dance-gestures.

Rameau's chamber cantatas: The eighteenth-century grand motet

In common with most composers of his generation Rameau contributed to the thriving French cantata production described earlier in the chapter. Only seven cantatas by him are known to us; five, *L'Impatience, Aquilon et Orithie, Les amants trahis, L'Orphée* and *Thétis*, belong to a period approximately between 1715 and 1722. *Le berger fidèle* dates from the late 1720s – it was performed at the Concert français on 22 November 1728 when it was described as a *'nouvelle cantate'*, while the *Cantate pour le jour de la fête de Saint Louis* possibly dates from the mid-1740s. No less than Campra, Rameau successfully blended French *délicatesse* with Italian vivacity, often incorporating a prominent instrumental obbligato. *L'Impatience* contains three affecting 'airs' with lively Italianate figures for the bass viol, *Thétis* two splendidly virile examples of the composer's developing dramatic powers, *L'Orphée* an infectious and lively *'air très gai'* and a poignant monologue, *Les amants trahis* an unexpected comic element and *Le berger fidèle* three beguiling and well-contrasted 'airs'. This early exercise of operatic skills doubtless stood the composer in good stead later on.

Rameau's contribution to the literature of the *grand motet* is small but significant. Although the *grand motet* was very much a product of the *grand siècle* of Louis XIV's reign when it was closely associated with the Versailles court chapel, it remained popular, especially as a concert piece, well into the eighteenth century. As we have seen the great master of the form was Delalande, who continued to compose and to revise his *grands motets* during the early years of the eighteenth century. Between 1725 and 1770 nearly six hundred performances of motets by the 'Latin Lully', as one of his contemporaries described Delalande, were given at the Concert spirituel. Among Delalande's gifted successors were Campra, Charles-Hubert Gervais (1671–44), Rameau and Mondonville. Campra and Gervais became responsible for sacred music at Versailles following the deaths of Delalande and Bernier. Campra's contemplative style is often resistant to the growing secularization of the Regency and later; his *grands motets In Convertendo* (1703) and *De Profundis* (1723), a *Messe de Requiem* (c.1722) and a *Miserere* (1725), though not without leanings towards operatic declamation, afford examples of affective writing comfortably on a level with that of his stage works. Gervais, who like Campra was a skilled opera composer, excelled with brilliant extrovert gestures, as we find in his *Te Deum* and Latin motet *Exaudiat Te*. In the south of France Jean Gilles (1668–1705) made important contributions to the *grand motet*, especially in his ability to complement the Latin texts with apt and touching musical expression – but it was his *Messe des Morts* above all which established his reputation. It was first performed in Paris at a Concert spirituel in 1750, and remained in the repertory for many years. It was also performed both at Rameau's funeral in 1764 and Louis XV's in 1774.

We know of only four *grands motets* by Rameau, and of these only *Quam Dilecta* and *In Convertendo* have survived complete. The *Laboravi*, consisting of a musical setting of a single verse, was printed in Rameau's *Traité de l'harmonie* as an example of fugal writing, but was probably part of a larger work. Rameau's motets probably date from c.1712 and seem to have been chiefly intended for concert performance; *Deus noster refugium*, which lacks only a *récit*, is probably the earliest and may have been written for the 'Lyon Concert' society. Each of the motets contains music of interest – an elaborate chorus with instrumental ritornellos in *Deus noster refugium*, the opening haute-contre (high tenor) solo, a trio for soprano, tenor and bass with its Italianate unison string ritornellos and the final chorus of *In Convertendo* are all impressive in their technical assurance and depth of feeling – but when *In Convertendo* was revived at the Concert spirituel in 1751 it was unfavourably compared with the *grands motets* of Mondonville. 'Mondonville has not been dethroned and Rameau's rivalry has but increased the esteem, in which his motets are held,' wrote the Abbé Raynal in the *Nouvelles littéraires*. Yet the comparison was perhaps hardly fair, for *In Convertendo* was very heavily revised for the 1751 performances.

Mondonville brought this phase of the *grand motet* to a summit with twelve works in a form which outwardly had changed little since Lully and Dumont. Sometimes his feeling for orchestral colour and transparency of texture approaches, even equals that of Rameau; this we can find in the bass *récit* of his most celebrated motet, *Venite exultemus*, where oboe, bassoon and strings provide a lucid, light-textured accompaniment to the voice. Elsewhere, as, for instance, in the 'Elevaverunt flumina' from *Dominus regnavit*, Mondonville unites choral virtuosity with vivid textual illustration, as we might expect from a resourceful and popular opera composer.

HIPPOLYTE
ET
ARICIE,
TRAGEDIE
de M.ʳ Pellegrin
mise en Musique par M.ʳ
RAMEAU;
Représentée pour la premiere fois
le premier Octobre 1733.

Title page of Rameau's opera *Hippolyte et Aricie* (1733)

Rameau's operas

Rameau was fifty years old when his first opera *Hippolyte et Aricie* was performed. By then he had had ample opportunity to familiarize himself with Lully's operatic style and with that of the post-Lullian generation. Two further 'tragédies-lyriques' followed during the 1730s: *Castor et Pollux* (1737) and *Dardanus* (1739). Of these, *Hippolyte*, with its effective libretto by Simon-Joseph de Pellegrin (1663–1745) based on Euripides and Racine, is perhaps the best sustained. Especially rewarding is the declamatory strength of Theseus's two extended monologues (Acts II and III), the counterpoint and chilling modulations of the second of two trios for the three 'Fates' (Act II), Phaedra's air 'Cruelle mère des Amours' (Act III), the contrapuntal chorus 'Que ce rivage retentisse' (Act III), Hippolytus's poignant air, 'Ah! faut-il, en un jour' (Act IV), Phaedra's

183

terrible confession, 'Non, sa mort est mon seul ouvrage' (Act IV), and the elegiac orchestral chaconne (Act V). *Castor et Pollux*, which includes one of Rameau's most affecting and best-known airs, 'Tristes apprêts', and *Dardanus* contain music hardly less fine than *Hippolyte*, yet they do not possess the dramatic cohesion or the almost unrelieved atmosphere of grand and sombre tragedy which suffuses Rameau's first opera. In each, Rameau adheres to the Lullian formula of an overture, prologue and five acts containing recitatives, airs, choruses and dramatic 'symphonies'. In *Hippolyte* the instrumental music is more closely related to the action than in several other of Rameau's operas, and this, too, serves to strengthen dramatic continuity. *Dardanus* contains 'symphonies' which rank among the finest of the kind that Rameau ever wrote – the chaconne (Act V) is an outstanding example – but the opera suffers from an indifferent libretto, and even in its drastically revised version (1744) fails to match either *Hippolyte* or *Castor et Pollux*.

The two remaining stage-works of the 1730s are *opéra-ballets*. The more celebrated of them, *Les Indes galantes*, was staged in 1735, *Les Fêtes d'Hébé*, another masterpiece of the genre, in 1739. These works and the many *opéra-ballets* which followed gave Rameau greater opportunity than the *tragédies* to develop his outstanding abilities as an orchestrator. In a country where instrumental concertos established themselves only gradually the operatic 'symphonie' was considered of particular importance, one contemporary of Rameau remarking that it should move an audience in much the same way as the poetry of Racine and Corneille. Rameau, with his advanced harmonic language, his imaginative and perceptive use of orchestral colour and his intellectual strength, was supremely well-equipped to achieve this.

During the 1740s and early 1750s Rameau was at the height of his powers, as a succession of masterpieces testifies. This period witnessed only one *tragédie-lyrique*: *Zoroastre* (1749), but in its five-act structure without a prologue it made a significant break with Lullian tradition. An unusual feature of this opera was its departure from the more common classical legendary sources. Instead the librettist, Louis de Cahusac (1706–1759) with whom Rameau collaborated on several other occasions, chose an ancient Persian context, focussing on the theme of good and evil. The result was not entirely successful due to the implausibility of the love relationship between Zoroaster and Princess Amélite, and in 1756 composer and librettist made substantial changes.

The remaining stage works of the 1740s show a pronounced bias towards the dance. Among the *opéra-ballets* are *Le temple de la Gloire* (1745) and *Les surprises de l'Amour* (1748), both of which contain a wealth of inventive music. *Naïs* (1749) is a *pastorale héroïque* whose prologue celebrated the Peace of Aix-la-Chapelle. Its slender plot enabled Rameau to concentrate on the divertissements, which contain an unusually rich variety of dances in the composer's headiest vein. *La princesse de Navarre* (1745) is somewhat different from these in its use of spoken dialogue. This *comédie-ballet* was commissioned for the wedding celebrations of the Dauphin and his bride Princess Maria-Theresa of Spain, and involved Rameau in an uneasy collaboration with Voltaire who also provided the libretto for *Le temple de la Gloire*. Different again in form is *Pigmalion* (1748), the second and perhaps finest of several *actes de ballet* consisting of a continuous plot confined within a single act. The piece was more successful with the public than almost any other of Rameau's dramatic works – so much so that the composer wept with joy at its reception – and it contains some affecting and vigorous music.

Still more dramatic and affecting, however, are two full-length operas, *Platée* (1745) and *Zaïs* (1748), a *comédie-lyrique* and *pastorale héroïque* respectively. The two forms differ from a typical *opéra-ballet* in their use of a continuous plot and in being generally cast in fewer acts than the *tragédie*. *Platée* like *La princesse de Navarre* was staged at Versailles in honour of the Dauphin's wedding. Four years later it was revived at the Paris Opéra, and in 1754 once again, when the *Mercure de France* described the opera as 'the composer's masterpiece'. This mordant tale, concerning a nymph of unprepossessing appearance who aspires to a marriage with the god Jupiter, is in the fairy-tale tradition; but it is also a parody of French opera conventions, drawing from Rameau some of his most engaging and playful music. Platée herself, a travesti role, is particularly well catered for with two airs of affecting beauty, the *ariette badine* 'Que ce sejour est agréable' (Act I), and 'A l'aspect de ce nuage' (Act II). The opera is further endowed with a wealth of engaging choruses and 'symphonies' among which a storm (Act I) and an extended chaconne (Act III) are particularly impressive. *Zaïs* contains music of great originality, nowhere more so than in its overture depicting the original chaos and the creation of the world. Opinion, however, was not universally favourable: 'I consider that the overture paints chaos so well that it is unpleasant,' complained one of Rameau's contemporaries, 'for this clash of elements ... cannot have composed a very agreeable concert for the ear; happily man was not yet there to hear it; the Creator spared him such an overture which would have burst his ear drums.' Rameau's characteristically colourful scoring unusually calls for a 'tambour voilé' or muffled drum.

If the 1750s were on the whole less productive for Rameau than the previous decade, they witnessed nevertheless the composition of several more *actes de ballets*, a three-act *pastorale héroïque*, *Acante et Céphise* (1751), whose supernatural plot with a good fairy, a wicked genie and a magic castle inspired Rameau to write splendidly vigorous and colourful music, as well as providing for the first time in his music independent parts for two clarinets; and there were some important revivals, notably *Castor et Pollux* (1754), *Zoroastre* (1756) and *Hippolyte et Aricie* (1757), all of which were skilfully revised to accommodate the simpler, more melodic taste of the mid-eighteenth century.

The Enlightenment and the close of the Baroque period

The 1750s may be regarded as a decade of change which profoundly affected French artistic and intellectual life. The 'Enlightenment' as it is known, or *siècle de lumières* as it was termed in France, was a European movement, one of whose greatest achievements was the publication of the *Encyclopédie, ou Dictionnaire raisonné des sciences, des arts des métiers*. The first book of this colossal enterprise, under the supervision of Denis Diderot (1713–84) and Jean d'Alembert (1717–83), appeared in 1751, and its publication was the earliest among several events in the first half of the decade to have significant bearing on French music. The *philosophes*, as the literary men, scientists and theorists of eighteenth-century France were known, did not confine their attention to rational and intellectual issues but also addressed themselves to the subject of human emotions. In his *Discours préliminaire* to the *Encyclopédie*, d'Alembert criticizes the present state of music, and urges composers to arouse the human passions with vivid imitation of nature. Diderot also saw the function of music as one of imitation, yet ultimately was forced to concede an element of mystery. An anonymous author of the time, writing of Rameau, illustrates what was now expected: 'I have never heard the overture to [Rameau's ballet] *Pygmalion* played, without imagining myself in [the sculptor] Le Moine's studio. I would picture this gifted artist, chisel in hand, chipping away at a marble block; from it would emerge a Venus.' This overture met with wide approval, and some years later Rameau himself is said to have been delighted by performance on the organ by his champion and fellow Dijonnais, Balbastre.

Debates on the respective merits of French and Italian music which had begun in earnest some fifty years earlier were now resumed. Marin Mersenne in his *Harmonie universelle* (1636–7) had been among the first French writers to discuss their differences, and a partisan view had been expressed at the beginning of the eighteenth century by François

Raguenet in his *Paralèle des italiens et des français en ce qui regarde la musique et les opéra* (1702). Raguenet favoured the Italian style, thereby prompting a defence of the French by Jean Laurent Le Cerf de la Viéville in his *Comparaison de la musique italienne et de la musique française* (1704–6).

During the 1730s and 1740s Paris was the forum for a lengthy dispute concerning the respective operatic merits of Lully and Rameau. The 'Lullistes' were conservative, deploring any departure from the time-honoured operas of their paragon, whereas the 'Ramistes', or 'Ramoneurs' (chimney-sweeps) as they were sometimes mischievously known, championed the complexities and innovatory character of Rameau's music. Not until 1752, when Friedrich Melchior Grimm, a German critic resident in Paris, published his 'Lettre sur *Omphale*' (*Omphale* being a *tragédie-lyrique* by Destouches, revived in that year) attacking the older style and lavishing praise on Rameau, was the balance finally tipped in favour of the 'Ramistes'.

Two further events of significance to the development of French opera occurred in the same year. In spring the Swiss philosopher and contributor to the *Encyclopédie*, Jean-Jacques Rousseau (1712–78), wrote the text and music of his one-act opera – or *intermède* as it is described on the title-page of the score – *Le Devin du Village*. Rousseau, whose musical education had been unorthodox, had once been an admirer of Rameau; but Rameau's dismissive assessment of the younger man's musical ability some years earlier had soured relations. Like Diderot, d'Alembert and others, Rousseau rejected the conventional sentiments expressed in classical tragedy, seeking instead simplicity, spontaneity, true emotion and the triumph of virtue over corruption, the keynotes of the period to follow. Rousseau had encountered Italian music in Venice during the early 1740s and modelled *Le Devin du Village* on the Italian intermezzo.

Between the completion of Rousseau's *Le Devin du Village* in spring and its performance at court in the autumn of 1752 came the other significant event: a true Italian intermezzo, Pergolesi's *La Serva Padrona*, was staged at the Opéra after a performance of Lully's *Acis et Galatée*. It was not the first time that this piece had been played in Paris, but now its performance by an Italian troupe known as the 'Bouffons', under the direction of Eutachio Bambini, sparked off an argument which was to become a celebrated pamphleteer war, the 'Querelle des Bouffons', a somewhat ill-defined confrontation between 'le coin de la Reine' (supporters of Italian music, among whom were Rousseau, the *Encyclopédistes* and the French Queen), and 'le coin du Roi' (supporters of

French music, who included Mme de Pompadour and the King). Although superficially inconsequential, the argument, and above all Pergolesi's intermezzo, opened the minds of French dramatic composers to themes other than ancient myth or legend (p. 158).

In the following year the Théâtre de la Foire-Saint-Laurent staged *Les Troqueurs* (The Barterers), a one-act *intermède* inspired by *La Serva Padrona* and written by the French composer Antoine Dauvergne (1713–1797). To tease the opposing faction Dauvergne's identity was at first withheld and the music attributed to a nameless Italian composer living in Vienna. Only after the pro-Italian camp had expressed delight in the piece was the truth of its authorship disclosed. Dauvergne's 'opéra bouffon' is skilfully composed with an effective blend of 'symphonie', da capo aria and divertissement. The action is carried by a fluent handling of 'recitative semplice' or continuo recitative which increasingly established itself in France from this time. Rameau himself is said to have admired *Les Troqueurs*, allegedly remarking: 'If I were thirty years younger I would go to Italy and Pergolesi would be my model. But when one has turned sixty one must stay as one is.' However, neither a growing taste for such lighter, simpler entertainment nor Rousseau's well-known condemnation of French opera in his *Lettre sur la Musique Française* – somewhat surprising after the considerable success of *Le Devin du Village* – stood in the way of acclaimed revivals of two of Rameau's masterpieces, *Castor et Pollux* and *Platée*, in 1754, soon after which the 'Bouffons' left Paris.

In the last years of his life Rameau produced two major works, a comédie-lyrique, *Les Paladins* (1761), and his fifth and final *tragédie en musique*, *Les Boréades* (1760). *Les Paladins* though richly endowed with graceful airs and beguiling 'symphonies' is dramatically weak. *Les Boréades*, on the other hand, belies the composer's advanced age with its assured and inventive orchestral writing, its colourfully evocative divertissements, and its gestures towards new fashions in music. It was rehearsed in 1763 but abandoned in the same year. The work remained unperformed during Rameau's lifetime, and only in recent times has it been heard. The extent of Rameau's extraordinary gifts is at last receiving the recognition it deserves. He represents the apogee of the expressive eloquence which French musical language can command at its best. The subtle declamation, vivid dances full of beguiling gestures, inimitable grace and rhythmic diversity appealed greatly to the English, but even more to German composers and audiences. In Germany, meanwhile, rigorous technique was brilliantly complemented by the rejuvenating textures and styles of the French court.

11

Musical synthesis: eighteenth-century Germany

$\mathbf{A}$RTISTIC LIFE IN GERMANY during the eighteenth century was the very antithesis of that which prevailed in France. French cultural activities centred on the Versailles court and, to an ever-increasing extent, the fashionable milieu of Paris. German culture, by contrast, had no such focal points and little in the way of uniformity, since not only were the German-speaking peoples divided in their religious faith – the north Protestant and the south Catholic – but they were also politically fragmented. Nevertheless, as we have seen in Chapter 4, a wholly indigenous element, that of the Lutheran hymnody, with its binding force throughout sacred as well as much instrumental music, gives German music of the late Baroque its distinguishing profile. The political fragmentation promoted vigorous competition among the numerous lay and ecclesiastical principalities, many of which had been granted sovereignty. Princes and bishops, Protestant and Catholic alike, chose elegance or ostentation as a means of displaying their wealth and importance. Versailles was their first model, then Vienna, as the Habsburgs acquired further prestige as a result of decisive victories over the Turks. Rivalry resulted in the creation of magnificent buildings, gardens, painting, sculpture and music, by no means always the product of German artists. Austria, with its close ties with Italy following the Treaty of Utrecht, imported Italian artists of every kind during the eighteenth century; Germany commissioned Italians to build churches and welcomed both French and Italian musicians to its courts. The contribution of these visitors to the art of Germany and Central Europe can hardly be overstated, since not only was their artistic skill often of the first rank, but their ability to absorb into their work the spirit of the milieu in which they lived created fresh interpretations of forms largely conceived in Italy and France.

The importation of foreign styles to German art was nothing new. Palestrina had been an uncontested model to composers early in the seventeenth century and was to remain so in southern Germany for considerably longer, and Schütz, above all, achieved a synthesis of the Venetian concertato style and the Lutheran hymnody. In the first half of the eighteenth century the union of often seemingly irreconcilable forms continued, with many features of Italian and French music being absorbed into German stylistic tradition.

Germany's principal courts and trading cities also played a significant role in determining musical developments and shifts in emphasis. South Germany, largely dependent on its courts for artistic endeavour, was of less importance during the eighteenth century than northern and central Germany, where growth in trade and the emergence of Prussia as a great power gave rise to a wealthy, influential middle class.

It was nevertheless three south German composers who introduced French and Italian instrumental styles to Germany. They were Georg Muffat (1653–1704), Johann Caspar Ferdinand Fischer (c.1670–1746) and Johann Sigismund Kusser (1660–1727). Muffat is in many respects the most interesting of the three. He was of Scottish ancestry, French-born, but regarded himself as a German. During the 1660s he studied with Lully in Paris, later visiting Vienna, Prague, Salzburg and in the early 1680s Rome, where he studied with Bernardo Pasquini (1637–1710) and heard Corelli's concerti grossi, yet unpublished. The profound effect of Muffat's French and Italian studies is witnessed in four important collections of his music. In 1682 he published his *Armonico tributo*, consisting of five 'sonatas' in which concertino and *tutti* passages are clearly differentiated in the manner of Corelli's concertos; Corelli's influence is evident, too, in the absence of any set pattern of movements, and in certain features such as 'walking' bass parts and fugal writing. In his last work, the *Ausserlesene Instrumental-Musik* (1701), Muffat included revised versions of the 'sonatas' of *Armonico Tributo*, adding six new concertos also based on Corellian principles. Between these two Italian-dominated collections Muffat published two others in which he paid tribute to the French style. These were the *Florilegium primum* (1695) and the *Florilegium secundum* (1698), consisting of orchestral suites in which the five-part string texture reflects French practice at the time. Hardly less interesting than the music itself are the prefaces which Muffat published with each collection. Those of the *Florilegia*, printed in Latin, French, German and Italian – indicative in this of the composer's wish to preserve an accessible record of what he had learnt – afford valuable insight to French performing styles of Lully's time with their detailed information concerning bowing, and characterization of movements and their relationship with a wide variety of dance-measures – that element so important in Baroque music.

Kusser, who like Muffat studied with Lully, was successful as an opera composer and director, first at the court of Brunswick-Wolfenbüttel then at Hamburg, where he also introduced operas by foreign composers, including Steffani. Kusser published four sets of orchestral suites between 1682 and 1700, and is credited with being the first to preface each dance-sequence with a Lullian French theatre overture.

Fischer contributed to the dissemination of French orchestral music with his collection of eight suites published in 1695, *Le journal du printems*. Fischer's working life was spent as *Hofkapellmeister* to the Baden court, and he adheres to French custom in his five-part string writing but introduces a dash of colour with the occasional use of two trumpets. The music, though less contrapuntal than that of Muffat, is similarly inventive in its engagingly contrasted dance-measures; the elegantly constructed *passacailles*, or variations over a ground bass, are especially noteworthy.

The concerto in north Germany

While Muffat, Kusser and Fischer provided German composers of the next generations such as Fux, Telemann and Bach with models for the orchestral suite, Muffat, as we have seen, additionally introduced South Germans to the Corellian concerto. The form, however, did not penetrate central and northern parts of Germany until around the second decade of the eighteenth century, by which time the Venetian concertos of Albinoni and Vivaldi were offering rival models, with a greater element of solo virtuosity. Almost all later German Baroque composers took the Venetian concerto as their model, while at the same time introducing features of their own music and that of France.

An important musician for the development of the Baroque concerto is Georg Johann Pisendel (1687–1755). Pisendel joined the Dresden court orchestra in 1712, officially becoming its *Konzertmeister* (leader/director) in 1730. More significant than his musical legacy – only seven violin concertos and four concerti grossi are known to us – is the fact that he studied in Ansbach with Torelli and later in Venice with Vivaldi, acquiring along the way a reputation as the foremost German violinist of his generation – indeed, Vivaldi, Albinoni and Telemann dedicated pieces to him. Pisendel imparted the fruits of his Italian encounters to his fellow German musicians through his compositions and in his performances at Dresden of Venetian sonatas and concertos, some of which he re-orchestrated to accommodate the forces of the court band, adding wind parts.

Apart from Bach and Telemann the leading German composers of concertos were Johann David Heinichen (1683–1729), Christoph Graupner (1683–1760), Johann Friedrich Fasch (1688–1758) and Gottfried Heinrich Stölzel (1690–1749). Heinichen's sphere of activity encompassed not only instrumental writing but also opera, and it was this which took him in 1710 to Venice, where he may have met Vivaldi. During his period as *Kapellmeister* at the Dresden court Heinichen enriched its opera repertory as well as cultivating the Venetian concerto style; in this he was supported by Pisendel, who had brought with him from Venice a collection of Vivaldi's concertos. Heinichen was an excellent theorist, and his treatise *Der General-Bass in der Composition*, printed in Dresden in 1728, was widely praised. It was probably the theatrical and philosophical range of this work which, according to Burney, prompted his contemporaries to dub him 'the Rameau of Germany'.

Graupner, although like Heinichen an opera composer, was more prolific as a composer of concertos, suites and symphonies, whose subtle instrumental colours and textures are distinctive features. Like Telemann with whom he was on friendly terms, Graupner wrote skilfully for a wide variety of woodwind instruments including treble recorder, flute, oboe, oboe d'amore, bassoon, and various sizes of chalumeau.

Graupner, and to a greater extent his pupil Fasch, incline towards the early Classical style in many of their concertos – that is to say, they show an interest both in the three-movement sinfonia style of Vivaldi and in the techniques of the early Mannheim symphonists such as Johann Stamitz (1717–57). Fasch shares with Graupner an interest in woodwind textures, often using the instruments in pairs episodically within *tutti* sections of a movement. Stölzel favoured equally the concerto grosso and the solo concerto, approaching in the former a manner more closely resembling that of Bach than of his other contemporaries. His 'concerto grosso a quattro Chori' in D major for two groups of trumpets, woodwind and strings affords a fine example of this neglected composer's style. Bach rated him highly, including his keyboard Partita in G minor in *Das Clavier-Büchlein vor Wilhelm Friedemann Bach* (1720).

Another talented composer of the period, though he left only one concerto, is Jan Dismas Zelenka (1699–1745). Zelenka was born near Prague, but spent most of his working life at Dresden, where he was engaged as a bass player and where he eventually became *vice-Kapellmeister* of church music. In his sacred vocal music, and above all in his instrumental pieces, which include six trio sonatas for two oboes and bassoon, and five orchestral *capriccios*, he reveals a highly distinctive style full of novel ideas, often requiring almost startling virtuosity, and flavoured with a piquancy derived from Central European folk tradition.

Solo instrumental music

As in orchestral forms, so too in the sphere of solo instrumental music were German composers susceptible to French and Italian styles. The instrument which took pride of place in Germany approximately between 1650 and 1750 was the organ, and it was this period which witnessed the greatest development in organ music. Following in a tradition established by Weckmann and Tunder, a younger generation of north German composers brought organ playing and composition to a level of virtuosity hitherto unequalled. The most important Lutheran organist-composers of the generation before Bach were Georg Böhm (1661–1733), Vincent Lübeck (1654–1740), Dietrich Buxtehude (c.1637–1707) and his gifted pupil Nicolaus Bruhns (1665–97). Further south, Friedrich Wilhelm Zachow (1663–1712) in Halle, Johann Kuhnau (1660–1722) in Leipzig and Johann Pachelbel (1653–1706) in Nuremberg made distinctive contributions to the organ repertory with their treatment of fugues and chorale techniques.

The principal forms explored by the German organ composers were the toccata and organ chorale. Buxtehude excelled at both, at the same time realizing the brilliant potential of the instruments built by north German craftsmen. A vivid element of display and entertainment is inherent in his toccata-like *praeludia*, where exuberant virtuosity on the one hand and discipline and restraint on the other illustrate one of the fundamental paradoxes of Baroque expression.

Buxtehude is no less skilled in his fugal writing and in the three main types of organ chorale – variation, fantasia and prelude. His fugues are tautly constructed and expertly crafted, often possessing striking subjects, while his chorale fantasias such as *Wie schön leuchtet der Morgenstern* (BuxWv 223) extend the traditional improvisatory element in a virtuosic manner. The short chorale preludes which probably prefaced the congregational singing in the Lübeck liturgy are elaborately ornamented in the upper voice *cantus firmus* (chorale melody) and contain a rich vein of fantasy and lyricism. Buxtehude's three well-known organ works, the *Ciaconas* in C minor (BuxWv 159) and E minor (BuxWv 160) and the *Passacaglia* in D minor (BuxWv 161), are based on *ostinato*, or persistent, repeated melodic phrases, and so provide a link with southern German and Italian traditions.

The forms which attracted German harpsichord composers were

chiefly those of the suite, the theme with variations and, later in the seventeenth century, the sonata as modelled by Corelli. The concerto, too, was adapted to the solo keyboard medium, notably by Johann Gottfried Walther (1684–1748), Bach's cousin, and by Bach himself.

We have already seen in Chapter 4 that Froberger established a pattern for the German keyboard suite consisting of allemande, courante, sarabande and gigue. While keeping approximately to this plan, composers of the following two generations extended it, mainly with French dances, such as menuets, bourrées, gavottes, chaconnes, and variations. Kuhnau in his two sets of *Neue Clavier-Übung* (1689/92) furthermore introduced each suite with a prelude, and seems to have been one of the first German composers to do so. Fischer adopted a similar practice in his *Musicalisches Blumen-Büschlein* (1696). Six of the eight suites of this collection provide early examples of fully fledged French orchestral dance-suites transferred to the solo keyboard. Fischer's pioneering outlook is reflected in his *Ariadne musica* (1702), in which twenty preludes and fugues for organ explore twenty modern keys in circles of fifths made available by approximations of equal temperament proposed by Kuhnau, Andreas Werckmeister (1645–1706) and others. *Ariadne musica* is an important forerunner of Bach's *Well-Tempered Clavier* for which it may have been a model. Some of Fischer's most colourful keyboard music is contained in his last publication, *Musicalisches Parnassus* (1738). Its nine suites bear the names of the nine Muses, and consist of a wide variety of French dances prefaced in all but one instance by imaginative, idiomatically written preludes. The exception is the second suite which begins with a French overture, a form in which Fischer had already proved himself skilled. This movement together with an extended *Passacaglia* in D minor from the Suite No. 9 are among the most impressive pieces of the set.

Three of the most skilled composers of ornamental variations and variations on a ground bass were the leading organists Buxtehude, Böhm and Pachelbel. Towards the end of the seventeenth century the form of the secular variation on a dance melody was adapted by organ composers, who substituted a chorale melody as the basis of variations. Böhm was notably resourceful in his chorale 'partite', as they were called, probably intended for harpsichord, while Buxtehude's skill in variation technique is brilliantly displayed in the thirty-two secular variations on *La Capricciosa* (BuxWv 250). Pachelbel contributed to the art of ornamental variation with his *Musicalische Sterbens-Gedancken* (1683), containing variations on chorale melodies in suite form, and *Hexachordum Apollinis* (1699) which he dedicated to Buxtehude. Six manuscript *ciacconas* (chaconnes) provide examples of Pachelbel's gift in writing variations on a ground bass.

The earliest harpsichord 'sonata' seems to have been composed by Kuhnau who included one in his collection of suites, *Neue Clavier-Übung* (1692): 'Why should one not be able to achieve such things [sonatas] on the Clavier as on other instruments?' he wrote in the preface. Kuhnau followed this anthology with two others consisting entirely of sonatas, the *Frische Clavier Früchte* (1696) and the six programme sonatas of the *Musicalische Vorstellung einiger biblischer Historien* (1700).

Sacred music. Buxtehude and the Lutheran cantata

Protestant church music of northern and central Germany in the late seventeenth and early eighteenth centuries was directly influenced both by changing religious attitudes and developments in music itself. In 1675 the father of Pietism, Philipp Jacob Spener (1635–1705), published his *Pia Desideria* which contained the essence of Pietist ideology. It placed emphasis on the Scriptural word, and on not merely believing in Christ but also living a Christ-like life. Although Pietism had little influence on orthodox Lutheran church services it coloured the devotional life of the individual by encouraging subjective thought and an intensification of personal faith. Orthodox Lutheranism and Pietism retained in common an unquestioning faith, but this was soon to be challenged by the *Aufklärung*, or Enlightenment, which proclaimed a combination of belief and reason as the source of Divine revelation.

The music of the Protestant Church, meanwhile, was as receptive to Italian and French influences as were secular instrumental forms. A growing taste for virtuosity in singing and playing in secular music was shared by composers of sacred music, who recognized in virtuoso techniques a new means of celebrating the faith with a vivid and moving elucidation of the text.

By the mid-seventeenth century the cantata – a term seldom used by composers for sacred pieces at this time but which modern writers have applied to such works made up of independent movements – was beginning to replace the motet and sacred concerto as the most important form of Lutheran church music. Linking the older and newer forms were the concerted pieces developed by composers such as Tunder, which incorporated both the text and melody of a chorale. The varied cantata techniques employed by late seventeenth-century composers can be found in the music of Buxtehude, Nicolaus Bruhns, Johann Schelle (1648–1701), Johann Philipp Krieger (1649–1725), Kuhnau and Zachow.

Following the death of Tunder, Buxtehude was appointed to succeed him as organist of the Marienkirche at Lübeck in 1668. His official duties, unlike those incumbent upon most of his fellow-organists in similarly important churches in northern and central Germany, did not require him to provide much in the way of vocal music, yet well over one hundred sacred vocal pieces have survived. Some of these were performed at the Communion services at the Marienkirche, some may have been occasioned by more intimate gatherings, while others may have been intended for the celebrated Lübeck 'Abendmusiken'.

The Abendmusik, held in the Marienkirche, was an early manifestation of German public concert life. When the series began is uncertain, but during Tunder's early term of office it consisted principally of organ recitals, gradually expanding to include small-scale pieces with voices and instruments. The concerts were funded largely by the wealthy middle classes, whose growing importance throughout northern and central Germany influenced the spiritual and intellectual life of the late seventeenth and eighteenth century. Buxtehude extended the scope of the Abendmusik to include repertory for vocal and instrumental soloists, chorus and instrumental ensemble to be performed at its gatherings five times a year.

Buxtehude's cantatas occupy middle ground between the chorale concertato style of the previous generation and the early cantatas of Bach. Texts were usually compiled from biblical passages, hymns, and the rich legacy of miscellaneous German devotional poetry of the first half of the seventeenth century. These were treated by Buxtehude in various ways. Sometimes, as in the awe-inspiring *Wachet auf, ruft uns die Stimme* (BuxWv 100) for three-part vocal texture with strings, bassoon and continuo, Buxtehude keeps to the verse pattern of the hymn, in this case by Philipp Nicolai, though making but slight reference to its associated melody. In *Jesu, meine Freude* (BuxWv 60), on the other hand, he treats Johann Franck's six-verse hymn as a set of variations, matching musical ideas with textual content in a manner recalling the song-variations in Scheidt's *Tabulatura Nova* (1624). Another of Buxtehude's cantatas, *Fürchtet euch nicht* (BuxWv 30), mingles poetry with biblical quotation, while the masterly *Alles, was ihr tut* (BuxWv 4) draws upon poetry, hymn and biblical text. Buxtehude's skill in combining disparate text elements is matched by the way he draws together instrumental sonata, concertato style, aria and chorale, providing an attractive model for the following generation of cantata composers. In his development of the hymn-variation technique, his choral and instrumental writing, which reflect Italian methods acquired above all through Schütz, and his combination of chorally sung biblical text with solo or ensemble pieces, Buxtehude provided the young Bach with important models. Some of Buxtehude's vocal music, at least, Bach must have heard during his visit to Lubeck to meet the elder composer in 1705.

In 1700, with the publication of *Geistliche Cantaten* by Erdmann Neumeister (1671–1756), the Lutheran cantata was given new definition. In his preface Neumeister, a Hamburg poet and theologian, while firmly identifying the term 'cantata' with Lutheran sacred music, wrote that 'a *Cantata* seems nothing other than a piece from an opera, put together from *Stylo Recitativo* and arias'. Neumeister's first publication consisted of Bible paraphrases, but later collections which appeared from 1711 included both Bible text and hymn verses. Neumeister's texts provided complete cycles of cantatas for the church year, closely allied to his own sermons, and were taken up by almost all the northern and central German *Kantors*. They were attracted not only by the dramatic qualities intrinsic to recitative and da capo aria but also by Neumeister's discerning blend of orthodox congregational faith and Pietist emphasis on the individual soul. Among the first to embrace Neumeister's ideas were Zachow in Halle and, to a lesser extent, Kuhnau in Leipzig; but it was composers of the next generation such as Graupner, Telemann and, above all, Bach who exploited them most thoroughly.

Bach: early life. Weimar years (1708–17)

Johann Sebastian Bach (1685–1750) was born at Eisenach, in the central German territory of Thuringia, close to the Harz mountains. His family had lived and worked as musicians in this part of Germany since the mid-sixteenth century, and apart from his prodigious talent and the various positions reflecting it, Bach's musical activities were very similar to those of his forebears. His family name was associated with music almost throughout central Germany, and family pride played an important part in the make-up of his character. He traced his family tree, the *Ursprung der musicalisch-Bachischen Familie*, and assembled the precious anthology of music by earlier generations of Bachs, the *Alt-Bachisches Archiv*.

At the age of ten Johann Sebastian was orphaned and taken in by his elder brother at Ohrdruf, Johann Christoph, who gave him early instruction in keyboard playing. Probably in the spring of 1700 Bach was sent north to Lüneburg to continue his musical education at the Michaelisschule. Among the important events in his life at this time were his acquaintanceship with Böhm at Lüneburg, an opportunity to hear the organ playing of the aged and renowned Johann Adam Reincken (1623–

1722) at the Catharinenkirche in Hamburg, where he had been organist since 1663, and another to hear French orchestral music at the court of Celle. By 1703 Bach was a court musician at Weimar, but in the same year he accepted the post of organist at the Neukirche at Arnstadt. Clashes of temperament between Bach and the Arnstadt consistory foreshadowed difficulties of a similar nature which lay in store at Leipzig, and by October of the same year he was travelling north to Lübeck with four weeks' leave from the consistory to hear Buxtehude's organ-playing. That a month's absence became almost three did little to improve Bach's relations with his employers. In 1707 he moved to Mühlhausen as organist of St Blasius, and it was here that he wrote his earliest cantatas, *Aus der Tiefen rufe ich* (BWV 131) and *Gottes Zeit ist die allerbeste Zeit*, '*Actus Tragicus*' (BWV 106). Another, *Gott ist mein König* (BWV 71), was composed in honour of the Mühlhausen annual town council election in 1708, and was to be the only cantata of which both text and music were printed during Bach's lifetime. These early cantatas did not conform to Neumeister's model, as set by his recently published collection, but more closely adhered to established tradition at the time, incorporating elements of motet, strophic aria and chorale as practised by Buxtehude and various of Bach's Leipzig predecessors such as Sebastian Knüpfer, Johann Schelle and Johann Kuhnau. Even at this early stage Bach showed a mastery of form and a skill in colouring text with affecting musical images which matches that to be found in the later cantatas.

In 1708 Bach returned to Weimar, taking up duties first of *Hoforganist*, then in 1714 of *Konzertmeister* as well. In the early years organ music rather than cantatas occupied his time. At Weimar Bach wrote prolifically for the organ, drawing upon all that he had assimilated so far, mainly of north German tradition, but also of Italian and, to a lesser extent, French styles. Buxtehude and Böhm were important influences in Bach's earliest organ pieces, whereas those of the Mülhausen period onward are marked by a greater expressive individuality and the emergence of a weightier, fully mature style. These qualities are apparent above all in the impressive *Passacaglia* in C minor (BWV 582), the first part of whose *passacaglia* theme is identical with one in André Raison's *Livre d'orgue* (1688), and in Bach's own *Orgel-Büchlein* (BWV 599–644). Bach assembled his *Orgel-Büchlein* (Little Organ Book), excepting one piece (BWV 613), between 1713 and 1716. Later at Cöthen he added a title-page inscription indicating its partly didactic function: 'wherein an inexperienced organist is given guidance in various ways of treating a chorale [hymn], as well as becoming competent in the use of pedals, which are treated in the chorales therein as entirely obbligato'.

The Weimar years witnessed Bach's preoccupation with the Italian concerto, especially the Venetian solo type developed above all by Vivaldi. Its influence on Bach's personal style can hardly be overstated, for his awareness of its formal possibilities gave scope to his own vitally imaginative musicianship and technical ability. The concertos that resulted are unsurpassed at the period. The early fruits of the encounter can be found in both the solo keyboard pieces and the later cantatas of the Weimar years. It was probably during the middle years of his employment that Bach made solo keyboard arrangements for harpsichord and organ of concertos by Vivaldi, Telemann, Alessandro Marcello and Johann Ernst, the young nephew of his employer, Duke Wilhelm Ernst of Saxe-Weimar. Among the most successful of these are three for harpsichord and two for organ from Vivaldi's earliest set, *L'estro armonico*, printed in 1711 in Amsterdam, one of the leading centres of music publishing.

Bach's Weimar cantatas, though comparatively few in number are of considerable interest and formal variety. The earliest of them, *Nach dir, Herr, verlanget mich* (BWV 150) and *Christ lag in Todesbanden* (BWV 4), though consisting of self-contained movements, are not of the Neumeister type (p. 197) but closer to central and north German traditions. Luther's Easter hymn *Christ lag in Todesbanden* is a strikingly effective example of a chorale-cantata 'per omnes versus', that is, in which each verse of the hymn is set to a variation of its associated melody.

At Weimar in 1713 Bach performed his first secular piece, *Was mir behagt, ist nur die muntre Jagd* (BWV 208), in honour of the birthday of Duke Christian at neighbouring Saxen-Weissenfels. The Weimar diocesan secretary, Salomo Franck, provided Bach with an attractive version of the legend of the goddess Diana. The arias, recitatives and ensembles which comprise the score are colourfully orchestrated with recorders, oboes, bassoon, horns, strings and continuo, evoking an enchanted pastoral landscape. Another secular cantata, *Weichet nur, betrübte Schatten* (BWV 202), for solo soprano, whose pastoral poem provided the background for a vernal masterpiece, may also belong to this period.

It was possibly towards the end of 1713 that Bach wrote his most elaborate church cantata of the Weimar period. The origins of *Ich hatte viel Bekümmernis* (BWV 21) are uncertain, but the likelihood is that Bach submitted it as an example of his work when applying for the post of organist at the Liebfrauenkirche in Halle in December of that year. This beautifully constructed cantata is unique among the Weimar works in falling into two parts. The text, probably by Franck, is based mainly on verses from the Psalms but also on the Epistle for the Third Sunday after

Trinity: 'Cast all your cares upon Him, for He careth for you'. This is the central theme of the work, drawing from Bach an astonishing range of musical affects. Among many striking features of the work are the poignant opening Sinfonia, the fugal choruses, and the theatrical nature of a dialogue between Jesus and the Soul at the beginning of Part Two. The inspiration for this duet, and several others similarly cast which were to follow, seems to have derived from opera, and particularly, perhaps, from the opera which thrived at Hamburg.

It was at Weimar that Bach used Neumeister's texts for the first time. One of the settings, *Nun komm, der Heiden Heiland* (BWV 61), is notable for the skill in which he united the form of the French overture with Lutheran chorale in the opening chorus. Among other cantatas of this period in which Bach explored a variety of forms are *Weinen, Klagen, Sorgen, Zagen* (BWV 12), later to become the basis of the 'Crucifixus' of the Mass in B minor, *Widerstehe doch der Sünde* (BWV 54) for solo alto, with five-part string texture in its opening movement and a bold harmonic design, *Komm, du süsse Todesstunde* (BWV 161) with its skilful treatment of Hassler's choral melody, effective writing for two recorders, and poignant evocation of the departing soul in the work's alto arioso, and Bach's only surviving cantata for Palm Sunday, *Himmelskönig, sei willkommen* (BWV 182).

By 1717 Bach's reputation as an outstanding organist was firmly established. He had been one of three musicians chosen to examine the new organ at Halle in the previous year, and had been described by Johann Mattheson in the preface to *Das beschützte Orchestre* (1717) as 'the famous Weimar organist'; but following the death of the Weimar *Kapellmeister*, Johann Samuel Drese, in December 1716, the Duke appointed Drese's son Johann Wilhelm as his new *Kapellmeister*. By then, however, Bach had been offered a similar post, and a better paid one, at the Calvinist court of Prince Leopold at Cöthen.

Cöthen years (1717–23). Brandenburg Concertos, instrumental collections

At Cöthen, for the first and only time in his life Bach assumed responsibilities which required nothing in the way of church music from him. His new employer, Prince Leopold, was musical – he had studied with Heinichen among others – and was a capable bass singer as well as able to play the violin, viola da gamba and harpsichord. By the time of Bach's arrival as *Kapellmeister* in December 1717 the court orchestra was able to boast some sixteen players, not to mention the gifted prince.

Autograph of the beginning of Bach's sixth *Brandenburg Concerto* in B flat major (1721)

The orchestral cornerstone of Bach's Cöthen years is the collection of six concertos assembled as the result of a 'command' from Christian Ludwig, Margrave of Brandenburg. Bach may well have met the Margrave in Berlin early in 1719 when he was negotiating the purchase of a new harpsichord for Leopold. The six *Brandenburg Concertos* or *'six Concerts Avec plusieurs Instruments'* as Bach himself described them, made demands far in excess of the modest musical resources of the Margrave's establishment – a clear suggestion that the composer intended his brilliantly diverse anthology to be played by the excellent band at Cöthen of which he himself was director. Only two French horn players would have had to be engaged as guests in the first of the six concertos. Bach's autograph of the Brandenburgs is dated 24 March 1721, but their composition almost certainly extends over a longer period embracing the later Weimar years. Indeed, movements of the Concerto No. 1 seem to have served as an introduction to the secular cantata of 1714: *Was mir behagt* (BWV 208). The colourful variety of instrumental groupings in the Brandenburgs is almost without precedent; and in the Concerto No. 5 Bach furthermore prepares the ground for the keyboard concerto which later on he was to develop at Leipzig.

We cannot be certain that Bach also composed all his violin concertos during the Cöthen years. Although only three have been preserved in their original form (BWV 1041–3) there were evidently a great many more. Several have survived in later versions as harpsichord concertos, while individual movements from lost concertos are almost certainly contained within the body of Bach's cantatas. Two orchestral works, the Suites Nos 1 (BWV 1066) and 4 (BWV 1069), may have originated at Cöthen, but the remaining Suites, No. 2 (BWV 1067) and No. 3 (BWV 1068), were probably written during the 1730s – the evidence is inconclusive.

As well as concertos, various collections of instrumental music belong, at least in part, to Bach's six years at Cöthen: three each of sonatas and partitas for unaccompanied violin (BWV 1001–6), six suites for unaccompanied cello (BWV 1007–12), six sonatas for violin and obligato harpsichord (BWV 1014–19), thirty Inventions and Sinfonias for solo harpsichord (BWV 772–801), a collection of twenty-four Preludes and Fugues, *Das wohltemperierte Clavier* (Book I of the '48'), as well as the part-assembly of the six *French Suites* and six *English Suites* for harpsichord. The Partita in A minor for unaccompanied flute (BWV 1013) also in all probability belongs to this period, although the sonatas for flute and continuo (BWV 1034–5), flute and obbligato harpsichord (BWV 1030 and 1032), and for viola da gamba and obbligato harpsichord (BWV 1027–9), once considered as products of the Cöthen years, are almost certainly Leipzig compositions. Bach's originality, and his craftsman's and musician's knowledge of stringed and keyboard instruments, enabled him to pursue ideas and explore techniques with unprecedented virtuosity and learning.

Bach's productive and contented existence at Cöthen was clouded by two events. The first was the death in 1719 of his wife of twelve years, Maria Barbara, while Bach was at Carlsbad with the Prince. The second occurred in December 1721 when, just a week after Bach himself had taken as his second wife Anna Magdalena Wilcke, daughter of a court trumpeter, the Prince married his cousin Friderica, Princess of Anhalt-Bernburg. The Princess unlike her husband was not interested in music, and the creative friendship between Bach and the Prince was shortly brought to an end. Bach had already offered himself as a candidate for the post of organist at the Jacobikirche in Hamburg in 1720. In the autumn of 1722 he applied for the position of *Kantor* of the Thomasschule at Leipzig, Kuhnau having died in June. Among the five other candidates for the post were Telemann in Hamburg and Graupner at Darmstadt. Telemann, the most successful German composer of the time, was elected, but Hamburg, unwilling to let him go, improved his terms of employment and the Leipzig council was obliged to reconvene. Graupner was next favoured, but was unable to secure his release from Darmstadt. Bach, meanwhile, had performed his two *Probestücke* or test pieces (BWV 22 and 23) in the Thomaskirche on 7 February; on 22 April 1723 the council unanimously agreed on his appointment and in May he took up his duties.

Bach at Leipzig (1723–50). Cantata cycles, Passions, oratorios

Although difficulties with the Leipzig authorities eventually brought the composer disillusionment, an astonishing burst of creative energy in the early years of Bach's appointment suggests that the wide range of activities open to him offered challenges which he was more than ready to accept. As *Kantor* of the Thomaskirche and Leipzig's *Director Musices*, Bach was in charge of music for the four principal churches and also for municipal occasions such as the annual election of the town council. Between 1723 and 1729 Bach composed three complete annual cycles of cantatas for the church year (according to his obituary as many as five annual cycles existed; but if so, two have been lost). He began his first cycle almost at once, with two cantatas of impressive dimensions for the first and second Sundays after Trinity (BWV 75 and 76). These and virtually all of Bach's Leipzig sacred cantatas were intended for performance at the principal Sunday service, the *Hauptgottesdienst*, and on feast days. Only during Lent and the last three Sundays in Advent were they omitted from the services; the cantatas were sung in the city's two main churches, the Thomaskirche and the Nikolaikirche, on alternate Sundays.

The cantatas formed an integral part of the Lutheran liturgy in Leipzig. Their texts were usually related to the appointed Gospel, and they were sung after the Gospel-reading, before the sermon; sometimes a second cantata, or the second part of a cantata, might follow the sermon. Bach himself would have directed the choir and instrumentalists, probably not from the organ, which would have been played by the regular organist, but perhaps occasionally from the harpsichord. The first year's cycle (1723–4) consisted partly of revised Weimar cantatas and partly of newly composed works. Some of these were on a more modest scale than the works of the impressive second cycle (1724–5). In this, Bach devised a new type of cantata related to the earlier German settings of chorale texts 'per omnes versus', in which the chorale melody, sometimes unaltered, sometimes modified, was retained in all verses. In Bach's new scheme, a significant contribution to cantata form and one carefully planned from the outset, the first and last verses of a chorale were set unaltered while the intervening verses were paraphrased in recitative and aria. The melody associated with the hymn forms the basis of the elaborate chorale fantasia with which these cantatas begin, while the last verse is a simpler, chordal setting of the chorale melody, often strikingly harmonized by Bach.

Among the many outstandingly original cantatas of the Leipzig years, Cantatas Nos 75 and 76 have already been mentioned as impressive. Of equal merit in the first annual cycle are Cantata No. 105, a profound, grief-laden piece; No. 119 with its resounding opening chorus, skilfully incorporated into the framework of a French overture, and its beguiling tenor aria evocation of Leipzig's boulevards of linden trees; No. 95 with its two hymn-tunes deftly woven into the opening chorus, a third sung by a solo soprano with a playful accompaniment of unison oboes d'amore, and a lively virtuoso tenor aria with pizzicato strings; No. 60 which possesses one of Bach's most boldly harmonized chorales; and lastly, No. 65, a radiant Epiphany piece with an opening chorus resonantly scored for horns and with a processional character.

Bach's virtuosity in the second annual cantata cycle is such that singling out individual works is even harder. In the order in which they are heard, the chorale cantatas Nos 93, 101, 78, 8, 130, 114, 5, 180, 115, 62, 133, 111, 92, 127 and 1 from this series are masterly in the cohesive strength of their construction and in the depth and variety of their musical expression. Towards the end of this remarkable cycle Bach all but abandoned the chorale-based form, but continued almost unfailingly to produce works of outstanding quality. Among them are nine set to texts by the Leipzig poet Christiane Mariane von Ziegler whose Pietist-inclined sentiments, reflected in a spirit of tenderness and heartfelt emotion, seem to have had particular appeal for the composer. Especially noteworthy, perhaps, are Cantata No. 108 with its expressive aria for tenor and solo violin; No. 87 whose darkly coloured tonal scheme provides strong contrast with the work's only major key movement, a radiant siciliano for tenor, and No. 68 with its elegiac opening chorus and celebrated soprano aria, 'Mein gläubiges Herze' (My heart ever faithful). No. 85 with its pastoral tenor aria projecting the image of Jesus, the Good Shepherd, though not one of von Ziegler's texts, is no less lyrical.

The cantatas of the third annual cycle and those which followed it at irregular intervals contain a comparably rich variety of styles in which Bach interprets his texts. One of the most deeply felt is Cantata No. 198, a 'Trauer Ode' or Funeral Ode by the Leipzig teacher and poet Johann

Christoph Gottsched, of whom Ziegler was a disciple. It was written to commemorate the electress Christiane Eberhardine who died in 1727, and who had remained a staunch Protestant after her husband, Augustus the Strong, Elector of Saxony, had been obliged to embrace the Catholic faith on his ascent to the Polish throne. Among the great wealth of masterly cantatas composed from the mid-1720s are No. 45 with its invigorating, tautly constructed opening chorus and theatrical bass arioso, and No. 88 with two strikingly contrasted images, of a hunter and a fisherman, in the opening chorus.

Although the cantata occupied the most important musical position in the Lutheran liturgy, motets, canticles, oratorios and Passions were also sung. Bach may have completed as many as five Passions, but only two, the St John and the St Matthew, have survived complete. The German dramatic oratorio Passion had developed during the mid-seventeenth century in works by the Hamburg *Kantor* Thomas Selle and by Schütz. While Schütz's masterpieces were unaccompanied, however, Selle uses instruments throughout, interspersing the Gospel narrative with hymns and reflective texts. This type of oratorio Passion gradually spread from Hamburg to other towns of northern and central Germany, but had been introduced to Leipzig only in 1721 by Bach's predecessor, Kuhnau. Thereafter a tradition was established that Passions were performed annually, alternately between the two main churches, at Vespers on Good Friday.

The earlier of Bach's two complete Passions, the St John (BWV 245), was first performed in the Nikolaikirche in 1724. Its subsequent history, however, is complex, since Bach prepared no less than four versions of the work, of which material for three has survived. The chief differences appear between the 1724 version and the version Bach performed at the Thomaskirche in the following year. Many of the alterations which he is reputed to have made for a third version (1728–32) are lost, while the fourth, on which he worked intermittently during the last years of his life, closely resembles, and indeed largely reverts to the first version. The St Matthew Passion (BWV 244), 'the great Passion' as it became known among members of the Bach family, probably dates from 1727, and was revived at least twice during Bach's life.

Broadly speaking the components of both the St John and the St Matthew Passions can be placed under distinct headings. Firstly, there is the narrative element in which the Evangelist (tenor) and Christ (bass) play the central role. In each Passion the Evangelist is accompanied by *continuo semplice*, but whereas in the St John Christ is similarly accompanied, in the St Matthew his direct speech is accompanied in all but one passage – that which occurs immediately before his death – by sustained strings, which according to older tradition form a 'halo' around him. Secondly, there is a lyrical and contemplative element provided by the arias, which reflect on the events of the Gospel narrative and are to some extent a response to Pietistic devotional attitudes. Thirdly, there is an element, at once meditative and communal, provided by the chorales, the traditional hymn-tunes of Bach's time, with which congregations would certainly have been familiar through the Leipzig and Dresden hymnbooks. Fourthly, there are the choruses, which occupy a position somewhat akin to those in ancient Greek drama, commenting on events and often emphasizing their significance with considerable, indeed at times startling dramatic force. An instance is provided in the St Matthew Passion by the full *tutti* outburst in Part II, 'Wahrlich, dieser ist Gottes Sohn gewesen', a climactic, almost overwhelming reaffirmation of the Christian faith.

The forces which Bach required to perform the St Matthew Passion are greater than those which he assembled for almost any other of his compositions: two choruses, two orchestras, each with its own continuo organ, a group of soprano voices to sing the 'cantus firmus' or hymn melody of the monumental opening movement, and an ensemble of soloists – though these in fact would simply have been the strongest singers from among the assembled voices of Bach's choirs. With resources such as these Bach, with genius and masterly intuition, was able to emphasize the dialogue-character of Picander's text and create a cohesive drama of profound and sustained intensity.

Bach compiled three oratorios at Leipzig during the years 1734–5. The distinction between this form and that of the Lutheran cantata is chiefly that whereas the cantata lacks a unified plot, the oratorio relates a sequence of events, sometimes incorporating biblical narrative, within a self-contained plot. The most extended of Bach's works in this form is the Christmas Oratorio (BWV 248) which he assembled largely from material borrowed from earlier secular cantatas, but which is nevertheless a unified work, carefully structured, opening and closing with the same chorale melody, differently treated. New recitatives, chorales and several choruses were added, and its six parts, each roughly corresponding in length and layout to a church cantata, were performed in sequence on the first three days of Christmas 1734, the Feast of the Circumcision, the Sunday after New Year and the Feast of Epiphany 1735. Later in 1735 Bach assembled two shorter oratorios, the Easter Oratorio (BWV 249) and the Ascension Oratorio (BWV 11); these, too, made extensive use of music belonging to earlier secular cantatas, as indeed, Bach was later to 'parody' the alto aria of the Ascension Oratorio as the 'Agnus Dei' of the Mass in B minor.

Short masses, motets, Magnificat

In 1733 Bach dedicated a 'Missa' or 'short mass' consisting of a Kyrie and Gloria to the Elector of Saxony at the Dresden court. In this work, which was eventually was to become the basis of the great B minor Mass (BWV 232), and in four more 'short masses' (BWV 233-6) probably assembled later in the 1730s, Bach once again demonstrates his skill in the art of 'parody'. Each of these Missae borrows extensively from the cantatas, perhaps offering an insight to earlier music which Bach himself considered of particular merit. Apart from the 1733 Missa, in whose accompanying letter the composer requested the Elector's patronage (eventually granted in 1736), Bach's intentions for the Missae remains in doubt; a mass of this kind could be sung either at a Lutheran service or at a Catholic one such as that customarily held in the Dresden court chapel. During the last years of his life Bach turned to the 1733 Missa once more, adding to it a 'Credo', 'Sanctus' (with 'Osanna' and 'Benedictus') and 'Agnus Dei'. His purpose in compiling a complete Catholic mass is not entirely clear; evidently it was not for liturgical use, though he may have wished to create a model, or indeed a monument. While the music was not conceived as a unity, the scale, proportions, tonal scheme and rich stylistic variety of the whole exert an overwhelming power over the imagination of the listener.

Occupying a smaller place in Bach's sacred vocal music are six motets and a Latin setting of the *Magnificat*. Four of the motets are for double chorus while a fifth, *Jesu, meine freude*, is a five-voice setting of a hymn by Johann Franck. The sixth, BWV 118, is alone in having independent parts for wind instruments. The authenticity of a seventh, BWV 230, has been questioned. Bach prepared two versions of his celebrated Latin *Magnificat*. The first, in E flat with four Christmas interpolations (BWV 243a), was sung at Leipzig on Christmas Day 1723. The second, a revised version in D major (BWV 243), omitting the Christmas interpolations, dates from the late 1720s. This joyful, brilliantly scored work differs from the cantatas in its exclusion of recitative, its avoidance of da capo aria, its Latin text, and its reintroduction of the opening thematic material in the final chorus.

The astonishing productivity already mentioned as stemming from Bach's exacting responsibilities as *Kantor* during the 1720s went alongside aggravation and disappointment caused by conflict with the Leipzig authorities. Far from accepting criticism, some of it justified, for failing to discharge certain of his duties to the letter, Bach responded with a Memorandum, dated 23 August 1730, in which he stressed the inadequate musical resources at his disposal, at the same time outlining his requirements 'for a well-regulated church music'.

The Leipzig 'Collegium Musicum'

Difficulties such as these probably encouraged Bach to diversify his activities during the 1730s. In 1729 he was offered the directorship of a *collegium musicum*. Founded by Telemann in 1702, it was one of two such musical societies in Leipzig, made up mainly of students but including professional musicians. An announcement in Lorenz Christoph Mizler's *Neu eröffnete musikalische Bibliothek of 1736* states that 'there are always good musicians among [the participants in the society's concerts], so that sometimes they become, as is known, famous virtuosos. Any musician is permitted to make himself publicly heard at these concerts, and most often there are such listeners as know how to judge the qualities of an able musician.' Gatherings of this *collegium musicum* took place in coffee-houses owned by Gottfried Zimmermann, in winter at one in the Catherinenstrasse, in summer in the garden of another on the outskirts of the city. Bach's two periods of office were 1729–37 and 1739–c.1744, and it is probable that his harpsichord concertos, several of his secular cantatas such as the *Coffee Cantata* (BWV 211) and perhaps the orchestral suites were included in the society's ordinary concerts. At least half-a-dozen cantatas, in addition, were performed between August 1733 and October 1736 by Bach and the *collegium musicum* in honour of the Dresden court and the new Elector, Friedrich August II, to whom Bach had already offered his Missa in the hope of securing a court title. The cantatas performed at the special concerts include BWV 213–15 and 206.

Later years

Apart from directing the *collegium musicum*, Bach was active during the last twenty years of his life in composition, in compiling and revising his music and as an organ recitalist. He retained his interest in instrumental craftsmanship, an aptitude which had long been developed in the Bach family, examining and inaugurating organs and playing a lively part in the development of Gottfried Silbermann's pianos. In 1731 Bach published the first part of his *Clavier-Übung* or 'Keyboard exercises', consisting of six Partitas for harpsichord (BWV 825–30), five of which had been published separately at intervals between 1726 and 1730. Part II of the *Clavier-Übung*, containing the *Italian Concerto* (BWV 971) and the *Overture in the French Style* (BWV 831), both for solo harpsichord, appeared in 1735. Part III, consisting of organ pieces, was published in 1739: it contained the Prelude in E flat (BWV 552) and its five-part fugue, often known as the 'St Anne', twenty-one chorale preludes (BWV 669–89) and four duets for keyboard without pedals (BWV 802–5). In 1741 or 1742, Bach published as Part IV of the *Clavier-Übung* his *Aria with Divers Variations* (BWV 988), better known as the 'Goldberg Variations', and in the early 1740s completed Book II of the '48' Preludes and Fugues.

In August 1742 Bach performed what was probably his last secular cantata. In that month Carl Heinrich von Dieskau received allegiance as new lord of the Kleinzschocher estate on the outskirts of Leipzig, and Bach was commissioned, probably by Picander, author of the libretto and a government official answerable to the new landowner, to provide musical entertainment. This he fulfilled with his 'Cantata burlesque', or *Peasant Cantata* (BWV 212), in which a courting couple is sympathetically and sometimes humorously portrayed. Folk-song and dance-rhythms play a part in Bach's delightful score; both here, and to an even greater extent in the bass aria of another late cantata, *Dem Gerechten muss das Licht* (BWV 195) for a wedding, Bach demonstrates his skill in handling the new 'galant' idiom of the close of the Baroque period.

During the 1740s Bach (p. 160)performed sacred music by many of his contemporaries, among them Handel, Telemann, C.H. Graun and his predecessor at Leipzig, Kuhnau. He revised and assembled into a new manuscript the '18' chorale preludes (BWV 651–68) for organ, and arranged the six chorales (BWV 645–50), all but one (BWV 646) from earlier Leipzig cantata movements, which were printed by Johann George Schübler in 1748–9. In 1747 Bach joined Lorenz Mizler's 'Korrespondierende Societät der musicalischen Wissenschaften' (Corresponding Society of Musical Learning), but after submitting his canonic variations for organ on *Von Himmel Hoch* (BWV 769) as a sample of his science he seems to have taken little further interest in it. (Mizler had earlier defended Bach against the anonymous criticism of the theorist and composer Johann Scheibe, who had accused him in his periodical *Der critische Musikus* of May 1737 of being out of touch with new ideas, and of excessive artifice and ornament.)

In May of 1747 one of the most celebrated occasions of Bach's life occurred. This was his second visit, in the company of his eldest son, Wilhelm Friedemann, to Frederick the Great's court at Potsdam near Berlin, where his second son, Carl Philipp Emanuel, was harpsichordist. His eldest son described his reception at court:

One evening, just as [the King] was getting his flute ready, and his musicians were assembled, an officer brought with him a list of the strangers who had arrived. With his flute in his hand the King ran over the list, but immediately turned to the assembled musicians, and said with a kind of agitation, 'Gentlemen, old Bach is come.' The flute was now laid aside; and old Bach, who had alighted at his son's lodgings, was immediately summoned to the Palace ...

During the visit Bach tried out several of Silbermann's new fortepianos in the palace, executing a fugal improvisation on a theme provided by the King himself. This was the ingenious fugal three-part 'ricercare' which Bach informed the King he would print.

When he returned to Leipzig Bach set about an altogether larger project consisting of not one, but two keyboard ricercares, in three and six parts, assorted canons and a trio sonata for flute – the King's instrument, violin and continuo. This was the 'Musical Offering' published at the end of September 1747 as *Musikalisches Opfer*.

Although in declining health, Bach remained active almost throughout the last two years of his life. In 1749 he repeated a performance of his satirical cantata *Phoebus und Pan* (BWV 201), made revisions to various works and involved himself in preparing his *Art of Fugue* (BWV 1080) for publication. This didactic, profound and very beautiful work, whose fugues are all developed from a single theme, had probably been composed between 1740 and 1745. Bach left no specific instrumental requirements for the performance of the *Art of Fugue*, though he seems at least to have envisaged a solo keyboard as one possibility. By the late 1740s Bach's eyesight had deteriorated, and two operations by an English eye-specialist (who later operated on Handel) were only partially successful. When the composer died, after a stroke, on 28 July 1750, the engraving of the *Art of Fugue* was incomplete, and this has left us with unanswered questions concerning the order of movements, and whether or not Bach completed the quadruple fugue. According to C.P.E. Bach his father died while working on this final, complex piece, but it seems likely that Bach would by then already have drafted its essentials, and that some material was lost between his death and the publication by his two elder sons in 1751.

Telemann

Although Bach was recognized as a fine keyboard player and composer during his lifetime, above all in his native Germany, he did not enjoy the popular acclaim granted to his friend and contemporary, Telemann.

Georg Philipp Telemann was born in Magdeburg in 1681 and became the most successful composer working in Germany during the first half of the eighteenth century (p. 159). During a long and astonishingly productive life Telemann acquired an international reputation as a composer while at the same time playing a full part in the musical developments taking place around him. In 1701 he travelled to Leipzig to enrol at the university, meeting the sixteen-year-old Handel in Halle on the way. After some four years of study, during which he was active as a composer as well as founding the *collegium musicum* of which Bach later became director, Telemann accepted his first appointment, as *Hofkapellmeister* to Count Erdmann von Promnitz. The Count's taste in music inclined towards France, and it was probably in the two years during which Telemann served him that he composed many of his orchestral suites in the French manner. Count Erdmann's residence was in Moravia where Telemann encountered the folk-music of the region 'in its true barbaric beauty', as he himself expressed it. The deep impression made by Polish folk-rhythms lasted throughout Telemann's life, and they became a distinctive element, together with those of France, Italy and Germany, in what Quantz termed the 'mixed style', for, as he explains:

> If one has the necessary discernment to choose the best from the styles of different countries a mixed style results that, without overstepping the bounds of modesty, could well be called the German style, not only because Germany came upon it first, but because it has already been established in Germany for many years, and flourishes still, and displeases neither in Italy, nor France nor in other lands.

Johann Joachim Quantz (1697–1773) who thus characterized German music was an accomplished flautist and composer whose most celebrated pupil was Frederick the Great. His *Versuch einer Anweisung die Flöte traversière zu spielen* (Essay of a Method for Playing the Transverse Flute) was published in Berlin in 1752. This treatise discusses wider musical issues than its title implies, providing then as now an invaluable guide to style, taste and technique in the mid-eighteenth century.

Telemann left the Count's employment in 1707 and in the following year took up the position of *Konzertmeister* at the little court of Eisenach. It was here, in all likelihood, that he met the young J.S. Bach, to whose second son, Carl Philipp Emanuel, he stood godfather. Four years later, in 1712, Telemann moved again, this time to Frankfurt-am-Main as director of the city's music, *Kapellmeister* of the Church of the Barefoot Friars and director of a *collegium musicum* for which he organized weekly public concerts. Here he extended an already varied repertory of suites, cantatas and assorted chamber music with operas, a Passion oratorio to a text by Barthold Heinrich Brockes, and concertos. Brockes's Passion oratorio with its Pietistic reflections upon biblical narrative became one of the most popular texts of its kind, and was set by many composers including Keiser (1712), Handel (1715/16), Telemann (1716), Mattheson (1718), Fasch (1723) and Stölzel (1725).

In 1721 Telemann made his final move, when, as the eighteenth-century English music historian Sir John Hawkins reported, 'the city of Hamburg, desirous of having such an extraordinary man amongst them, prevailed on him to accept the place of director of their music' (*A General History of the Science and Practice of Music*, 1776). The post was that of 'Kantor of the Johanneum and Director of the Five Main Churches'. Hamburg with its prosperous trading links was one of the most influential cities in Germany. Music and literature thrived in this strongly patrician environment, and it was here that Telemann was able to respond fully to cultural developments taking place around him. Hamburg, furthermore, was a leading centre for music publishing, and this is reflected in three enterprising publications launched by the composer between 1725 and 1733. The earliest was a cycle of twenty-seven chamber cantatas, *Der harmonische Gottesdienst* (1725), to which he later added two further volumes, making seventy-two cantatas in all. In 1728 Telemann issued the first instalment of what is regarded the earliest music periodical, *Der getreue Music-Meister*, which he promoted by subscription. Issued fortnightly, the publication ran profitably for nearly two years, containing not only vocal and instrumental pieces by Telemann but also music by other composers, among them Bach, Pisendel and Zelenka. Telemann's third publication was purely instrumental. The *Musique de Table* (1733) or 'banquet music' was organized into three anthologies, each of which contains an orchestral suite, concerto, quartet, trio, continuo sonata and short orchestral conclusion. Among the many subscribers to this project were Handel from London, Quantz from Berlin, Pisendel from Dresden and Blavet from Paris.

By now Telemann's reputation had extended well beyond his native Germany, and in the autumn of 1737 he set out for Paris. He stayed for about eight months, was accorded the honour of hearing his music performed at the celebrated Concert spirituel, for which he had written his *grand motet* 'Deus judicum tuum', and took out a 'Privilège du Roi' entitling him to publish instrumental works there. Among the most admired of his compositions were six Quartets which had been published first in Hamburg in 1730, then, without his consent, in Paris in 1736. Telemann followed these with six *Nouveaux Quatuors* for flute, violin, viola da gamba or cello and continuo, published in Paris under his Privilège in 1738. This later set, like the *Musique de Table*, attracted subscribers from all over Europe, the most illustrious being J.S. Bach.

When Telemann returned to Hamburg in the summer of 1738 he took up his official duties with renewed vigour. About 1739 he published one of his most consistently rewarding anthologies of chamber instrumental music under the title *Essercizii Musici*. At the same time he continued to produce new cantatas and Passions for the churches, and music for public concerts which he promoted with ceaseless energy. Notwithstanding this busy schedule the mid-1750s witnessed a fascinating rejuvenation and change of direction in Telemann's music. There began an Indian summer of creativity which lasted almost until the end of Telemann's life. Between the age of seventy-five and eighty-five he produced a significant body of music whose orginality is in some cases more striking than anything he had previously produced. To an increasing extent he seems to have interested himself in musical and literary developments taking place around him. He had become a member of Mizler's 'Corresponding Society of Musical Learning' in 1739, and contributed several articles. He was also an industrious personal correspondent, and since 1739 or even before, had exchanged letters with the Berlin composer Carl Heinrich Graun (1704–59) in which he discussed, above all, French and Italian styles in music and the relationship between music and text. The Berlin musicians expressed interest in Telemann's music, and it was perhaps in part this vital link with a younger generation of composers which stimulated the large-scale vocal and choral works of Telemann's old age. Many of these employ texts by poets two generations younger than the composer, some of them barely on the threshold of their careers.

Among the many works by Telemann belonging to the period between 1755 and 1765 are several which possess outstandingly original features. The most widely performed of them was the Passion oratorio, *Der Tod Jesu* (1755). The text, completed in the previous year, was provided by Carl Wilhelm Ramler (1725–98), a Berlin poet and academic. He followed a newly developing concept in oratorio, in which dialogue and narration were largely dispensed with in favour of a more 'lyrically' developed account. In the following year Telemann first performed *Die Donnerode* (1756). This dramatic cantata, in whose text Ramler also had a hand, became so popular among Hamburg concert-goers that about 1760 the composer added a second part. In 1757 Telemann directed the first performance of his cantata *Die Tageszeiten* with a text by Wilhelm Friedrich Zachariae (1726–77). To each of its four sections is allotted a different time of day whose particular character Telemann evokes in music which sometimes foreshadows Haydn's *The Seasons*. The sections are scored for solo soprano, alto, tenor and bass respectively, with a brief chorus at the end of each.

The year 1759 witnessed no less than three major works from Telemann's pen: his St Mark Passion, one of forty-six Passion settings which he performed at the rate of one a year during his long tenure of office in Hamburg; the festive cantata *Das befreite Israel*, and the little oratorio *Mirjam and deine Wehmut* for which Telemann used part of Klopstock's epic poem 'Der Messias'. In all there is vitality and freshness of outlook.

The 1760s were hardly less productive, seeing the completion of four further substantial works by Telemann. These were the oratorios *Die Auferstehung und Himmelfahrt Jesu* (1760) set to a text by Ramler, and *Der Tag des Gerichts* (1762) to a text by Wilhelm Alers, a former pupil of the composer; a serenata, *Don Quichotte auf der Hochzeit des Comacho* (1761) to a libretto by Daniel Schiebeler, a twenty-year-old Hamburg poet, hardly known at the time; and a dramatic cantata *Ino* (1765), for whose text Telemann once more turned to Ramler. In *Ino*, a beautifully crafted piece for soprano and an orchestra of flutes, horns and strings, perhaps unrivalled by anything he had previously written, we find the octogenarian composer striving for new means of expression, infusing and refreshing a fundamentally Baroque style with characteristics of the newly emerging early Classicism. His eagerness to keep abreast of the times is further confirmed by his choice of texts, for in Ramler, Alers and Schiebeler he had found poets who reflected the intellect, rational clarity and integrity of the *Aufklärung* (Enlightenment).

Telemann occupied a central position in German musical life and was almost universally admired by his own and younger generations of composers, poets and theoreticians. Hardly a musical form was left untried by him, hardly an aspect of musical life developed in which he did not play a part. In his own music he frequently demonstrated his skill in blending older contrapuntal discipline with features of the new 'galant' style, and more than any other composer of his generation he provided a link between older styles and the progressive Berlin school which developed after 1740 under the patronage of Frederick the Great.

The light and graceful style cultivated by composers centred on Berlin, Mannheim, and other musical centres soon challenged the weightier, more elaborate style of the Baroque period. Now the emphasis was placed increasingly on pleasing melodies simply accompanied, rather than on learned disciplines such as fugue. With such challenges as these the established craft of Baroque style was gradually brought to an end.

Acknowledgments
Select Bibliography
Illustration Sources
Index

Acknowledgments

This book would not have been written without the advice and encouragement of many friends and colleagues whom I warmly acknowledge. I would like particularly to thank the following: Pierluigi Petrobelli who made valuable suggestions at the outset of the project; Barry Millington who approached me to embark upon it and who took an interest in all stages of its preparation; Jonathan Freeman-Attwood who has tirelessly read the book in its final stages and given much practical help; Lorenzo Bianconi who kindly showed me unpublished material relating to the first two chapters; Eric Cross, Peter Czornyj and Graham Sadler for reading sections of the book and making invaluable comments; William Christie, Graham Dixon, Laurence Dreyfus, Stanislav Heller, Edward Higginbottom, Marie Leonhardt, François Pilastre and Richard Wigmore for their interest and encouragement; Elizabeth McKim for her index; Kate Bertaut for expeditious word processing; Ann Stevens for her patient and constructive editing; and my wife, Alison, for almost a decade of much needed organization, word processing, and support.

Select Bibliography

Abraham, Gerald (ed.), *The New Oxford History of Music*: Vol. 6, 'Concert Music', Oxford 1975 and 1986.

Anthony, James, *French Baroque Music*, London 1974 (rev. 1978).

Arnold, Denis, and Nigel Fortune (eds), *The New Monteverdi Companion*, London 1985.

Arnold, Denis, *Monteverdi* (rev. Tim Carter), London 1963, 1990.

Basso, Alberto, *Frau Musika: La Vita e le Opere di J.S. Bach*, Turin 1979, 1983 (2 vols).

Bianconi, Lorenzo, *Music in the Seventeenth Century*, Cambridge 1987.

Blume, Friedrich, *Protestant Church Music*, London 1975.

Boyd, Malcolm, *Bach*, London 1983.

——, *Domenico Scarlatti*, London 1986.

Boyden, David, *The History of Violin Playing*, Oxford 1965

Bukofzer, Manfred, *Music in the Baroque Era*, New York 1947.

Dart, Thurston, *The Interpretation of Music*, London 1954.

David, Hans, and Arthur Mendel, *The Bach Reader*, New York and London 1945 (rev. 1966).

Daw, Stephen, *The Music of Johann Sebastian Bach: The Choral Works*, London 1981.

Dean, Winton, *Handel's Dramatic Oratorios and Masques*, Oxford 1959.

Dean, Winton, and J. Merrill Knapp, *Handel's Operas 1704–1726*, Oxford 1987.

Dent, Edward J., *Foundations of English Opera*, New York (repr. 1965).

Deutsch, Otto Erich, *Handel, a Documentary Biography*, London 1955.

Dixon, Graham, *Carissimi*, Oxford 1986.

Dreyfus, Laurence, *Bach's Continuo Group*, Yale, 1987.

Drummond, Pippa, *The German Concerto*, Oxford 1980.

Dürr, Alfred, *Die Kantaten von Johann Sebastian Bach*, Kassel 1971 (2 vols).

Dürr, Alfred, *Zur Chronologie der Leipziger Vokalwerke J. S. Bachs*, Kassel 1976.

Fiske, Roger, *English Theatre in the Eighteenth Century*, Oxford 1973.

Geiringer, Karl, *Johann Sebastian Bach: The Culmination of an Era*, New York 1966.

Geiringer, Karl and Irene, *The Bach Family*, London 1954.

Girdlestone, Cuthbert, *Jean-Philippe Rameau*, London 1957 (rev. New York 1969).

Glover, Jane, *Cavalli*, London 1978.

Hitchcock, H. Wiley, *Marc-Antoine Charpentier*, Oxford 1990.

Hogwood, Christopher, *Handel* (with chronological table by Anthony Hicks), London 1984.

Hutchings, Arthur, *The Baroque Concerto*, London 1961.

Isherwood, Robert M., *Music in the Service of the King: France in the Seventeenth Century*, Cornell 1973.

Kerman, Joseph, *Opera as Drama*, New York 1956.

Kirkpatrick, Ralph, *Domenico Scarlatti*, Princeton 1953.

Lewis, Anthony, and Nigel Fortune (eds), *The New Oxford History of Music*: Vol. 5, 'Opera and Church Music 1630–1750'.

MacClintock, Carol, *Readings in the History of Music in Performance*, Bloomington, London 1979.

Mellers, Wilfred, *François Couperin and the French Classical Tradition*, London 1949 (rev. 1986).

Newman, William S., *The Sonata in the Baroque Era*, N. Carolina 1959 (rev. 1966).

Palisca, Claude V., *Baroque Music*, Yale 1968 (rev. 1981).

Petzoldt, Richard (tr. from the German by Horace Fitzpatrick), *Georg Philipp Telemann*, London 1974.

Pincherle, Marc (tr. from the French by Christopher Hatch), *Vivaldi Genius of the Baroque*, London 1957.

Price, Curtis, *Henry Purcell and the London Stage*, Cambridge 1984.

Sadie, Julie Anne (ed.), *Companion to Baroque Music*, London 1990.

Sadie, Stanley (ed.), *The New Grove Dictionary of Music and Musicians*, London 1980 (20 vols).

Selfridge-Field, Eleanor, *Venetian Instrumental Music from Gabrieli to Vivaldi*, Oxford 1975.

Smend, Friedrich, *Bach in Köthen* (tr. John Page, ed. Stephen Daw), Berlin 1951; St Louis 1985.

Smither, Howard, *A History of the Oratorio*, Chapel Hill 1977 (2 vols).

Spink, Ian, *English Song: Dowland to Purcell*, London 1974.

Stiller, Günther, *Johann Sebastian Bach and Liturgical Life in Leipzig* (tr. Herbert J.A. Bouman, Daniel F. Poellot, Hilton C. Oswald, ed. Robin A. Leaver), St Louis 1984.

Strohm, Reinhard, *Essays on Handel and Italian Opera*, Cambridge 1985.

Strungk, Oliver (ed.), *Source Readings in Music History*, New York 1950.

Talbot, Michael, *Vivaldi*, London 1978 (rev. 1993).

——, *Tomaso Albinoni: The Venetian Composer and his World*, Oxford 1990.

Terry, Charles Sanford, *Bach: a Biography*, London 1928 (6th ed. 1967).

——, *Bach's Orchestra*, London 1932 (4th ed. 1966).

Tunley, David, *The Eighteenth Century French Cantata*, London 1974.

Westrup, Jack A. (rev. Nigel Fortune), *Purcell*, London 1980.

Williams, Peter, *The Organ Music of J.S. Bach*, Cambridge 1980/1984 (3 vols).

Wolff, Christoph, *Bach: Essays on his Life and Music*, Harvard 1991.

Young, Percy M., *Handel*, London 1946.

EIGHTEENTH-CENTURY SOURCES

Avision, Charles, *An Essay on Musical Expression*, 1733. (Facsimile edition, New York 1967)

Burney, Charles, *A General History of Music*, London 1776–1789 (4 vols).

Hawkins, Sir John, *A General History of the Science and Practice of Music*, London 1776 (reprint, 2 vols, New York 1963).

Mattheson, Johann, *Das neu-eröffnete Orchestre*, Hamburg 1713.

——, *Der vollkommene Capellmeister*, Hamburg 1739.

North, Roger, *Roger North on Music* (ed. John Wilson), London 1959.

Quantz, Johann Joachim, *On Playing the Flute* (ed. and tr. Edward R. Reilly), London 1966.

Illustration Sources

Index

Bold page numbers indicate main reference or composer's biography. *Italic* page numbers refer to illustrations